The Book
of
Psychic
Symbols

Melanie Barnum

About the Author

Melanie Barnum is a psychic, medium, intuitive counselor, life coach, workshop presenter, and hypnotist who has been practicing professionally for more than fifteen years. She was a VIP Reader at Psych-Out, a gathering of the nation's foremost psychics organized by Court TV. Melanie is also an Angelspeake Facilitator, and a member of the National Guild of Hypnotists (NGH) and the International Association of Counselors and Therapists (IACT). She lives in Connecticut.

Please visit her online at MelanieBarnum.com.

Interpreting Intuitive Messages

The Book
of
Psychic
Symbols

Melanie Barnum

Llewellyn Publications
Woodbury, Minnesota

First Edition
Fifth Printing, 2015

Book design by Donna Burch
Cover illustrator: Lola and Bek/The July Group
Cover design by Lisa Novak

Llewellyn Publications is a registered trademark of Llewellyn Worldwide Ltd.

Library of Congress Cataloging-in-Publication Data
Barnum, Melanie, 1969–
   The book of psychic symbols : interpreting intuitive messages / Melanie Barnum. — 1st ed.
      p.   cm.
   Includes bibliographical references (p.   ).
   ISBN 978-0-7387-2303-7
1. Signs and symbols. 2. Symbolism (Psychology) I. Title.
   BF458.B376 2012
   133.8—dc23
                          2011047316

Llewellyn Publications
A Division of Llewellyn Worldwide Ltd.
2143 Wooddale Drive
Woodbury, MN 55125-2989
www.llewellyn.com

Printed in the United States of America

Dedication

This book is dedicated to my husband, Tom, and my amazing daughters, Molly and Samantha. Without the unconditional love and support of my incredible family, this book never would have been possible. They have taught me that, for all of us, being psychic is normal, exciting, and pretty darn cool!

Acknowledgments

Following your heart is not always an easy thing to do, especially when you are going against what is considered the norm in society. Having incredible teachers and like-minded peers has helped propel me toward the life I know I was born to live.

Over fifteen years ago I was gently guided—actually more like shoved, by forces I couldn't see or touch—into pursuing a psychic career. This push jump-started me on a quest to fulfill this tug on my soul, which was clearly something greater than I'd ever experienced. Luckily, I was not the first to travel this path. A great many individuals with incredible gifts have paved the way for all of us to tap in to the natural intuition that is part of our birthright. All I can say is, Thank You!

I have been fortunate enough to participate in many workshops and events with amazing people who have unknowingly influenced my psychic world. These incredible earth guides deserve appreciation. I've studied with, and often played with, remarkable intuitives and readers such as Sonia Choquette, John Holland, James Van Praagh, Elizabeth Harper, Brian Weiss, David Morehouse, Raymond Moody, Kathleen Deyo, and Rachel Pollack.

Authors in the intuitive field also deserve praise and gratitude, as I took their stories to heart and at times compared my life with theirs to help me understand what I was experiencing. There have been so many over the years, including those I've studied with, but I will try, with my feeble memory, to include them! Jeffrey Wands, Colette Baron Reid, Terry Iacuzzo, Terry and Linda Jamison, Sylvia Browne, and John Edward have shared their lives through the pages of their books. Their honest and often hilarious narratives encouraged me to share my story.

A big thank you to everyone who has publicly acknowledged their psychic gifts. For the most part, we are not the crazy ones! We are simply following a path we have no other choice but to follow. I hope my book influences at least one more person to "come out" with their intuition and be open about who they truly are. We have the power to change the way we interact in the universe.

Contents

Introduction:
Who I Am and What I Do

"I understand what you are saying, but none of it makes sense!" my client Anna said to me as she sat in my office. "I'm *not* traveling to Africa, and I'm definitely *not* moving out of the country!"

We were in my office, and I was giving Anna a psychic reading. She was looking at me as if I had two heads. The information I was receiving psychically was not ringing true for her. Anna, together with her life partner, Sis, owned a thriving deli and a catering business. They were in no position to pack up and leave the United States, nor did they have any desire to do so.

"It sounds crazy. I realize that," I answered, "but I have to share it with you as I get it."

I was receiving psychic symbols, pictures in my mind, as I was talking with Anna. What I saw was the American flag being taken down off of a flagpole with a different flag being raised in its place, though I couldn't decipher the country of origin for the new flag. I also saw a cartoon image of a map with dotted lines jutting out of the country. After that I saw elephants and a dry landscape. In the background were giraffes.

"Do you have any aspirations to go on a big game hunt or a safari? I'm feeling you connected to animals in a major way, though I don't feel your intentions are to harm them," I continued.

"No, but that's all right. Don't worry about it," she replied, the look of disbelief now coupled with a look of amusement on her face.

"Just be open to the possibility that this can happen, and happen within a couple of years," I urged, chuckling, and we moved on to other topics.

Almost two years later to the day, I heard from a mutual friend that Anna and Sis had indeed packed up their household and moved to Canada. They moved so that Anna could attend veterinary school. Not only was she changing her career and becoming a vet to take care of domestic animals, she also went on a safari in Africa to learn about large-animal medicine!

The symbolic impressions I had received during her reading were dead on. I only needed to interpret and believe in them. Though Anna and I couldn't imagine what I was telling her would actually happen, she recognized the accuracy of the symbolic predictions when they did indeed come true. Symbols are everywhere; we need only appreciate their value.

I am psychic. I am a medium. I'm pretty normal. All my life my brother teased me about being average, liking Top Forty music, and wearing pretty much what everyone else wore. Average is where I'm comfortable, where I fit in. To me, being psychic is pretty normal, too. After all, everyone has some intuitive ability.

According to the *Microsoft Encarta College Dictionary*, being psychic means I am "somebody supposedly sensitive to supernatural forces; a person who is, or is believed to be, sensitive to nonphysical or supernatural forces." The dictionary also defines a *medium* as "a person believed to transmit messages between living people and the spirits of the dead."

I never saw dead people or angels or anyone who wasn't supposed to be there. I don't remember ever seeing people as colors or hearing their thoughts. I don't remember wondering why my dead relatives were hanging around, or why my animals that had passed came back to visit. I didn't have a horrific car accident, and I was never struck by lightning. I have never died only to be reborn again. None of that ever happened to me.

I didn't have anything that profound or that painful to begin my career as a psychic medium. Mine is a simple story. One day, in the 1990s, I felt as though someone hit me over the head, and I heard the words, "You need to do this work now." I just stood there, looking around. "What the heck was that, and where did it come from?"

Here I was, the mother of a new baby and a wife in a new marriage. I had just opened a new business, a children's consignment store, after quitting my job as the controller of a company. I knew intuitively that corporate life would never make me happy. I also felt an overpowering need to be home to mother my daughter. I had no further explanation of this new career path other than those life-altering seven words: "You need to do this work now." *What the hell did it mean?*

I've always been able to read people's energy, so I thought maybe that's all it was. I did believe that I'd had some kind of primitive intuitive ability since childhood. But there was a nagging in my gut, my intuitive chakra area, my solar plexus, telling me, "That's not it." The more I tried to justify it, the more I understood, again intuitively, that like it or not, this was what I needed to do. "*You need to do this work now*" was the beginning of a whole new world, for me *and* my family.

I currently have a private practice in Ridgefield, Connecticut, and the more I practice, the better I'm able to carry out the work I was directed to do! I offer a wide range of healing and intuitive modalities such as psychic readings, hypnosis, mediumship, life coaching, past-life regression, reflexology, and Reiki. In addition, I regularly conduct phone sessions and teach on a variety of subjects, including intuitive development, goal attainment and prosperity, understanding symbolic meaning, manifestation, and hypnosis. I help people communicate through mediumship with their friends and loved ones who have crossed over and even work with friends and families of murder victims. I am lucky to work with people from all different walks of life and who live in different areas of the world. I tune in psychically and access their potential to help them become aware of the possibilities that will present themselves in their future and assist them in understanding their past.

I work differently with each client, depending on what my intuition tells me and what the person is hoping to get out of the session. To tune in, I sometimes utilize a psychic resource known as *psychometry*. Psychometry works on the premise that all objects, especially pictures and other personal items, hold energy and all energy can be read, intuitively. I also employ the use of a variety of divination cards such as tarot, angel, or rune cards. The pendulum, an object or crystal on the end of a string or chain, is another psychic instrument I keep handy and one that I like to use when helping children. Known as *dowsing*, it's a tool kids are naturally curious about and open to. Other times I simply access their energy or auric field by talking with them and synching our vibrations naturally, enabling me to receive symbolic messages for them.

But all of this didn't happen instantly. Like everyone else, I had to work for my supper. I always valued qualifications, and this was no exception. I believed that if I didn't have letters after my name, no one would take me seriously—that if I didn't have the right credentials, I wouldn't be worthy of the work I do. I knew it would be hard enough putting myself out there in a field most people viewed as phony without having at least some schooling to back me up. There was no way I was going to hang out a shingle that said, "Psychic!"

I set out to learn all I could about intuition. Over the years I've been lucky to have worked with teachers individually and in groups, in person and long distance. Some of the teachers were obscure, and some were so famous that I could only work with them as part of a group of hundreds. As I started my training, I also practiced. For years I offered free sessions over the Internet so I could "test" my new talents. I found that I could access the symbolic messages regardless of where the people were physically. As these sessions became increasingly accurate, I started offering in-person readings. So began my career as a practicing psychic and medium.

As my confidence connecting to the spiritual realm grew along with my psychic ability, I was able to work on a much deeper level. I recognized how vital symbols were to extrasensory communication. I also noticed patterns or routines—things I was doing to prepare myself for each session.

Everyone who does this work has their own way to get ready for each gig. I like to turn the music up full blast in my car and sing at the top of my lungs. This helps me relax, and through this relaxation I connect to the universal energies more easily, my senses becoming more in tune with the higher vibrations from the other side. I'm then able to access the symbolic messages I'm sent. Some professional psychics or mediums practice meditation before their sittings or sessions. Others literally throw off their shoes and walk barefoot in the grass to ground them energetically to the earth. There is no right or wrong way to prepare; the only criterion is to do something that feels right.

I am now conscious of adding water to my fountain or lighting additional candles around my office or reorganizing my desk or the crystals and decorations I have throughout the room. I used to worry I was wasting the time I should have used to meditate. Now I understand that I *am* meditating. This mindless housekeeping balances my energy so I'm not processing anything, not thinking too hard. Instead, I am tuning in to my surroundings. This helps me to recognize, almost unconsciously, when there are any energies that change my environment or any messages that are being symbolically communicated.

After one of these "meditative" moments, I did a reading for someone who was very interested in becoming a screenplay writer. I knew from the bottom of my core that he needed to be in the healing field. I even told him I saw him working in a hospital and that he would go to medical school. I explained I symbolically saw healing hands and a hospital, and I felt he was the giver of the energy, not the receiver, which meant he would be a healer. He laughed and told me he loved the reading, at least the rest of it. I laughed, too; I knew he didn't have a chance against his true calling. Sure enough, last I heard he was in nursing school. Okay, so not exactly a doctor, but pretty close to it.

Being present to facilitate the flipping of the switch for clients is a huge part of what I love. Communicating with the other side and helping people understand their own intuitive abilities is my passion.

Teaching others to be aware of their everyday symbols and synchronicities makes me happy. Understanding your own symbols can make
you happy, too.

What to Expect and Why You Need This!

You've picked up this book for a reason. Possibly, you are interested in
developing your existing knowledge of psychic symbols or you may
have discovered a new desire to explore a previously untapped intuitive ability. Either way, you'll find that within these pages is a key to
unlocking wisdom that's been there all along. No amount of meditation or spiritual practice can fully prepare you for living intuitively.
You must also develop your understanding of psychic symbols to access your metaphysical connection to the other side. By opening up
this relationship, you will become increasingly self-aware. Chapter 3
will help you apply this new awareness.

You can look to this book as a digest directed toward self-
improvement. By reading the chapters straight through, you will gain
an understanding of psychic symbols: what they are, where they come
from, how they appear, and what they mean in all different contexts,
including dreams, messages from the other side, and even tarot cards.
You will acquire much-needed insight into an ever-present symbolic
world. Following the exercises at the end of most chapters will reinforce this new awareness, which will enable you to continue your life
more passionately and with greater depth.

Alternatively or additionally, you can use this book as a practical
guide, something to be absorbed repeatedly over time. By reading all of
the chapters and then utilizing this book as a simple handy reference
to the numerous symbolic impressions you receive every day, you'll
have an easy-access source for answering all of your questions. If you
are like me you soak up information through tactile means, or actually
doing rather than simply reading about doing. This is how I created
the symbols glossary. Some of the symbolic interpretations come from
common knowledge and books I have read, but I've gathered most of
the insight through my own intuitive experiences and workshops I
have attended. You may find doing the numerous exercises frequently

will enhance your new experiences and your understanding of psychic symbols. Once you've done all the exercises, you'll be ready to manifest your true desires, and chapter 12 will teach you how simply you'll accomplish this.

You'll need a number of different journals or sections in a journal. Those of you more comfortable with technology may prefer to use your computer instead. Practice all the exercises and record your experiences. You may be amazed when you look back in your journal at all you've written. By recording everything it becomes easier to recognize synchronistic events, which are discussed in chapter 11.

Organized in a practical and uncomplicated way, each chapter contains a new or different method to look at symbols and how they are interspersed in our lives. You are afforded a unique opportunity to construct your own journal through the various exercises, including developing and creating a personal symbols reference section in chapter 9. There are chapters introducing intuitive awareness as a necessary partner to comprehending psychic symbols. Sometimes, in order to truly recognize psychic symbolism, one has to understand how one's senses see, hear, or feel the symbolic information as it comes through. You'll learn all about these "clair" senses in chapter 4.

Opening our metaphysical connection to the astral plane becomes easier when we understand how our physical bodies connect to our spiritual bodies. Chapter 6 shows us the role chakras and auras play in this development and how we can contribute to our own well-being. Chakras and auras often present through color, and chapter 5 describes the meanings within colors symbolism.

There is a basic symbols glossary you can use as a reference manual to help answer or interpret almost any symbol you can imagine. Looking up the meanings to symbols in this cipher dictionary is easy and can become a practical, everyday tool. Symbols received while sleeping will be easier to translate by using the methods and ideas set forth in chapter 10, entitled "Symbolic Dreams." You'll learn how to interpret these stories that enter your psyche on a nightly basis more easily and more accurately than you ever imagined. You'll come to realize that dreams are more prevalent and packed with more relevant information than you may have previously believed. Sometimes a dream is just our mind's way of working out the day's events, but often they are images and words from another plane of existence.

Passed down through centuries of art, culture, and divination, tarot cards hold many archetypal images. Once mystical and otherworldly, their meanings are now accessible to even the extreme novice. Using this book will familiarize you with the symbolic meanings on the tarot cards. You will find that every time you see a divination card, symbols will present themselves. While focusing on the information presented in the tarot card section, chapter 8, you will allow these new discoveries to become part of your life.

Symbols are around us every day, regardless of our religious, spiritual, and cultural beliefs. Chapter 7 teaches us that we have the capacity to be both devout as well as spiritual, and also shares the interpretive dualities many religious symbols hold. Once we realize we are encouraged to understand the intuitive impressions we are presented with, it becomes less challenging to open ourselves to everything God and the universe have to offer.

This gift of awareness comes with the understanding that you are opening your mind to the possibility that everyone is capable of interpreting and living through symbolic messages. These gifts come from a variety of sources, and in chapter 2 you'll explore where this symbolic information comes from. Whether you are a beginner or an expert you'll learn to interpret the differences between the symbols from angels, spirit guides, and deceased loved ones. Receiving their assistance allows us to discover who we are, and more importantly, who we are capable of being.

How will you know which method to use to tune in to your intuition? That's the easy part: whatever feels right! We are all predisposed to certain talents. Some of us grow up to become famous professional football players and some become concert violinists. Others, like me, experience the magic of channeling divine guidance and symbolic messages so we can connect and help others to interact with the other side. We all have natural intuition; reading these pages will teach you how to use it.

Overall, think of this book as a guide to communicating and comprehending life in a new symbolic way. Allow this information to help you manifest what you truly desire in life. You will never view these metaphysical pictograms in the same manner as before. Instead, by introducing yourself to the extensive information in this book you will be armed with a new understanding of the extraordinary meanings of everyday objects. This new awareness will expand your thoughts, ideas, and dreams for the rest of your existence.

1

Why Are Psychic Symbols Important?

Decoding the Language

Symbols are around us every day. They are present in dreams and when we're awake. They are the sometimes secret and sometimes widely acknowledged cryptograms that are interspersed throughout our lives whether we recognize them or not. We are all capable of receiving psychic information, but we need to comprehend it. Think of yourself as a turntable: you know, one of those old machines that played actual vinyl records. What would happen if the information being sent to you was streaming in through an incompatible USB computer cable? How could you possibly connect to the data, let alone interpret it? It's the same with psychic symbols. To understand information from the other side we need to have a universal language.

Take that one step further and add in the interdimensional concept. It's like trying to tune in to a radio station to hear the music without any static; but that station isn't just down the street, it's in a whole other plane of existence. In order to receive messages and accurately understand them we need to be on the same frequency.

It is in this same spirit or principle that we use intuitive symbols. With a comprehensive alphabet we are able to connect to our psychic ability. Using this alphabet we can tap into our extrasensory perception and tune in to our natural intuition. Language is a funny thing. You can create your own alphabet, but if no one else understands it, there is no point to having it. The very purpose of language is to be able to communicate with each other. This allows us to share our needs, our wants, and our demands—the stories of ourselves. It is because of this ability to communicate that we have civilization, a society of people sharing commonalities.

"The limits of my language means the limits of my world," wrote Ludwig Wittgenstein, the Austrian philosopher who understood that without communication he would be alone amidst a pool of confusion. With no cohesive transfer of ideas, progress would be severely hindered. The same is true with psychic language. There has to be a key to decode the messages from the other side. If we have no way to conceptualize thought, how can we interpret the information we are being given psychically? We use symbols as a way to express ideas or thoughts, physically or metaphysically. This organization of shapes, sounds, colors, tastes, and images forms what we know to be a highly developed yet simple collection of psychic symbols. With these symbols we can open up our extrasensory perception, or ESP, to communicate with the other side. We can receive assistance from spirit guides, angels, and deceased loved ones. By becoming aware that this help is available we can live a much fuller and more informed existence.

Sometimes a Coffee Pot Really Is Just a Coffee Pot

You will see hundreds of symbols every day without even realizing it. Think about your journey through life and what you do on a regular basis. You wake up, and perhaps think about that morning cup of java that you so desperately crave to get those bones up and out of bed. What picture springs to mind when you imagine that magnificent elixir: Is it a steaming mug? Perhaps a bag of coffee beans? Maybe a coffee pot? Or possibly you smell the coffee, a rich aromatic scent wafting through your senses even though the pot is not yet brewing. Maybe you taste the coffee, your special brew of dark roast mixed with a bit of cinnamon and nutmeg.

That first inkling of recognition of the drink you so desperately crave is your symbol for coffee. This is not because you've just discovered it while reading this book, but because it has always been there. This may be a universal symbol, or it may be yours and yours alone.

The coffee pot is a real-life item. So, you may be thinking, "Okay, but that's not a psychic symbol," and you're right, in a way; sometimes a coffee pot is just a coffee pot. The important thing to understand here is the sky doesn't have to open to recognize a symbol. The simplest everyday objects can be part of your indispensable spirit communication language. In order for you to understand your psychic messages, you have to recognize the many symbols being presented to you. These paranormal images are only good if you are able to make them out so they are offered in a way you can identify.

Carl Jung, the noted Swiss psychiatrist and founder of analytical psychology, talked about what he coined the "collective unconscious," where primitive images and memories are stored. He believed all humans shared in this pool of knowledge. He concluded that through these primordial images and memories everyone can access this universal or common warehouse of information by tapping into the unconscious.

As Jung put it in his book *Man and His Symbols*: "But symbols, I must point out, do not occur solely in dreams. They appear in all kinds of psychic manifestations. There are symbolic thoughts and feelings, symbolic acts and situations."

One of the first times that symbols became significant to me was when I was doing a psychic reading for a woman named Jen, who asked me whether or not she was going to stay with her husband. I immediately saw a house built into the side of a cliff, but not just any cliff. It was a red-rock cliff, like in Arizona. I could see this house clear as day as if it were a photograph. But it wasn't something I saw *outside* my mind or physical body; it was in my mind's eye, *inside* my head like a thought, as if I were imagining it. The structure was modest: a single-story ranch house with a great big porch running the entire length of the front as if it were shooting out of the landscape. It was almost the same color as the red rocks, with a darker metal roof. On the front porch were two rocking chairs. Although I couldn't see anyone in the chairs, I could tell they were rocking.

Of course I asked Jen whether they had a house in Arizona or had plans to move there. She looked at me like I had two heads. She had no idea what I had just seen in my mind, so I explained it to her, thinking maybe it was a vacation spot or something they hadn't yet considered.

"No, absolutely not," she said emphatically. "Can you please just answer the question? Am I going to be with my husband or not?" she demanded.

Well, okay then, I thought. I tuned in and saw the house again, and this time the rocking chairs were a little more pronounced. Then it hit me.

"Aha! You are going to be together." I understood. I explained to her that apparently this was my new symbol for a couple that would be together. She didn't really care much about my new psychic reference, but she was happy to hear about her marriage. I realize now that every time I see the rockers rockin', the relationship will carry on.

Some years ago I was chosen to be a VIP reader at an event in New York City what was billed as "the largest gathering of psychics ever." This event, called *Psych-Out*, was put together by the *Psychic Detectives* television show on the Court TV channel. There were over a hundred psychics there, raising the energy of the entire exhibition hall. I discovered a lot about symbols that day.

I did a quick reading for one of the producers of the show, a young woman who lived with her boyfriend at the time. After seeing in my mind what we concluded was her apartment, she became comfortable enough to ask me about her relationship. She stated that she and her boyfriend were having a difference of opinion about something they were unsure they would be able to overcome.

Right away I saw eggs in my mind's eye: regular white eggs, dropping one by one to the floor, and breaking apart as they hit. I described the gooey mess and asked, "Were you discussing this in your tiny galley kitchen? I see them falling on the floor."

She replied, "Yes, but we weren't eating eggs ..."

"Okay, do you normally have eggs? Are you or your boyfriend expert omelet makers? Do you have allergies to eggs? Do you at least like eggs?" I asked laughing, not yet understanding what I was seeing.

"No ... I'm sorry, I don't know what you're talking about. Neither of us have any allergies that I know of ..."

"All right, but I keep seeing it. It's not going away. This means it's significant in some way," and then, like the rocking chairs, it clicked. It was not white chicken eggs falling. It was so much more than that.

"Are the eggs symbolic in some way? They are dropping and breaking steadily: drop, drop, drop, over and over again."

"Oh, wow! The discussion we had was about having children. I told him I was getting nervous that we were waiting too long to have kids and my eggs were dropping and going to waste," she exclaimed.

"Well, I see you utilizing those eggs, and soon!" I told her and we laughed for a good ten minutes.

Many times people will see very distinct or easy-to-reference symbols like birthday cakes for birthdays or wedding rings for marriages or infants for a new baby. Symbols will not always carry the same meaning for other people. Essentially, everyone is unique, so their references for things may be different. Sometimes eggs are simply eggs.

Discovering the language of symbolic messages will open you up to a new dimension of reality. "Like everything metaphysical, the harmony between thought and reality is to be found in the grammar of the language," as Ludwig Wittgenstein put it. Whether you've decided to pursue offering readings to others or you're just attempting to understand your own inherent abilities, you may discover intuitive occurrences have already happened in your life. By the end of this book you will know without a doubt exactly how to translate your psychic symbols.

Exercise: What This All Means To You!

Give yourself about a page in your journal for each of the topics that follow. Be sure to write down only the thoughts that are initially invoked with each heading. Don't try and rationalize or overthink it. This will help you record what's truly meaningful.

Turn to the first page. At the top of the page, write the word *Intuition*. Then, write whatever thoughts come to you about intuition. Include your beliefs, your doubts, and any flashes of intuition you may have experienced. Also, record any psychic readings you may have had that were significant.

On a fresh page write down *Symbols*, and use this space to list anything you think of when you hear the words *symbol* or *symbolism*. It is not necessary to know the exact definition right now; just record what it means to you in this moment. Be sure to include any times of symbolic importance in your life.

Next, on a clean page, write the word *Psychic*. What does this word mean to you? Write down any feelings you may have about the word *psychic*. Is the word alone evoking any deep-seated beliefs either for or against this term? Record any psychic events or memories you have.

After you are done with that, on a new sheet write the words *God*, *Religion*, and *Afterlife*. If you find you want to separate these words onto different pages, by all means do. These opinions can be life-altering. Be sure to give yourself enough space to do them justice.

Finally, start a fresh page with the words *What I Do!* and begin writing what it is you do in this existence at this current phase of your life. You can possibly include here your work or your career. Also, if you're like me, a huge part of what you do may include parenting and taking care of family. Include also what you do for fun. What do you enjoy?

If you've been honest in your writing you may find some interesting themes throughout your new journal pages. You may even have experienced a new understanding of or appreciation for your beliefs or the things you do.

Take a minute to revel in your values, in your principles. They are your thoughts; be proud of who you are. You've just taken your first step of many toward living symbolically.

2
Where Symbolic Messages Come From

Rudolf Steiner writes of guardian angels and spirits in his book *Guardian Angels: Connecting with Our Spiritual Guides and Helpers*: "Their existence is a spiritual and scientific fact which can be fruitfully researched and studied through clairvoyant means. Furthermore, working consciously with these entities can assist each of us in fulfilling our evolutionary goals."

As Steiner suggests, we have a plethora of angels, ascended masters, spirit guides, and deceased loved ones to assist us symbolically on a daily basis, all of whom are important facets of the spirit world. While each category of helpers is fully capable and available to support us, there is an order to the symbolic information we receive. Deceased relatives share many personal messages with us, while spirit guides help direct us in life, and angels tend to be around for life lessons and emergencies. Ascended masters work in the background, helping guide us gently toward enlightenment.

All of the messengers have one thing in common: they are operating out of pure unconditional love. It is this love that we feel when we are making the right decisions, and this love that we experience when we ask for help. This universal love comes from God, the divine, the other side. God, or whatever name you use to identify God, is the universal light, the pure love, the essence of all there is and all there will ever be, and this energy is being shared with us. This divine energy is what drives all of the communication from angels, guides, deceased loved ones, and ascended masters toward us. Their job is to help us become beings of love ourselves and be present to facilitate our journey through life by sending us assistance through symbolic messages.

Those messages are usually sent as intuitive impressions. If you have ever seen a medium perform, you may recall they often pause for a moment before speaking or take a break between sentences. This is so they can understand whatever messages they are getting. Often it is to sort out the images they are seeing in their third eye or psychic eye or to hear the messages metaphysically. Receiving psychic messages from the other side is not like opening a newspaper and reading the headlines. Almost always the information is vague and needs to be interpreted.

When you go to a gallery event where a medium is "on stage" in front of anywhere between five to thousands of people, they do their readings for the lucky few because they are guided or directed to. They are like radios picking up sound waves from the other side. Frequently these messages are sent from deceased loved ones; this is who the audience is there to connect with. These relatives, alive and well on this other metaphysical plane of existence, show up to comfort the living, the people who are there hoping to receive a message.

Sometimes the messages are trivial yet helpful, as was the case when we were visiting my mother in the hospital before she died. We were looking for a parking space in a full parking garage.

"Mommy, not here, go around!" yelled my daughter Molly.

"But the parking garage is full, honey," I replied back.

"No, Mommy, I just asked Mima and she told me to keep going. Around the next corner there is someone pulling out!" she insisted. Mima was her paternal grandmother who had passed a few years earlier.

"All right, let's try it," I told her as I continued to drive to the next level.

And then I saw it, exactly what she was talking about. There was a car backing out of the perfect parking spot, directly across from the elevator. This was perfect, except, wait ... there was a car in front of me waiting to pull in.

Darn, she was doing pretty well, I thought about Molly connecting to Mima.

"Oh well, Molly Bug, next time you'll have to tell her to bring you to the space where someone else isn't going to pull in first," I joked with her.

"Just WAIT!" she told me impatiently.

"All right, Bug, but that car is ..." I began.

"That car is what?" she asked.

"That car is driving right past the spot," I replied with my jaw on the floor as the car in front of us continued exiting down the parking garage.

"I told you, Mommy. Mima never lies," she said with a smile, and all was right with the universe again.

Deceased Loved Ones

As Molly proved, dead relatives are lining up to communicate with their loved ones, but it is very difficult for the medium or psychic to understand them. Their energetic frequency is much higher than human beings. The medium has to try and tune in to that channel to talk to the spirits. Remember the example of the turntable and the USB cable? It is a very fine energy wave that needs to be tuned in to in order to connect.

These deceased family members are here for a reason, though, so they are going to keep trying to get through to us. Whether it's a professional medium or a regular everyday person, the dead relation is going to use whatever means necessary to communicate so they usually employ the use of symbols. They may send a birthday cake to let you know they are acknowledging or sending happy birthday wishes. Or, they may send roses to let you know they love and care for you.

Reaching out to their living families and friends, deceased loved ones are key transmitters of psychic symbols and are an important line of communication in the paranormal infrastructure. The information they send us may not be earth-shattering, but to a child missing his or her mom it can mean the world! After all, everything's relative (pun intended).

Friends and family members share our lives with us. They are there to experience monumental moments as well as daily events. They are the people we tell our secrets to and the people we go to for advice. When we lose a job, they are there to hold our hands and comfort us. When we get a new boyfriend or girlfriend, they jump up and down with us, giggling with excitement as they teach us how to drape our arm over our date's shoulders using the secret yawn. And when that relationship ends, they stay up all night, commiserating with us with damp tissues and a pint or two of Ben & Jerry's Chunky Monkey, or they take us out to the batting cages to console us with the crack of a ball hitting wood. They are the people we are closest to, with whom we can be ourselves and to whom we can expose our real personality.

Just as was the case when they were here on earth with us, friends and family are there on the other side to help us work through or celebrate events. We receive similar advice from them as we asked for or were given when they were alive.

Occasionally, these deceased loved ones are sending apologies or messages of love because they've done something in life that was less than acceptable or they know they've hurt someone and never had a chance to rectify the situation while they were physically present in body as well as spirit. They may simply want us to know they see us grieving and are sorry to have caused us pain.

Victims of foul play may also come through to assist in the arrest or capture of their tormentors or even murderers. When a passing is quick or unexpected, especially because of an egregious act of violence, the soul of the deceased may not even understand they are gone or comprehend they are no longer present, and they appear to us because they are confused. They may also need to use us as a conduit to bring their attacker to justice.

The spiritual plane is filled with all of our old loved ones, ready and willing to help us the same way they used to, just from a different place. When we receive symbolic messages regarding everyday occurrences or special occasions, they are the senders of those communications. They are the metaphysical helpers we are interacting with.

Angels

Unlike our relatives on the other side, angels have never walked the earth in a physical body. They exist purely in a metaphysical plane to help us with every area of our lives. They are a direct line of assistance from God. When you receive messages from angels you'll know; they leave behind energy of pure love. Angels show up in time to save you from something or someone and disappear just as fast. These beautiful creatures from God will not speak to you out loud, nor will they usually send you images. They instead will act swiftly to alert you to potential danger or protect you from harm. Despite the fact that they don't use human voices, they are able to communicate telepathically, although most accounts of angelic encounters are silent.

Most often, with angels, you will receive psychic guidance to keep you on your life plan, or life itinerary. They will gently lead you, or if the case merits, forcefully, physically, or spiritually maneuver you toward your life goals. An angelic presence may pull you to safety after a dangerous accident. You were not supposed to leave your earthly body yet, and this is their way to keep you in alignment. Angels may come to you as you are driving, to steer you in a new direction, possibly showing up in human form with stunning and even glowing skin. As Sylvia Browne puts it in her book *Phenomenon: Everything You Need to Know about the Paranormal*: "Angels are quite literally illuminated from within by the loving, sacred, perfect light of their Creator, which is their essence."

If you psychically see a shimmering form, pay attention to this symbol; it is there to help you. If you see a symbolic angel, it may be a warning of danger ahead or, alternately, overwhelming love and support. Consider any other symbols you may receive with the angel to help you determine the meaning.

Ascended Masters

Ascended masters are enlightened beings who have worked endlessly throughout history, with no personal ego or individual agenda, to help humanity. Ascended or ascending to the highest levels of spiritual awareness are miracle workers such as Jesus, Mother Mary, Siddhartha Buddha, Kwan Yin, etc. These incredible souls were once people who lived on earth but are held in the highest regard as having attained all of the answers to life's lessons. They are revered for their spiritual wisdom and knowledge.

Many of these masters are hailed in the Buddhist religion as *Bodhisattvas*. As one definition phrases it, a Bodhisattva is "a soul who, through compassion and altruism, has earned the right to leave this world of suffering and enter Nirvana, but has chosen instead to stay on Earth to instruct others until all beings are enlightened." (This definition is from a woman named Sucheta, on her webpage "About Kwan Yin.")

Although they have died physically, there is no definitive answer as to whether ascended masters reincarnate. Most believe masters are in service to all of humanity from the other side. Their main line of assistance is to bring spiritual awareness, peace, and enlightenment to the human race. It is quite normal to feel their love when channeling symbols that have to do with reaching higher states of consciousness, although it is common to confuse them with angels and other spirit guides.

These enlightened souls had a purpose while living and they continue that purpose upon dying. They are available to help us, and though they are revered as incredible beings, their path is plain and simple. Their desire is to open us up to love and the very essence of love and all love has to offer, because it is through that love we will become spiritual and enlightened beings.

People who receive wisdom or act as a conduit to share the knowledge of the ascended masters will experience a feeling of illumination, almost an ethereal feeling of being out of their bodies. This is because the energy is so incredibly buoyant and light that it's as if the person channeling is being fully supported and gently lifted while graced with their presence. Ascended masters are part of a very high frequency. I find I personally don't often act as a medium for their specific messages; instead, I am more in tune with the more grounded energies like guides and deceased loved ones.

Spirit Guides

Spirit guides have, at one time, lived a human existence, though they have been part of the other side for many generations. Rather than reincarnate, they remain there by choice—learning and gaining as much wisdom as they possibly can in order to better aid us. Sonia Choquette, an amazing psychic, author, and teacher, communicates this to us in her book *Ask Your Guides: Connecting to Your Divine Support System*: "…While angels have never had an earthbound experience, most spirit guides have had at least one, so they understand firsthand the particular trials and challenges that we face as humans."

As Sonia suggests, spirit guides help with practical matters and angels handle the big dilemmas. Just like our friends and relatives from the other side, spirit guides use symbols to communicate with us. Symbolism is the easiest form of communication to transcend the distance between this world and the paranormal world.

Many people wonder whether their spirit guide is their dead mother or father or best friend. Spirit guides are generally around for a long time on the other side, building up wisdom and knowledge to help you through your current lifetime or many lifetimes. One's parents are usually alive when one is born, when one comes into this world, so they normally would not be your spirit guides.

Your mother or father can help you when they cross over, but you really want to stick to asking them for help with what they know best. For example, I would never ask my mom for help with my finances, as she lived in financial crisis her whole adult life. I might instead ask her for the gift of money because she was very generous, always helping others if she could. I might also ask her for direction if one of my children were complaining about not feeling well or having aches and pains, because she spent over forty-five years as a very well-respected critical care nurse.

Using our ESP, or extrasensory perception, we are able to understand their messages, provided we recognize them as representations. Like the birthday cake example, there are many common images, almost like a shared language among the many entities from the other side. Spirit guides use these images to assist us with just about anything we need. "The purpose of spirit communication is to help us rediscover the wonder, the awe, and the power that is available within our life," Ted Andrews writes in his book *How to Meet & Work with Spirit Guides*. As Mr. Andrews states, they are trying to help by directing us so we may live a more fulfilling and loving existence.

Messages from the other side are available to us daily; we just have to speak the symbolic language. It is inevitable that you will receive support from your helpers many times throughout your life. The hardest part isn't getting that help; it is simply accepting they are helping you.

We receive information from all of the types of messengers on the other side, each at various times. We may develop more of a rapport with one sort of communicator over the other, but we are still available to interact with the others. This can feel challenging at times because the transmission of symbolic messages originates from different sources and is therefore sent in a variety of ways. But being open to the myriad of symbolic images, no matter how or from whom they've developed, is what allows us to communicate.

When I am getting ready to do a reading for someone, I ask the universe for all positive energies to come through to help me bring messages to my client in a clear and concise way that my client will understand. I also assert I will not allow anything negative to be sent to me or my client unless it's something that will help them in the future or assist them in moving beyond or letting go of something in their past. In order for this to work, I not only talk to dead people, but I also have to pay attention to any of the spirit guides who may come through. Often I'll feel a sense of love around the person and know they are protected by angels.

As a practicing psychic I receive questions all the time. Commonly, I'm asked, "Who are my guides? How do I know their names? Do they have anything for me? What do they want to give me?" The exercises that follow will help you discover the answers to those questions and teach you how to use energy to protect yourself from any negativity that might otherwise be present.

Exercise: Connecting to Your Guides for Symbolic Messages

Open to a clean page in your journal and write in big letters the word *Guides*.

One of the most important steps to spirit communication of any kind is to protect yourself energetically before you begin.

Bring your journal to a quiet location. It can be somewhere in your house or your yard or even out at a park. Just go and be somewhere that is peaceful to you. Get comfortable. Sit or lie down; make sure you are free from restrictive clothing or anything that will prevent you from breathing deeply. Close your eyes.

Begin taking deep breaths, in through your nose and out through your mouth. Observe how your belly area goes up and down when you are inhaling and exhaling. Pay attention to your breath: in and out, in and out.

Now, imagine a beautiful white light all around you, surrounding you like a bubble. Imagine feeling the brightness of this light on your face, warming your skin like the sun.

Slowly reach out your hands, fingers pointed up, palms directed away from you, and see yourself pushing this bubble of white protective light further and further out. Expand your circle of protection until you are comfortably surrounded, with enough space to move around inside of the protection but far enough away that you feel secure that no one is going to get too close to you. Let your hands rest back down again, keeping the bubble of light surrounding you.

Now, notice how your body feels; pay attention to the way it feels lighter and more relaxed than before.

Imagine being at the beach, on the warm golden sand. Feel the warmth of the sun on your skin. Feel the soft, powdery sand beneath your toes. Listen to the gentle waves lapping at the shoreline and hear the birds as they sing overhead.

There is a beautiful, gentle, calming presence coming closer and closer, and with every step the presence takes toward you, feel yourself becoming lighter and more at ease.

This is one or more of your spirit guides. Let them come into full view. You can see what they look like. You see what color hair they have if any. Notice what their clothing looks like or any jewelry they may be wearing. Look at the color of their eyes and their skin.

When you are comfortable, ask them, in your mind, what their name is and wait for their response. If you don't understand your guide, or if they were too quiet, ask them to speak more clearly and loudly so that you can hear them. Give yourself a good minute or two and listen in your relaxed state for their answer. If you still don't hear their response, ask them to write their name for you in the sand so you can read it.

Feel yourself there, in the sand, with your guide. Imagine that your guide has a gift for you. It may be wrapped up neatly in a box, or unwrapped; it may be small or even large. Open your hands and arms and accept this gift. Thank your guide.

Look and see what your guide has given you. Is it something tangible that you can hold? Is it symbolic? Or is it something figurative; did they give you information or direction about something in your life? Ponder this gift and what it could mean. It may be something as simple as a pen or as complicated as the name or description of your next romantic partner.

Notice what the gift looks like, what it sounds like. Experience how the gift feels, if you can hold it in your hands or physically touch it. Make mental notes about every part of your gift. If you still don't understand the gift, ask your guides to explain it to you. Once again, thank your guides for what they have given you.

Next, while in this relaxed state, ask your guides for their assistance. Use this connection to request their help for something you are struggling with in your life or something you want in your life. Let them know that you appreciate any guidance or direction they may give you or any help they can share with you now. Ask them for support in the next few days or even weeks.

Again, say thank you for coming to you and making their presence known.

When you are ready, take a deep breath and open your eyes. Know that you can repeat this exercise often, but don't do it constantly. Part of what makes us human is being present and grounded in our physical selves.

Write down anything that you received: your guide's name, appearance, and the gift or gifts they have presented you with. Take a moment to note what your gift was, and what it meant to you. It may have more than one meaning or make you think of multiple things. Be sure to write down any feelings the gift evokes. Also, record any requests for help.

Jot down any images or thoughts that appeared symbolically to you—possibly that you didn't realize were symbols until now. List any words you associated with these images during your meditation. Include any additional thoughts or meanings that come to mind now. Be sure to include both old and new translations for whatever symbols you were experiencing.

You can refer back to this exercise whenever you need direction or help to assist you in calling forth your guides. You may notice that different and additional guides show up to support you.

3

Understanding and Applying Your Intuition and Symbolic Messages

Intuition

Everyone is born with natural intuition, the capacity to tune in to higher energetic vibrations from the other side. This sixth sense is part of our birthright as human beings. We are created to be intuitive and to be open and fully capable of receiving those little intuitive nudges. Just as not everyone who plays baseball will end up playing for the New York Yankees, not everyone is meant to be a professional psychic. While some need to interpret symbols for themselves, others are intended to excel and develop their talents and become channels for others who aren't. Having this incredible gift of receiving intuitive symbols should never be taken for granted or allowed to be ego-based. When this happens, we shut out the love we need from the divine and instead tune in to the negative energies. Influence from these lower vibrational energies will cause us to be blinded to the truth of the divine essence; we will be shadowed by energy that works to hinder or even harm us and those around us.

Being able to access symbolic communication comes with the responsibility of understanding that we are all connected, we are all one; there are no spiritual boundaries. It is this belief that affords us the opportunity to be present for others, and relate to others on the same level. Negativity can create an illusion that we should be on a pedestal above everyone else because we have the ability to predict the future or know the outcome of events. This is a false illusion, and the clarity of our psychic impressions will undoubtedly become increasingly less accurate as we ascribe to this notion. When intuitive messages are translated out of or from our ego, it can cause confusion and inaccuracy. Coming back to the essence of pure unconditional love, the divine, free-from-ego-based beliefs will ground us and allow us to be honest and precise with the messages we receive.

You may not be psychic or want to offer professional psychic readings. More often than not, you are interested in learning more about intuition because you want to understand how to recognize and utilize symbolic information you receive. It doesn't matter whether the symbols are of a significant or trivial nature; either way, they are important. Otherwise, these messages wouldn't be sent to you.

Accepting and Applying Symbols

What should we do with these symbols? That's easy. Whatever you want! You are a being with free will. Free will helps propel you along your path by making choices. It is up to you whether you want to act on whatever impressions your guides and helpers send to you or whether you wish to ignore them. Sometimes, you may not even recognize that you are acting on them. But if you consider how you're making choices in your day-to-day life, you will easily acknowledge you are listening to some form of inner guidance system, otherwise known as intuition. Accepting your intuition does not force you to give up your right to have freedom to choose; rather, it helps you make more informed decisions. At the same time, recognizing you are capable of symbolic communication does not entitle you to more assistance or intuitive gifts than anyone else. It merely gives you a great opportunity to utilize those gifts to their fullest potential.

Every day we have to make choices about which direction to go in our lives or which path to take. When we are hungry we need to decide if we are going to make something to eat or go out to a restaurant for dinner. If we see in our imagination or our mind's eye the golden arches of McDonald's, it may be a symbolic clue to go out. But if we see our dining room table laden with dishes of food, we can assume we are better off sharing the meal with our family at home. The reasons are not always clear and may not even be important. Occasionally, the messages are imperative, however. For instance, you may get the symbol to stay home (the family meal at the dining room table), because perhaps if you were to go out you would get food poisoning or even get into a car accident on the way home. Or, less critically, it may simply be that during dinner preparations you'll strengthen the bond you share with your children. While we don't always know why we get the messages, we can be sure of one thing: they are always there.

The movie *The Adjustment Bureau*, which stars Matt Damon, gives us an interesting perspective on choice. Its premise is that "The Chairman," assumed to be God, controls our life plan, and if we deviate from that plan the world is suspended until the beings, or "caseworkers," who work for The Chairman can make adjustments to correct the path we've chosen. In other words, in the movie, everything is predestined. In real life, fate is real but destiny has many outcomes. Simply put, we have the ability to mold our destiny. Certain points in our lives are fated, but it is up to us how we get there. We need to choose which direction to take to lead us to any predetermined parts of our lives, including our final human act of dying. By paying attention to the symbolic impressions we receive, we are able to make informed choices or decisions based on what will produce the best outcome or the greatest result.

When I was looking for a new house with my family I picked up numerous symbolic messages. I saw the color brown and I heard the word *Mountain*. I smelled the woods and I felt secure and private. We looked at many houses and even went so far as to put in offers on two of them. They all fit the descriptions: brown, on a mountain or had Mountain in the street name, and backed up to the woods, which created privacy.

The only difference was these first two felt off. They were beautiful houses on gorgeous wooded property, but they made me feel psychically ill. This was a clairsentient symbol that something was wrong. I was symbolically being warned these would not be the right homes for our family.

The last house, the smaller and oldest of the three, felt comfortable like a warm blanket. This was the right home for us; I symbolically felt the blanket wrapping around me. My husband, while a little bummed out that I didn't feel right in the larger and newer houses, understood how important it was to listen psychically to my senses, and he agrees we picked the right place. I appreciate even more that we listened to my intuition, as the worsening economy has hit us hard and the larger homes would have also carried a much larger mortgage. By paying attention to all of my clear senses I was able to understand the symbolic messages I was getting with absolute clarity, and I am convinced that the other houses, while beautiful and enticing on the outside, would not have worked for us and may even have caused us grief. By just listening to my inner guidance system I was able to apply the symbolic communications I was given, and it helped us avoid what could have been a disastrous situation.

Occasionally, we are given symbolic messages as a warning. Imagine hearing the song "Dirty Diana" by Michael Jackson playing over and over in your head. Perhaps this symbolic communication is a warning for you to pass by Diana, a woman you will meet later, because a relationship with this person would be emotionally toxic. Alternatively, if you also hear "Jack & Diane" by John Cougar Mellencamp, it may be a symbolic message just to let you know you will meet someone named Diane or Diana who will be the love of your life. (Pay special attention if your name happens to be Jack!) It's always important to check in with all of your senses when you need clarification. Remember that you can always ask for another symbol to help you determine what the message is. In this example, you could check in to see how your body "feels" about the song you were hearing. Does it feel happy? Icky? Worried? Gross? Loving? Knowing how the symbol you are getting makes you feel intuitively will help you interpret how to use the messages you are receiving. (See also chapter 4, "How We Receive Symbols.")

Many people tap into or use their intuitive abilities without even realizing it, transcending the barriers of a perceived physical reality. By utilizing all of our senses we are creating a power that exceeds the mundane; it opens us to endless possibilities. By integrating with our spiritual or metaphysical selves we are able to recognize opportunities in a different and more fulfilling way. Often, we increase the frequency of receiving symbolic messages when we begin paying attention to the communications we are getting, adding to the unlimited benefits of tuning in to our psychic awareness. Thus, we are able to understand with greater clarity the psychic symbols we are being given.

Not everyone wants to be a conduit to the other side or is interested in facilitating a connection with the spiritual world for others. Going down this road can feel especially difficult when you are surrounded by people who don't believe in psychic ability or symbolic communication. It is quite common to find yourself trapped somewhere between wanting to believe in the symbolic language and thereby increase your psychic sensitivity and wanting to remove from your mind the images you clairvoyantly or psychically see. This is okay! Not everyone is ready to accept their gifts or to readily acknowledge, especially to other people, that they even have any intuitive gifts. However, being talented in this way enables us to be available physically and mentally to so much more in our community.

The symbolic journey is one that is ever-changing. True comprehension evolves through conscious and unconscious understanding, and as we allow this evolution to occur, our life progresses. We all have the intellectual capacity to understand psychic symbolism, but it is through curiosity or necessity that most of us turn to it as a source of help and illumination. This is easy when we are surrounded by people who are in synch with what we believe in. When we are able to share our symbolic curiosity with others who are like-minded, we are more comfortable disclosing our opinions.

A change in our belief system regarding intuition changes our perspective. Change causes disruption, which can internalize itself as fear.

When we are fearful of seeming different or we are afraid to stand out, our intellect or convictions can get lost behind timidity. Giving up this opportunity of becoming symbolically aware feels like the easy road, and while there is nothing wrong with wanting to play it safe, it does not help us to advance toward our highest potential of becoming the spiritual beings we were created to be. The path of least resistance is actually the spiritual path of symbolic wisdom and knowledge. Imagine intuitive energy as a river. This river flows through us and around us. When we try paddling against the current or in the rapids, it is very difficult. Paddling with the current, on the other hand, is easier, as the energy of the river actually helps propel us to the next peaceful resting place or stop along our journey. (See also chapter 6, "Chakra and Aura Symbolism.")

Intuitive development can be challenging in a town filled with minivans and soccer coaches; receiving symbolic messages can seem too far out of the box. There is sometimes a sense that the status quo or fitting in means conforming. I live in a small town that I love because people are very kind and there is a sense of community; everyone knows everyone else and my kids are safe and happy. While there are many different personalities and belief systems in this area, and some openly admit to believing in psychic ability, the majority of the community is religious rather than spiritual and is content in not rocking the boat. What I do as a professional psychic tends to create some disturbance in the water and cause waves, though I am generally accepted because everything else about me is pretty "normal" and thus the boat stays afloat.

What I've found somewhat comforting and at the same time perplexing is that most people, when introduced to what I do, will shy away at first. Then, after pondering, they will share with me an experience they had that piqued their intuitive curiosity. I can usually tell whether the person is attuned to their symbolic impressions or closed off to them almost immediately, though I don't try and persuade them either way. Staying objective instead of subjective allows me to remain balanced. Not everyone is ready to have their familiarity challenged by introducing the concept of innate intuition. I find that most people, after taking a moment to think about it, are generally interested in understanding symbolic communications, even if they're not ready to be public about their curiosity or their own natural aptitude. It's exciting for me to be present when they are ready to help me guide them toward their own personal awareness. We are like diamonds in the rough; we're made up of many different facets, including intuition.

About eight years ago I had someone named Annie try and persuade me to join her church. I politely thanked her repeatedly and agreed that while I wholeheartedly believed in God or a universal energy, I didn't feel I needed to attend organized services to pray. I did, however, encourage her to follow her own heart, and if going to this particular church made her happy, then by all means she should continue. When Annie persisted I went on to share with her my work and what I did believe, knowing full well she was not open to the spiritual conditions and methods (psychic abilities) I used to commune with God. As I intuited, she wasn't, and she ended the conversation.

Many years later, I saw Annie at the grocery store. This time, she conveyed her appreciation of the work I do, and congratulated me on my upcoming book. She told me she had recently lost her father and had been receiving symbolic impressions of his love and signs of his presence both intuitively and physically. She smelled him, and felt him around her. Her father also showed her he was there by sending her symbolic images of musical notes; a love of music was something they shared while he was alive. While insisting that she still went to and believed in her church, she asked if she could talk to me about her intuitive experiences sometime. I assured Annie my door was always open.

Annie wasn't originally open to the possibility of symbolic messages. She didn't believe that someone who talked to the other side or communicated using intuition was accessing something positive, pure, or holy. She worried that by playing with what she decided was hell's fiery lies she would get burned. Annie truly believed all psychic connections were the devil's work because that's what she was taught.

Luckily, the same person who introduced Annie to her loving church was now able to introduce her to the extraordinary channels of intuitive communication. Though still somewhat fearful, she is now able to look beyond and release the preconceived notions she once held. Annie can focus less on the destination stemming from psychic awareness and more on the journey she will travel.

Remaining open to psychic potential and symbolic messages helps us physically as well. Frequently when we are closed off to something, whether it is of a spiritual sense or not, we become unbalanced. This imbalance can manifest into disease or dis-ease in our bodies. When we deny our visions by shutting out the psychic images we see, we can create or manifest headaches or sinus infections. This is because we are disrupting the energy flow. When we try and ignore the gut instincts we have or the psychic feelings we get, we may experience weight gain, thus creating a physical barrier around our intuitive energy from the outside world. Though not always the case, many common diseases, mild and critical, including arthritis, fibromyalgia, irritable bowel syndrome, and even forms of cancer can stem from a breaking down of psychic energy within the psychical body. Often, these conditions can be alleviated and even cured with natural energetic and homeopathic remedies. At the very least, allowing symbolic communication clears the energetic channels and encourages rather than obstructs healing energy to flow along its natural pathway throughout the spiritual and physical form.

Preventing symbolic communication from helping you in life only hinders your natural evolutionary process; it impedes your ability to be everything you can possibly be. By listening and being mindful to the messages you receive, whether purposely or unintentionally, you increase your chances of becoming a more tolerant, knowledgeable, comfortable, and compassionate human being. Chances are you will even accept, appreciate, and like yourself more.

Not everyone wants to be psychic or exist purely through intuitive thought. You can, however, live a spiritual life without having to fully integrate psychic symbols as part of your focused daily routine. If you are concerned about what others may think, don't worry; you can be as private or as public as you'd like. Take a few minutes, as often as you want, to just sit and relax. Allow yourself to quiet down, internally as well as externally. I'm not saying you have to go into full "Om" mode.

Just take a couple of deep breaths and let yourself be open to hearing, seeing, and feeling. Your guides and helpers from the other side will send you symbolic impressions when you are ready. The more you open up, the more often you will receive these messages.

One of the most common and ordinary symbolic communications involves phone calls. When you think of someone it may be a symbolic message to get in touch with them. It can also be a message that they are trying to call you. If the phone rings, and you answer it and the same person you were thinking of is on the other end, know that it was your intuition alerting you that the person is thinking about you. It doesn't necessarily mean there is anything wrong or that they need anything from you—it can just be that they have sent out their energy to you and you felt it, intuitively.

Allowing yourself the mental space for symbolic impressions can assist you in sorting out your life in so many ways. If you are a youth coach (like me!), you might find you regularly receive intuitive information that can help you teach the children better. You may channel directions without even realizing it. Open yourself to that possibility. If you have a birthday coming up for a special someone, you may have a nagging idea that you need to get them a special present; pay attention to that thought. It is a symbolic message that you really shouldn't ignore! If you are at the store and you psychically see a glue bottle but can't figure out why, buy it! You'll be happy you did when you walk through the door and your spouse says he (or she) wished he had gotten hold of you because he needed you to buy glue for the project he is working on. Take it from me: paying attention to these little impulsive symbolic urges just makes life a lot less frustrating.

Take advantage of the symbolic messages you get; use them. No matter which avenue of sensory input you are receiving them through, they will help you make choices in your life that will expand your awareness beyond what you may have once thought feasible. Practice being open to them and appreciating them. Congratulate yourself on being available to the infinite possibilities you will discover!

The following exercise will help you see how far you have come in the evolution of your intuitive belief system. By remembering where you began, you will most surely be surprised at how far you've come! Know this: wherever you currently are on your symbolic path, it's only the beginning. By being present, in the moment, you'll find you have many more symbolic opportunities to come.

Exercise: Defining Terms to Understand Your Past and Present

On a new page in your journal write the words, *The first time I ever heard of the word "psychic," I was...* and continue by filling in the rest of the sentence. Include whatever information you remember. Where were you? How old were you? What did you hear? What did you see? Did someone else tell you something? Did you see something on TV? Did you have a personal experience? Did you feel something? Be sure to include everything you can possibly remember.

Continue doing this, replacing the word *psychic* with *intuition* and then *symbols*. You may find they were all part of the same situation or they were different. Either way, expand with as much information as you can recall!

After you are done, write down, *Today, I believe "psychic" means...* Or, *Today, I know this about psychic awareness...* and complete the sentence, interchanging *psychic* with *intuition* and then *symbols*. How far have you come? Further than you previously thought?

When you are done with that exercise, it's time to just be— be present and allow yourself to be in the moment. Sit quietly and let yourself be open to any impressions you may receive. You may find you feel something around you or even in your physical body. You may hear sounds or words, or see images. Whatever you "get" is fine.

Record whatever information you can discern amidst the noise and chaos that is bound to be occurring in your mind, any thoughts or impressions that jump into your consciousness. Remember that it's all right to go over the grocery list or what you have to do at work later. It's part of your natural state. Say thank you to that information and let it pass. However, pay attention to the little things that aren't normally there, the random stimuli that are floating through. Chances are they won't yet be full-on psychic impressions; instead, they will be your conscious mind trying to sort through everyday practicalities. You may even see images of people who are unfamiliar to you. This may happen because you passed them during the day, last week, or even last year. That, too, is okay. Just relax and be.

When you are done, look back at the entries in your journal. Does anything jump out at you? Do you recognize anything as a pattern? If not, that's okay. If so, good for you!

Think about symbolic impressions you may have received in the past. Did you listen to them? Did you acknowledge them? Why or why not? If you didn't, do you think you would have been better off if you had? Why or why not? If you did, do you think things would have worked better if you ignored them?

4

How We Receive Symbols

"Clair what? Clair who? What is Clair?" are commonly asked questions. Most people have heard of clairvoyance, but there are many "clairs." We all experience some form of psychic sense, though the majority of us will not draw on them all daily. "Clairs" are the collection of psychic senses known as *clairvoyance* (clear seeing), *clairaudience* (clear hearing), *clairsentience* (clear feeling), *claircognizance* (clear knowing), *clairgustance* (clear tasting), and *clairalience* (clear smelling). We have borrowed *clair* from the French language, meaning "clear," and it is through these clear senses that we receive all psychic information.

Imagine these senses are multidimensional interpretive layers within us. Distinguishing between each layer is not necessary to receive intuitive messages, but recognizing we're getting the messages is easier when we understand how we're actually communicating.

"Seeing" Symbols: Clairvoyance

Clairvoyance is "clear seeing." Seeing flashes of colors or images is the most common way to experience visions in your "third eye," that extrasensory energy center in the middle of your forehead. Similar to photographs or more distinct movie-like visions, these images can be very basic or extremely detailed. Additionally, these mental pictures may appear in color or be black and white.

Take, for example, the story about the rocking chairs on the porch of the Arizona house. I was almost positive that I was looking at a real house; I saw all of the details. However, being open to the possibility that it was representative in some way led me to the deduction that it was symbolic. I now have it in my toolbox; I know it is a blanket symbol for that ever-present relationship question.

Clairvoyance is the most common way to receive psychic symbols. As indicated by the egg story from chapter 1, being open to different metaphysical interpretations or meanings is extremely important. I could have continued on in vain, ignoring that it was not a literal translation. If I had not been open to other explanations, I might have even mistakenly convinced that young woman she had an undiagnosed egg allergy.

When we see things clairvoyantly we may experience a full vision and know exactly what it is. More often than not, however, we'll experience a flash of color or a snapshot. When this happens it becomes even more crucial that we understand the meaning behind those colors or images.

Have you ever played the game "Memory"? It's a game that tests your visual awareness. You look at a bunch of objects, either illustrations or physically present, and then try and remember everything you saw. You don't have an awful lot of time to study the objects. Instead, you have to look quickly and try and remember everything in order to succeed in the game.

Like the memory game, with symbolic messages you may receive just that little flash—an image that appears in your mind only for a quick second. These flashes may occur at any time, during the day or at night. They may be full-color, semi-colored, or black and white. Sometimes the images you see won't be like photographs. They will be more like line drawings or stick drawings: two-dimensional, un-shaded objects rather than three-dimensional. Quite often you'll find this is how geometric shapes, Asian writing, and old-fashioned drawings of things like fleurs-de-lis appear. Usually, you'll receive a mix of images. The key to understanding all of these pictures, no matter how they are presented, is to interpret them clairvoyantly as psychic symbols.

I was having coffee with my friend Tricia one morning. "So, what do you think? Is it worth going on the callback audition? Do you think there is a chance she'll get the part?" she asked about her twelve-year-old actress daughter.

Now, usually I don't do off-the-cuff readings; you never know what's going to come up when you are in a casual setting. I could just be guessing rather than truly channeling information. But for this friend it seems to work best this way. We will be talking about something totally unrelated and she'll sneak in a question out of the blue.

"Hmmm. I don't know. I'm seeing an older building, not the type I'm used to in the city," I tell her.

"That's right. It's in Brooklyn this time. Not Manhattan, and it is in an older building," she answered.

I told her I got a good overall feeling from this and that I thought they were going to like her, but she wouldn't be right for this project. I went on to say it would be beneficial to go; she might end up meeting the actual producer or director.

"All right, I wasn't sure, but I guess we'll go. It's just going to be a quick run in, and then back home," Tricia acquiesced.

"Good, and by the way, what does *Sesame Street* have to do with it?" I asked her.

She looked at me and her eyes opened wide. "Oh, wow! When we were there for the initial interview, we were in the hallway and I noticed a *Sesame Street* poster. I asked the casting staff why the poster was there, and they said that *Sesame Street* used to tape there years ago! How did you get that?"

"I saw a flash of *Sesame Street*! I think that's validation that you should definitely go on the callback audition! I have a feeling it will lead to bigger and better things," I told her.

"Yeah, I'd say so. Okay, I guess we're going!" Tricia replied, and she beamed that knowing smile.

Tricia had never really put much faith in psychic ability. Having a religious upbringing, she found comfort in her belief system, which did not allow much room for the paranormal. Now, however, she asks me for guidance in many areas of her life.

Our country is experiencing yet another recession, and unfortunately many people are being affected by this, including my friend Andee. "Do you think Scott will get laid off?" she asked one time while we were relaxing around her fire pit. It was mid-July, and a cool breeze was trying to chase away the mosquitoes.

I looked at her husband, Scott, and replied, "I think he will be fine. I see something happening around Halloween and something around Christmas, but everything will work out." What I saw when she asked was a jack-o'-lantern and then a Christmas tree. These are very definite symbols that not only point to the specific holidays, but also the time of year.

"Everything will work out," I continued, even though I saw these two events interrupting their tranquil lives.

Sure enough, around Halloween Scott received the information that he was being laid off right after Christmas. We don't always see what we want to see. I would have loved to have been able to tell them that he wouldn't lose his job. But I saw the symbols and recognized them for what they were. I also knew they would be just fine. As it turns out, his company did offer him a new job allowing him to keep basically the same position along with the identical benefits! Be honest with the symbols you see or feel; change is not always bad.

Keep in mind that sometimes what we see is not always as it appears. A client, Sonia, asked me one day, during a particularly stressful money week, "Do you see me getting a chunk of money anytime soon?" Now, what she meant was: did I see her getting a commission check in the near future?

"I'm not sure. I see two thousand dollars being deposited next month," I told her. I saw a banded stack of money with *$2000* written on it in my mind's eye.

"Okay...let's hope you're right!" she replied.

I was right...and I was wrong.

"Well, Melanie, I figured out what the two thousand dollars was," Sonia laughed. "I didn't get a commission check, but I took two thousand dollars out of an IRA and put it in my checking account."

Like I said, not always 100 percent accurate, but this is what I do. Not so glamorous when you get right down to it, but pretty cool all in all. I wouldn't trade it for anything. One of the most important aspects of clairvoyance is the ability to be honest with what you see. Just because it may not be what we want at the time, by recognizing the symbols for what they are, we can open ourselves up for new symbolic communication—new images for future progression.

Tuning in to your own clairvoyant capabilities will assist you in seeing the messages as they come. By doing the exercises in this chapter you'll learn the difference between how physical and metaphysical light appears through your third eye and how to psychically see symbolic images by bringing your awareness to that clairvoyant part of your intuitive self. You will also learn how telepathy, or mind reading, is different from clairvoyance, yet still plays a part in understanding symbolic imagery.

Clairvoyance Exercises

Write *CLAIRS* across the top of a new page in your journal, giving yourself some extra pages in between, to set your intention. Practice the exercises in this chapter and record them in your journal. Again, leave yourself plenty of room to record additional experiences so you can go back and do the exercises as often as you'd like.

Before you begin any exercise, invoke your powerful protection against any negativity by imagining a bubble of protective white light. Allow it to surround you and encircle you, giving you all the space you need to receive intuitive guidance and symbolic messages while protecting you from any negative energy.

Exercise 1: Opening Your Third Eye

There are many different ways to tune in to your third eye or your clairvoyant gifts. Lie down on your back in a dark location, so there is not light casting shadow across your face as you perform the exercise. Close your eyes and focus all your attention on your third eye—the spot between your brows in the center of your forehead. Notice any dots of light or presence of light in that area. Slowly, without casting a shadow, place your palm over your third eye. Notice if there is any difference with the brightness of the light, or if there is a change in what you see when you focus in on that spot.

Continue to practice this once a day, if not more. Eventually you will find that by concentrating on that spot you will become aware of a change in the coloring or the light, and possibly you will begin to clairvoyantly see images or flashes of pictures or symbols. Record your experiences in your "CLAIR" journal. Pretty soon you'll realize how easy it is for you to receive symbols clairvoyantly.

Exercise 2: Practicing with Zener Cards

Another wonderful exercise to test and enhance your clairvoyant ability to psychically see symbols is to play with Zener cards. Zener cards were developed by perceptual psychologist Karl Zener in the 1930s to experiment with ESP. He, along with colleague J. B. Rhine, a noted parapsychologist, conducted these experiments with his newly developed series of five cards. Each card contains a specific drawing: a hollow circle, a Greek cross (two even, perpendicular lines), three wavy vertical parallel lines (waves), a hollow square (four lines), and a hollow five-pointed star.

Get five blank index cards or cardstock paper. The paper must be thick enough that you won't be able to see through or see the indent of anything on the other side. Draw the five symbols, one on each card, in black ink: the circle, cross, waves, square, and star. Then get five additional blank index cards and use colors to draw each one. Red for the circle, yellow for the cross, green for the waves, purple for the square, and blue for the star.

Now, here comes the fun part. You can do this alone or with a partner. Shuffle either the black or the colored cards and lay them out, face down. Point to a card and say aloud which card you think it is. Do it again. Don't get discouraged. If you shuffle between each spread there is less of a chance of "tampering," because you'll start with five fresh cards each time. Another way to do it is to hold the cards and put one face down and intuit which card it is. When you use the colored cards you can also try and psychically see the colors to know which card is which.

Or, hold the cards, one by one, up to your third eye. Try and "see" each symbol clairvoyantly.

I like to use the cards with a partner. Have someone else shuffle the cards and hold one up. The great thing about doing it with a partner is that you can exercise your ability to see symbols clairvoyantly, telepathically, and clairaudiently all at once. Have your partner look at the card and send it to you with their mind. Have them see the shape, the color (if you're using the colored set), say the shape in their mind, and visually draw it with their own third eye. See how accurate you are.

Then you can have your partner randomly pick a card and not look at it. This cuts out the possibility of telepathy, because your partner hasn't seen it and therefore can't send the symbol to you.

Notice how accurately you see the various symbols with each different method.

Exercise 3: Anima Project

There are also ways to practice online. Currently there is an online endeavor, called the Anima Project (www.animaproject .org). The purpose of this free site is to study psychic phenomena and ESP. This is a great way to build your ability to see symbols clairvoyantly.

"Hearing" Symbols: Clairaudience

Clairaudience is "clear hearing." You might experience this "sixth sense" when you hear a song or a tune in your head or you hear a name whispered. This can be difficult to recognize. It often seems as though you are making it up because the sounds are coming from inside your head. Chances are you're not crazy. Celebrate the voices! You are a clairaudient being.

People who work with sound, like musicians, may perceive their psychic symbols clairaudiently because of their finely tuned natural sense of hearing. This is why many mediums blast music and sing at the top of their lungs before doing readings at gallery events. They are opening up their clairaudient abilities, getting ready to tune in. Hearing symbols doesn't necessarily mean you have to be musical. You might hear a note of music or a complete song, or you may just hear a word or grouping of words. Maybe you'll hear a sound that you can easily identify or you'll hear a name.

I did a reading about ten years ago for a woman during a psychic sensitivity training. I repeatedly received the name Pedro or Peter, and I felt a grandfatherly presence. When I kept telling her about him, she vehemently denied knowing anyone who fit the description. I continued, explaining he was showing me models and an attic where he and his dad used to build the models. Again, she didn't understand who I was referring to.

Now, usually when I psychically get information that keeps repeating I am pretty sure it's relevant. This time I was not so sure. The more I told her, the more she pulled away.

"Time's up!" said the teacher, and I reluctantly stopped the reading. When my session partner was called on, she told of my "mistaken identity" reading, insisting that I just hadn't tuned in at all. A little discouraged and also a bit embarrassed, I asked her what her grandfather's name was.

"Well, it's Pietro. Of course you can see why you were wrong!" she continued.

Of course I can see why I'm wrong. I mispronounced an Italian name! Please, let's give ourselves some leeway when working with symbols; we are only human, trying to connect to a supernatural frequency. Sometimes I only get the initials. Being psychic does not make us infallible or perfect, as evidenced by my Italian, but it does make life more fun. Don't be afraid to get things wrong; you are only a channel.

Clairaudience is not limited specifically to hearing music or even names. It may be simple words representing objects. For example, if you hear the word *radio*, it may suggest a regular radio used to play everyday music or it could be your symbol for your connection to the other side. A ringing telephone may signify a normal earthly call from someone, or instead it may be your symbol for spiritual communication. The way you interpret the words or clairaudient symbols is going to be based on your experience with them.

One of my favorite Christmas movies is the classic *It's a Wonderful Life*. In the final scene, the youngest daughter is being held in front of the Christmas tree by the family, amidst most of the town, and an ornament, a bell, begins to ring. She pronounces, "Teacher says, 'Every time a bell rings, an angel gets his wings.'" This famous line is one of the most powerful or widely recognized clairaudient symbols. Every time a bell rings, an angel gets his wings; what can be clearer than that? Now I think of angels whenever I hear the tinkle of a bell.

Recently there has been a spike of interest in the paranormal, including many television shows that search out and track down ghosts and apparitions. One of the ways they capture evidence is by using simple recording devices. They hope to record EVPs, electronic voice phenomena, which are voices of disembodied spirits or messages from the other side. These EVPs are generally only picked up by the digital recorders and are not physically heard. The frequencies these voices are coming through on can be measured with digital equipment and are different from the normal speaking frequency.

What's most interesting about this phenomenon is that people who excel at or have a propensity for clairaudience can also hear these

EVPs with their naked ears, psychically. Often, the EVPs come through with only one or two words, making it essential to comprehend what's being conveyed. For example, if such people hear the word *noose*, they decipher it as a symbol that the spirit was hanged, or if they hear the sound of a gun firing, that will become symbolic of someone shot to death.

In order to access our clairaudient abilities we need to first hear clearly with our physical ears. The exercises that follow will train you to focus on the sounds words make, and by extension the messages we receive through our psychic clear hearing. By learning how to really listen, we open ourselves to the invaluable gift of being able to hear answers from beyond our normal state of awareness.

Clairaudience Exercises
Exercise 1: Learn to Listen

Do you remember the game "Telephone" from when you were a kid? One person would make up a sentence and whisper it into the ear of the person closest to them. That person, in turn, would continue by whispering the same words to the next person and so on. With enough people you'd usually find by the time the loop reached the last person, it would sound nothing like the original sentence. Most often it would end with everyone laughing.

One of the exercises I have in my workshops is "Psychic Telephone." It's not that we play the game any differently; we just do regular old Telephone. The difference is the sentence we start out with. It usually involves some kind of clairaudient lesson to be learned, and ends up instead being a question on how to access clairaudience.

Next time you are together with a bunch of friends, try it. See how well you can listen with your physical hearing. It's even more difficult if you are out at a loud restaurant or a club. Pay attention to how much concentration is necessary to really hear and understand what is being said. Remember: in order to hear and receive symbols clairaudiently, you need to raise your vibration; you need to really focus.

Exercise 2: Hearing the Words

Do you like to sing? Do you like music? If so, great. You should love this exercise. If not, that's okay, too. You'll enjoy the challenge.

Sit down with a CD or an MP3 player or something that you can rewind on command. Press play and start listening to the lyrics. When you come to a part that is difficult to understand, rewind it and try again to interpret the words. Keep rewinding until you are sure you know what is being said. The more you practice being able to discern the sounds of our language, the easier it will be to recognize when you are receiving symbolic information clairaudiently.

Exercise 3: Hearing Clairaudient Messages

Put together a list of questions you have: questions about yourself, your family, your deceased loved ones, your spirit guides, and so forth. Leave enough space after each question to record any answers you may receive. Pick a quiet room with no distractions, no loud noises, and no interruptions. Bring your questions, a pen, and your journal.

Sit down and get comfortable. Take a nice deep breath. Now take another deep breath; inhale for the count of six and hold it for four seconds, then exhale to a count of eight. Do this a few times and allow yourself to relax even deeper.

Now, in this altered state of relaxation, begin slowly asking your questions, one at a time. Sit quietly and wait at least thirty seconds. During that time listen for any response. Notice if you hear anything, even if it sounds like it is coming from inside your head. You may hear a specific answer or you may just hear words or even sounds. You may receive words that are symbolic to help you understand the messages as opposed to full sentences. If you don't hear anything, ask the question again.

If you still don't hear a response, imagine you do. Sometimes, what we think is our imagination is really intuitive or symbolic guidance.

Write down any answers you received next to the questions. Also be sure to include any additional information you received, even if it wasn't in answer to any specific questions. Pay special attention to any symbolic sounds or words you heard. You may be surprised to record so much more than you originally thought you heard.

"Feeling" Symbols: Clairsentience & Claircognizance

Clairsentience, or "clear feeling," and *claircognizance*, meaning "clear knowing," are prevalent in all aspects of intuitive awareness. This is the most common form of psychic communication, but a somewhat unusual way to receive symbolic guidance. Clairsentience means you feel things. You may imagine you are touching something or your body may experience various sensations. Feeling temperature change is common; you may sense warmth to indicate a geographic tropical location or summer, or cold to direct your attention toward a cooler climate or time of year.

A sense of floating in water might be your "pool" or "ocean" symbol. You may even find that it makes you seasick, which could change the interpretation to "nauseated," though I hope you won't have too many of those feelings!

Claircognizance comes in the form of "just knowing" something, not really knowing how or why, but knowing it as certain as you know your own name. When you assign meaning to these knowing feelings, you may find that those same cognizant flashes will come back again, in the same way. Claircognizance may occur in conjunction with clairvoyance or clairaudience; seeing a symbolic image creates that knowing in your gut, or that psychic sound you hear suggests that the significant feeling you have means something. You may also feel physical ailments when you are reading other people. For example, if you feel a pain in your head, it's possible the other person has a headache. It could be taken even further to possibly connect to someone's tumor. If you feel pain in your knee, maybe it's because the person you're reading just had surgery to fix a torn anterior cruciate ligament. This can be because of the skiing accident they just had, symbolized by the pair of skis you saw in your clairvoyant flash.

Flashes of clairsentience or claircognizance can occur randomly. There may be times when you find yourself getting angry with seemingly no exterior motivation—until you realize that an injustice has occurred nearby that you weren't yet aware of. Or it could be that uncomfortable feeling you get when you walk into a party and everything looks okay, but on closer inspection you recognize a heated argument had just occurred. How about when you feel uncontrollable laughter coming on, the kind that doesn't feel like your own? You have no idea where it's coming from. Then, all of a sudden, you get a flash of your mother (who's on the other side) from when you watched a funny movie together. Again, this is a combination of clairsentience and clairvoyance. This feeling of out-of-control laughter may be your new psychic symbol for a funny movie, or it could be the way you know your mom is around.

You can also have a positive clairsentient experience for someone else. About ten years ago I did a reading for someone in a "ghost-busting group" who was having a problem in her home with her lights flashing on and off, causing her bulbs to constantly blow out. When I tuned in I could feel a presence there in the house, and I couldn't help laughing. I laughed so much that everyone in the group thought I was losing it.

I explained to them that I could see the foyer of this house and its rich décor of mahogany wood paneling lining the hall, complete with antique light sconces. I detailed the deep reds in the carpet and the length of the hallway as well. But, the most intriguing was the old woman I described. She had white Phyllis Diller–like hair, a three-quarter-length grayish-white flowing nightgown, and an uncontrollable laugh that reached right up to her blank eyes. She would run up and down the hallway, touching the lights. "Pop, pop, pop," they would go, off and on, blowing a bulb every so often, all while the old woman laughed hysterically.

What was so cool about this was I could "feel" her hysteria. The laughter seemed to take me over as well, as I tuned in to her. It was as if she unwittingly had superimposed her frenzied mood on top of mine. I didn't feel she meant any harm; it seemed that she was simply stuck in some kind of loop. It also felt like she suffered from dementia or senility.

"Aaaahhhh!!" she would yell, as she ran up and down the hallway, laughing and blowing the light bulbs. She continued this pattern until we helped her to move on, simply by continually telling her she could meet her loved ones if she moved into the light.

This was the first real time that I realized how incredibly important it is to notice clairsentience for what it is. I felt her hysteria. It wasn't as though I was completely taken over or that I "lost" myself, but I could definitely feel her emotion. I can still feel her energy to this day, and every time I do it brings a smile to my face.

Frequently, claircognizant experiences can relate to our mortality. This is when our sixth sense is more than just important; it is crucial to our survival. If we don't recognize these otherwise nonexistent occurrences we may ignore them all together. My friend Dave and I were having a conversation about intuition. He is an accomplished artist as well as a very talented musician. He told me that he loses time and gets "in a groove" when he is really "on" with his artwork and that he loses himself in his music.

More importantly he told me about the time he was walking through the streets of New York City, moving along from street corner to street corner. After traveling many blocks without a care in the world he stopped. He didn't know why he was stopping, but he knew he wasn't supposed to cross the street. This time, even though the light was on his side, he waited. Seconds later a car appeared out of nowhere and ran the red light, flying through the intersection feet from where he was standing.

Dave is convinced, as I am, that if he didn't have that precognitive thought, that clairsentient feeling, he would have been killed by the out-of-control car. Many people would call that pure dumb luck. Dave rec-ognizes it for what it was: pure intuition. He is positive that through his intuitive awareness he either foresaw something bad happening or he had help from his angels or guides and understood the message to stop.

Clairsentience and claircognizance are very grounded psychic senses. When you feel something psychically it is within, which means you are present and in your body. As you continue on your path you'll begin to notice when you feel as though your feet are rooted deeply into the ground beneath you and alternatively when you feel lighter or ungrounded. When I conduct readings I feel heavier when I'm connecting with my sentient and cognizant senses than when I am connecting to my clairvoyance or clairaudience. I usually get a little taller in my chair or feel myself stretching up toward heaven when I am trying to connect with my clear seeing and hearing senses. Being grounded helps you experience the emotions you are channeling through your clear feeling and knowing senses.

By practicing the exercises that follow you will learn that you can connect simply by grounding yourself and becoming one with the earth. You'll know what it feels like to be completely in your body and what your body feels like when you are in it. You will share with an-other person how their body feels to you and if there are any areas that need work, and the other person will do the same. Imagine a world where we could intuitively feel or even know exactly what ailments we had if we were able to symbolically understand there was a block in energy or a tumor present in our friend or colleague. This is possible. By practicing and opening your awareness, you are taking the first step toward comprehending these abilities.

Clairsentience and Claircognizance Exercises
Exercise 1: Grounding and Scanning the Body

For this exercise you are going to use the protection of the white light, and you are also going to ground yourself.

Sit down in a comfortable position and plant your feet se-curely on the ground. Take a deep breath: in through your nose, out through your mouth. Keep breathing like this until you fall into a natural rhythm.

Feel your feet on the floor. Pay special attention to the bottoms of your feet. Imagine there are roots growing from your soles, reaching down through the ground, all the way down. See these roots attaching themselves to a large boulder deep in the center of the earth.

Feel the earth's energy traveling all the way up these roots, into the soles of your feet. This energy moves up, now, through your calves, your knees, and your thighs. This beautiful grounding energy continues traveling up through your body into your hips and reproductive area, into your abdomen and your solar plexus. As this incredible energy moves up it clears away any negativity, any psychic debris that no longer belongs there, that no longer belongs to you. You can almost feel the warmth of the energy now, as it moves into your chest and your neck, releasing any tension from your neck and shoulders.

Imagine this beautiful, warm, grounding energy spreading out through your arms, your elbows, your wrists, your hands, and out the tips of your fingers. Feel this energy as it moves up, through your neck into your jaw and mouth muscles, relaxing them, releasing any stress or tension, letting it flow back down to the center of the earth to be recycled into positive energy. Feel this grounding earth energy moving up farther now, through your cheeks and into your eyes, your forehead, and third-eye area. Imagine this energy clearing the veil over your third eye. Feel this warmth as it fans out, bringing grounding energy all the way up, through your skull and your hair, to the top of your head.

Notice now how solid you feel, yet at the same time how light you feel, filled with this grounding energy. Allow this energy to surround you, flowing out of the top of your head like a fountain, creating a funnel of protection all the way around you.

Pay attention to how your body feels. Start with your feet and notice whether they feel as though they are where they normally are and if they are warm or cold or average temperature. Move over the rest of your body, including your organ system, and observe whether you feel any difference in temperature anywhere. Take as long as you want to continue your body scan, paying special attention to any differences in temperature.

When you are done ask yourself how you feel overall, whether there is any tension that needs addressing or any parts of your body you need to work on to help yourself feel more present, more relaxed. Notice if you feel any colors or any shapes or images while scanning any parts of your body.

Whenever you are ready, take a deep breath and open your eyes. Continue to feel yourself wholly grounded, helping you to come back into your body solidly and fully.

Sit for a moment until you feel ready to write in your journal. When you are prepared, record how the different parts of your body felt and whether you noticed any correlation with any temperature variations in any areas that need attention or any areas you may have been having trouble with. Also, be sure to include whether your overall body felt heavier or lighter throughout the meditation. Make sure to write down any symbols you received while scanning your body; colors, shapes, images, and the like.

Jot down any feelings you had about the overall exercise and whether you felt grounded or not. Include your level of comfort as well, and whether or not you liked the exercise and if it was easy for you to do.

Exercise 2: Practicing with Emotions

For this exercise you need a partner. Find someone who is willing to work with you and bring up different emotions.

Sit facing each other. Hold hands and close your eyes. Have your partner think of a time in their life they were very emotional or felt a very strong emotion. It can be any emotion:

happy, sad, angry, glad, hurt, comfortable, secure, scared, frightened, etc. Have them remember that feeling, that emotion. Tell your partner to consciously think of that feeling and allow themselves to experience that emotion now. Have them be aware of it twice as much, now, remembering back to that time in their life when they felt this emotion so strongly.

Give your partner about one minute to really begin sensing their feelings. Tell your partner you will be trying to feel their energy and to send their energy to you.

Now, allow yourself to begin feeling your partner's energy, coming right through their hands into your hands and into your body. Experience your partner's feeling, and allow yourself to begin to experience the sensations your partner is experiencing. Notice any symbols, sounds, colors, and the like that you feel while tuning in to your partner's energy.

You may immediately discover what emotion your partner is immersed in, or it may be more subtle. As soon as you truly feel what your partner is feeling, go ahead and share with your partner what you received. If it was what they were remembering, congratulate yourself. You now know what that feels like in your body, even when the actual emotion belongs to someone else. Additionally, you may now have a psychic symbol for that particular emotion or group of emotions. If you did not pick up what your partner was feeling, that's okay. You can try again. Take note, however, whether you were close: for example, mad and frustrated or comfortable and secure. Sometimes when we experience fear we are angry, or when we are comfortable we are happy. Notice if there are any correlations, and above all else pay attention to how this exercise made your body feel.

Continue this exercise until you are satisfied, or until you are tired, whichever comes first. Remember: using any of your "clairs" can be physically demanding, but claircognizance and clairsentience can really wipe you out, as they use your whole body.

Feel free to switch places with your friend. Quite often we find that we are better at either sending or receiving. Notice if this is true for you. Also, try this exercise with different people. You may find with one friend that you are more empathic and can connect to and read them, but you can't send them your energy as easily and vice versa with someone else.

Again, write down anything you noticed: what emotions were easier for you to interpret and what you felt like during each different session. Be sure to note any symbols that you felt, or that popped up during your exercises, and relate what emotion you were feeling when that symbol came up.

Most importantly, as with all of the exercises in this book, have fun. In order to live your truest, most authentic self, it is imperative that you enjoy yourself. You may experience a general feeling of catharsis; this is good. Allow yourself to feel, see, and hear everything you possibly can. This is the only way to achieve that sense of accomplishment that you so deserve.

"Smelling and Tasting" Symbols:
Clairalience & Clairgustance

Two of the less-referred-to, yet equally important, clear senses are *clairalience* (sometimes referred to as *clairolfaction*) and *clairgustance*. Clairalience is clear smelling and clairgustance is clear tasting. While we can receive symbolic information through these clairs, I've found the message is not always about the symbol we are getting; often it conveys a deeper meaning.

It is very common to smell perfume, flowers, or even cigars when connecting to deceased relatives, and in fact it is one of the most prevalent forms of communication loved ones have of letting you know they are around. Because of that I wouldn't assign the perfume my mother wore to symbolically represent "perfume." Instead, I would classify that scent as a symbol for my mom who has passed. By the same token, if I were doing a reading for a friend and that scent came through, I wouldn't automatically assume it was my friend's mother; I would investigate further by asking whether my friend's mother wore this particular perfume or whether my friend had lost someone known for this particular scent, or even if she knew or used to know someone who worked with perfume or even flowers.

The same holds true for cigars or cigarettes. My husband and I will often smell the scent of a very specific cigar when his father is around, whether we are together or in different locations when the scent appears. Unlike the other senses, clairalience and clairgustance are usually much harder to recognize as metaphysical; often we surmise the smell or the taste is physically present and we just ignore it.

My friend Kathy and I were chatting one day over coffee, and she brought up her son. "Kevin told me he is not going to go to the dance. He and his girlfriend broke up," she told me. "I wish he were going. It is a very special dance."

Right away I smelled flowers, more specifically roses. I was able to interpret that symbolic scent to mean Kevin would indeed be going to the dance, because my clairolfactory senses were picking up on the corsage he would be buying his new date. Checking in with my clairvoyance, I saw him placing the corsage on a girl's wrist, and I told Kathy what I had gotten using my clear senses.

The following week she was very excited to confirm my premonition that Kevin was going to the dance with someone new, and they had just placed the order for a white-rose corsage. Smelling the flowers had been the pivotal point in my off-the-cuff reading for Kathy and Kevin. Otherwise, I would have just felt I was seeing what could have been instead of what was to be. Often, we combine our senses to give us a fuller, more complete illustration of what we are symbolically receiving.

Occasionally, you may come across a cornucopia of clear senses to register one symbol. For example, my mother-in-law's name was Rose. I psychically know she's around because I symbolically see an image of a rose, hear her name, smell roses, and actually taste rose water. Using all of these psychic senses helps to really hit home the fact she's there. Luckily for me, I also feel her loving energy, which helps me discern between a regular "rose symbol" and my mother-in-law "Rose symbol."

Clairgustance is a popular form of communication from deceased loved ones as well. For example, my sister Tammy did a casual reading for me when I was about sixteen years old. She explained she saw me marrying a redhead and being comfortable and happy. Her main line of communication with the other side is her clairvoyance. She is extremely artistic and easily taps into this form of symbolic communication. However, she also used her clairgustance when she got the taste of hamburgers and hot dogs off the grill to confirm I would be happy and relaxed with my future family. Although clairgustance was not her dominant psychic sense, she could taste the food that was being cooked. The grill is now symbolic of a relaxed and content atmosphere.

Just because you have a more dominant psychic sense doesn't mean you shut off or close out other sensory input. More often than not, if someone from the other side is trying to send you a message, they are going to try whatever means necessary to aid in your understanding of it. Sometimes, this means creating more than one symbolic message to carry the same communication by using different extrasensory avenues.

This happened for me in a session with my client Roberta. She was concerned about her son Dean's performance at school and asked me if there was anything that would help him to help himself achieve the grades he wanted. Normally, I'd suggest hypnosis, which I use regularly to help children bring up their test scores. But, in this case, I immediately tasted the bitterness of pills and I knew he would be put on ADD (attention deficit disorder) meds to help him focus. Again, knowing the way I work, I didn't stop when I tapped into my clairgustory sense; I used my clairvoyance and saw two little white pills in his hand. This was just confirmation for me that I was right on track. Sure enough, when I talked to Roberta next she informed me that Dean had gone to a specialist and was doing wonderfully in school. He was much happier and more focused in class since he started taking his medication.

Clairgustance and clairalience are utilized in other ways as well. Some people have the ability to smell or taste death or disease and can advise others to seek medical attention before something actually happens or becomes life-threatening. Imagine smelling or tasting rotting meat or garbage; this principal scent or taste would be paramount to helping with early diagnosis of disease and should not be discounted for its unpleasantness. The smell of death may also accompany relatives and friends who have crossed over, and for some people this clairolfactory symbol is the first inkling they are being visited.

Much like the perfume and the cigars, there are many other symbolic tastes and smells that can accompany a visitor from the astral plane; the possibilities are endless. For example, maybe Cousin Anthony was known for being the pizza king, so you'll taste or smell Italian food to let you know he's around. Or perhaps Sanguita was known for her curried lamb, so you'll smell or taste Indian food when she's trying to say hello.

When it comes to clairalience and clairgustance, psychic symbols tend to delve deeper into personal significance or personal experiences. But remember that all symbols are presented in a way that you're able to recognize or understand. So, if you are trying to find a missing person and you keep getting the smell of Italian food, it's probably a safe bet it has nothing to do with your cousin Anthony and more to do with a different person of Italian descent or to an Italian restaurant that's relevant to the missing-person case. Symbols don't control what information you get; they help you understand the information that is presented in a way that is clearer and more comprehensive.

If you are like me, you'll find you receive symbols in many ways and usually in combination with each other. When I read for people I open all of my clair senses. This allows me to be a more fluid conduit for the symbolic information I am to give to my clients. This may not happen for you right away, however. Usually people who are just beginning to tune in will connect through one or two different clear senses but will develop their abilities as they practice their intuitive exercises. The more we practice, the better we become at deciphering these phenomenal cryptic messages.

The exercises that follow are specifically designed to help you assign symbolic value to various tastes and scents. By doing this you will be able to understand, with clarity, if these symbolic messages are sent to you from the other side, and what they mean. Synchronicity generally plays a part when working on developing your intuition, so be open to events, visitations, or other sensory experiences as they no doubt will present themselves to you!

Clairgustance and Clairalience Exercises

The next two exercises will best be accomplished by practicing together with a friend, and you will need some supplies. If the members of your family use perfume or cologne, spray a separate piece of paper for each person with their own scent. You will be using these later. If you have something from someone who's passed that still carries their scent, that can be added to the pile as well. Go outside and pick flowers or run to the store and buy some that remind you of your deceased loved ones or even your friends and relatives who are still alive. This can also be accomplished by using the oils or perfumes that smell like the particular flower. For example, I use lilacs for my mother because she loved them. Finally, gather any other sources for scents or smells you may want to use to practice with and have your friend do the same. Keep some of them hidden from each other for the purpose of the exercises.

Now, take out various foods and spices that you can use to tune in to your clairgustance. Interestingly, we use clairalience to help us understand our clear taste, so know that you will not only taste these foods, you will also smell them. You can take advantage of whatever you have in your kitchen, or you can turn it into an adventure and go on a scavenger hunt for different tasting and smelling foods in your area.

As always, get your journal ready and open to a new page.

Exercise 1: Foods and Spices for Clairalience

Using your clear smelling and clear tasting is no different from the other clairs when it comes to protecting yourself. Before you begin opening any of your psychic senses be sure to surround yourself with white light or ground yourself down deep into the earth. Go ahead and do this now, using the previous exercises to guide you.

We'll be focusing on clairalience for the first exercise, so gather up all of the "scents" you rounded up and bring them to a room close by or a different area if you are outside. Next, decide who is going to be the "psychic" and who is going to be the "helper." The helper is going to be in control of all of the scents and is going to decide which order to present them to the psychic. The psychic will need the journal or a piece of paper to record information.

The psychic: Sit down and get comfortable. Close your eyes, and take a deep breath.

The helper: One at a time, present the psychic with a different scented item, leaving time for the psychic to process each.

The psychic: As you are presented with each separate item, take note of the first impression you receive—the first thought, feeling, image, or sound you get. Open your eyes and record it in your journal. Be sure to include any names of people you may receive flashes of as well.

Continue this until you are done with all of the scent items and, if you want, switch places with your partner.

Next, we're going to focus on clairgustance, or clear tasting.

Follow the same process using all of the foods and spices, but instead of smelling them, have your partner put them in your mouth or hand them to you to put in your mouth. Be careful with any spicy or hot foods; you don't want to hurt yourself in this exercise!

Record every thought, emotion, person, and so on that you feel, imagine, hear, or see while tasting each food. After you've gone through all of your "tastes," switch places with your partner.

If you don't have a partner to work with you on this exercise, you can still practice it. One by one, take each object and smell or taste it with your eyes closed. Do the same thing as if you had a partner and record everything you received through your clear senses.

When you are all done, look at your notes. Do any of the scents or tastes bring thoughts, images, or feelings of loved ones who have crossed over or loved ones who are still alive?

Exercise 2: Tuning in to Your Tasting and Smelling Senses Using Locations

Another way to open up your clairgustory and clairolfactory abilities is to tune in to them psychically, rather than physically. Before you begin you'll need to write down a list of places that you are familiar with or you feel drawn to in some way. This can include cities, addresses, stores, countries, buildings, vacation spots, places of employment, and anywhere else you can imagine—as long as it's a physical location.

Go somewhere neutral, like a park or somewhere that you don't feel an attachment to. Get comfortable and protect yourself against any negativity by using your white light and your grounding meditations. The information you're looking for should be free and clear from any debris or bad energy in order to benefit from this psychic exercise.

Begin by taking the first place on the list and writing its name in an open area in your journal. Close your eyes and imagine what that location smells like to you or what you smell when you think about that spot. Do you taste anything? If so, does it taste dry? Wet? Sweet? Sour? Spicy? Salty? Does it have a texture? If you actually smell something, record it. If you see an image or hear something or even feel something, write that down, too. Remember that, as with all psychic senses, we are allowing ourselves to be open to using every one of them in order to increase our awareness in each of them. If you are thinking of Florida and you see the image of an orange, imagine what that orange smells like. By doing this you are taking it one step further and opening up your clairolfactory sense. Then imagine biting into that orange; doing so will help you train your clairgustory sense.

Continue this with each location you have listed and then go back and look at what you've written. Do the descriptions make sense? Can you still smell or taste them? From now on, whenever you think of somewhere you've just worked with, chances are you will smell or taste the location as well. Using these clairgustory and clairolfactory symbols can help you decide where to shop, go on vacation, send your kids to school, get a job, or anything else; take advantage of them! Practice any time you get a new scent or taste.

Exercise 3: Tuning in to Your Tasting and Smelling Senses Using People

Now that you've learned to tune in to your tasting and smelling senses with locations, you can do the same with people. Go through the same procedure; write down names of people who are still alive and those who have crossed over. Do your meditations and protect and ground yourself. Open up your clairgustance and clairalience and begin, one by one, recording what you receive to symbolically let you know you are tuning in to the other person's energy.

For example, my mother passed about four years ago. Every time I smell lilacs or taste beef goulash, symbolically with my clear senses, I think of her. This helps me to remember and stay connected to her. It also lets me know she's around.

List one person at a time. What do you think of? Notice whether it's more about tastes or smells. When you are all done, look over your journal and pay attention to the different symbols you received. Do they make sense? If you were working with people who have passed, are the scents or smells you recorded reminiscent of the time you spent together while they were alive? Or are they totally different? Have you ever smelled or tasted any of those symbolically before and wondered why?

Remember that there doesn't have to be one clairolfactory or clairgustory symbol per location or person; there may be multiple symbols. This is fine, as it provides even more guidance or clues to help you understand the symbolic communication you are receiving. Who knows: you may find that these clear senses will become the most prevalent form for understanding your messages from the other side!

Summing up the Clairs

Learning about what clair senses are and how they can play a part in your life can assist you in determining your dominant form of symbolic communication. Recognizing the symbolic messages that are sent to you is only the beginning of this process. Understanding you need to apply these messages is the rest.

When you receive symbolic impressions but don't know what to do with them, it can be frustrating. Think of every instance as an opportunity. Ask yourself, "Why am I getting this symbol? What does the universe want to share with me?" This will help you act in response to each symbol. If, for instance, you are at the beach and you receive an image of a jellyfish, it may suggest caution when swimming. Alternatively, if you are deciding whether to sign up your child for basketball versus swimming, you may actually smell the ocean. The swimming lessons are not being held at the beach, in an ocean, but symbolically it's a way to help you comprehend that swimming will be more fun or more beneficial for your son or daughter.

There are many different ways, as you've read, to experience symbolic messages, and many different reasons. You may want to learn how to connect so you can make better choices in life. Or you might be looking for another opinion to help make a decision. Also, you may be looking for answers to help heal pain or discomfort, or you may even be trying to help others with their lives. Possibly, you are looking to connect to those loved ones who have passed from this physical plane. What you do with the messages you receive is your prerogative.

But learning how to get them through various exercises opens up your ability to recognize them and gives you the opportunity to decide how you want to apply them to your life.

In order to trust your clear senses and the symbolic messages you receive, you need feedback. Many psychic teachers believe feedback is not essential, that's it more important to just let the information flow. While I agree you should not disrupt the flow of energy, I do feel it is invaluable to know if the information you believe you are getting is accurate or not. This helps to determine whether what you are receiving is truly symbolic communication or just your imagination. Having said that, the essence of using your intuition means you have to trust or believe what comes through. This means you need to let go of the outcome while you are tuning in. Knowing the outcome is not as important as being present for the journey.

When you work with a partner to develop your intuitive symbolic awareness, your partner has to be open to and not shut down what you share with them. If you tell them something, they cannot discount it straightaway. For example, if you tell your partner you got the initials MB, it might not immediately register. Let your partner walk away with those initials instead of telling you that you are wrong. Because you never know; MB may end up being the next person they see. If you are practicing on your own, you may not be able to validate everything you get, but eventually you will be more at ease with symbols and you'll know, intuitively, when you are on.

You've practiced tapping into your intuition through your different clairs, using each clair sense individually. The exercises that follow will help you utilize all of your clairs together, possibly helping you determine which feels most natural. Once you do the exercises you may find you will gravitate toward using the methods every day.

Exercise 1: Tuning in to Symbolic Messages through Psychometry

Psychometry, which is used to tune in to symbolic messages, is a form of extrasensory perception in which you hold an object and receive impressions about that object or the owner of the object. Objects retain energy. Holding an item in your hand assists you in tuning in to the energy of the person connected to that particular article.

Have a friend give you an item. Don't let your friend tell you where it came from or to whom it belongs. Usually, a photo or jewelry or something metal will work best, because these items tend to retain the most energy.

Without questioning anything, begin recording in your journal or on a piece of paper whatever impressions you receive. Do not censor the information you're getting, such as names, locations, dates, times, emotions, tastes, images, feelings, etc. These impressions may mean absolutely nothing to you but can mean everything to the person who owns the object.

Give yourself a few minutes to be sure you record everything you get symbolically. After you are done, check in with your intuition and see if there are any other messages or directions you need to give to your friend.

Now, it's time for feedback. Remind your partner that negativity will not be accepted. If you tell them something you symbolically received and they don't immediately understand it, that's okay. Explain they can "take the information home" with them and let it cook or develop. If it's important for them to know what it means they will get another symbol to connect it; otherwise, don't worry! After all, practice makes perfect.

As always, switch positions. Let your partner read your objects next. While your partner is tuning in, open up your own intuition and see what information you get at the same time. When you're both done, compare what you've written down and note if there are any similarities. Sometimes, tapping in together raises the vibrational energy even more than usual, and you just might get more than you expected!

If you don't have a partner you can always practice on random objects by holding something in your hand and tuning in to it. It is slightly less educational, however, because you won't have feedback to assess the accuracy of your symbolic interpretations. Don't let that discourage you though; all practice is great practice!

Exercise 2: Using Symbols through Remote Viewing

Remote viewing is something you can use to psychically travel to a different time and location and receive impressions from that time and location. A simple way to do this is to have someone place a picture, drawing, writing, or page from a magazine or a book into an envelope.

Next, you can either have your partner hold the envelope or put it down. Record every impression you receive, regardless of whether it makes sense to you or not. Ask yourself what you see, psychically. Then what you hear, feel, smell, and taste. Ask yourself if there are any prevalent colors or temperatures.

After you've written down everything you've received, open the envelope and take out the contents. Compare what you see with what you've recorded. Do not discount anything that at first doesn't seem to make sense. For example, if you wrote down something was really hot and it happened to be a picture of sunflowers, it makes sense! The sun is hot! If you said it looked like a cheetah, again, sunflowers are yellowish orange and brown and black, just like a cheetah! If you smelled the outdoors and the flowers were actually inside in a vase, that's okay, too. Sunflowers grow outside. The more you practice, the better you will be at deciphering your symbolic messages.

You can do this by yourself, without a partner, as well. Fill up five envelopes with different items. Mix up all of the envelopes and pick one random envelope at a time to work with. Be sure to record all of your psychic impressions. Remember: there are no wrong answers. Enjoy the process. You are learning how to tune in to your symbolic communications.

5

Color Symbolism

One of the easiest ways to interpret psychic symbols is by understanding what colors mean. Often, feeling or seeing color clairvoyantly is the first sign of recognition that you are receiving information. For example, if you get a flash in your third eye of a "purple" person it may be your symbol for someone who is very psychic. Alternatively, if you see in your mind that brown or black is mixed in with that purple, it could mean the person is closed off spiritually. Learning what colors stand for is paramount to comprehending those intuitive flashes.

For me, when I tell someone I "see" them as blue, this means I psychically feel the color blue all around them and I may also clairvoyantly see blue emanating off of their body, as part of their aura or metaphysical energy field. (See chapter 6, "Chakra and Aura Symbolism.") Occasionally, even though I've been practicing for years and have performed thousands of readings, it will still feel as though I am imagining the color. This too is okay; the imagination helps to open the senses. By feeling or seeing these colors psychically I'm able to interpret symbolically what I need to share with my client. Just experiencing the one color can help me understand so much about that person; it's as if I've received a paragraph of information for them. Thus, "seeing" a color can sometimes be more important and can transmit more information in that one symbolic message than having a spirit tell me something using other descriptors.

Often, children and adults are drawn to certain colors. This can manifest in a desire to wear a specific color or color group. When I was little, my mother used to call me the "Purple People Eater" because I loved to wear purple. What I wasn't aware of then, but I am cognizant of now, is that purple is a very spiritual and psychic color. It makes perfect sense to me that I wanted to wrap myself in and be immersed in this shade, as I am a professional psychic now. On some level, my intuitive sense helped me understand that by surrounding myself with purple it would add or enhance my intuitive abilities.

Children also express their desire to surround themselves with color by choosing what hue to paint on the walls of their bedroom. As grown-ups, we often find ourselves limiting the colors in our homes based on interior design cues, keeping many rooms neutral. Though they may not understand why, kids have a natural desire to spread their energy around their rooms using bright colors. Doing so not only helps to express their mental and emotional personality, but it also expresses their spiritual essence, which, unless shut down, can help them to retain and add to their natural intuitive ability.

Colors are a part of everyday life for most of the population and have the added benefit as messages, because they carry not only meaning but temperature and emotion as well. For example, blue is generally accepted as a "cooler" color, while red is "hot." As in, "I feel blue," this particular color is sometimes associated with feeling sad, lonely, or depressed, while red is associated with something sexy or exciting or even angry and full of rage.

Possessing emotion and temperature affords us the opportunity to metaphysically receive color in different ways. Seeing the color with our mind's eye or clairvoyance is common, but feeling the emotion or temperature using our clairsentience helps us understand what color we are psychically identifying.

Colors may also represent certain tastes. Red, again, represents heat. Using clairgustance, red may taste spicy. This can help if we are being directed to a certain restaurant or if we are being psychically directed to take care of our health by avoiding spicy food. White, on the contrary, may be represented by an extremely bland taste in your mouth, which may be a dietary necessity when recovering from surgery or from stomach problems. White or blue may also be sent psychically to suggest cold foods instead of hot foods, which would be represented by red.

Due to the variety of psychic senses we can use to receive colors symbolically, many metaphysical messengers choose this method to send us communications. Spirit guides, deceased loved ones, and angels will use whatever means they can to make it easier for us to comprehend what they are telling us. Luckily, these couriers of psychic messages recognize how we receive information and recognize the need to help us by presenting the data in different ways.

Mandalas

It is quite common to perceive isolated or individual colors in your mind's eye when deciphering a symbol or simply looking at someone. Frequently, though, colors will appear through artwork or design. One specific design is called a *mandala*. A mandala is a circular representation of spirit. Unlike the aura, which is the natural energy emitted from the body, the mandala is an artistic creation usually made by drawing or painting a picture loosely contained in a circle. It can be depicted in a myriad of colors and shapes and used as a tool to "read" your subconscious. Mandalas present a symbolic look or insight into your whole self, the essence of who you are and who you can be. Carl Jung viewed mandalas as affirming the value of the unconscious or the unconscious processes. Eastern religious traditions use mandalas as a meditation tool.

The symbols, designs, shapes, and colors that are present in the mandala are for you to decipher, whether you see a mandala clairvoyantly or you draw one yourself. You can also partition off your mandala to reveal different parts of your self: your past, your present, your conscious mind and subconscious. The upper part of the circle is your conscious mind and the lower part is your subconscious. The left side represents your past, parts of you that have helped to mold or shape you into who you are today. The right section represents your future, the potential of who you are to become. Blurred hazily down the middle, extending throughout the whole circle, is your present self, who you are today.

Understanding the Role of Colors

Colors play as big a role as objects or images when trying to interpret a symbolic message. Pay attention to the feeling you get with each hue. If you are receiving the colors as symbols, be sure to note whether the color was clear and true or whether it was muddied up or dirty in some way. For example, a bright orange can imply the person you are reading for has a healthy level of creativity and sexuality. Alternatively, if the color appears dull or not bright it may suggest that the person you're reading for is lacking any sex drive at all or is stifling all of their creative urges.

Listed on the following pages are basic color guidelines you can refer to, which may help you decipher colors or any symbolic artwork you receive. As with all the symbols described in this book, many of the symbolic interpretations are derived from both common knowledge and my own experiences and memories during my personal and professional life. Many of the descriptions will fit in with what you personally perceive colors to mean, but some won't. If they don't ring true, ask yourself, "Why not? Is there something I need to address in my own personal life that has struck a chord? Is there a definitive difference of opinion, or do the meanings overlap?"

You will find some of the descriptions contradict each other. That is normal, as some of the meanings are actually opposing ideas. Feel free to add your own unique symbolic references as well. This will allow you to really tap into your own intuitive sense to help you personalize the meanings behind the colors.

The exercises at the end of the chapter will help you to experience the different colors, whether you see them clairvoyantly, hear them clairaudiently, or feel them clairsentiently or claircognizantly.

After you read the meanings on the following pages, take a couple of deep breaths and close your eyes. Think about each color individually and notice what words, symbols, or feelings come to mind. While you are meditating, pay attention to any thoughts that pop up regarding a particular color. Open your eyes and write down what you get in your journal. Remember that there is no wrong answer.

Basic Color Reference Guide

Black: can indicate negativity; something that is dangerous or evil; may represent sin or sinners or evil or wrongdoers; may convey sinister or disturbing feelings; can indicate your subconscious or unconscious mind; black in the aura can represent a person's propensity for wrongdoing or for illegal dealings; when seen as directed toward someone can indicate hatred; as with "yin yang," can indicate the feminine; as with black and white, can represent one side of a story or right or wrong, or good or bad, or true or false, or the ability to see both sides of the story; as with black and white, can indicate the unconscious or conscious decision to only see black or white, instead of being able to see the gray or to read between the lines; can correspond to illness or disease; combination of all colors in a negative or positive way; can indicate the need to balance all chakras; may represent a void or missing piece

Blue: the fifth color of the rainbow, associated with the fifth chakra or the throat chakra, can indicate communication or may represent a teacher or someone who presents ideas through communication; can indicate a need to examine the thyroid gland; represents peacefulness or tranquility; blue in the aura may represent intelligence, wisdom, good communication skills, as well as spirituality and imagination; can indicate clairaudient ability; may represent male energy or young male or masculine energy; as in "feeling blue," can indicate depression or sadness; representative of emotions; can indicate a predisposition for idealism; may represent a need for water or to cleanse spiritually or physically

Brass: though similar to gold, it is not quite there, a tarnished version of gold (see *Gold*); a need for something to be polished or cleaned; a desire to reach the top; the need to remove any negativity; when seen in the aura may represent intelligence or obstinacy; may indicate the need to refine character; similar to "brash," can indicate rudeness or harshness; as in "tarnished," a false truth, or something or someone that is not true; can represent blending of two items together; the culmination of a wonderful accident; can refer to the Temperance card in the traditional tarot decks; the melding of items or people to form a new partnership or product; as in the brass ring, can represent reaching your goal, direction to or toward a goal, or attaining the prize or prized possession

Brown: as in the earth, can indicate someone who works with nature; may indicate the need to return to nature to ground oneself; clear brown can refer to someone who is grounded, someone who is hard-working or works hard outdoors; may suggest a back-to-basics method of approaching something; as in "down to earth," can represent a relaxed person or atmosphere; may represent nurturing or comfort or simplicity; in the aura may indicate something negative in the area of the physical body where brown is located, or some part of the physical body that needs attention; can indicate low energy or low levels of energy; as in age spots, can indicate knowledge and wisdom earned through time; may represent a feminine or mother energy

Fuchsia: can indicate a vibrant person; may represent someone who is positive or the positive aspects of someone; as in the Fuchsia plant, can represent someone who is connected to nature or someone who is grounded; can indicate someone who is unconventional or nonconforming to the general population; may refer to someone who wishes to stand out; a need for recognition or the need to be acknowledged; as associated to pink, can indicate a strong, positive love; may refer to someone who is committed to the idea of love or the ideal relationship; can represent someone who surrounds himself or herself with loved or adored objects

Gold: represents awareness; indicative of enlightenment or reaching the highest possible level of spiritual awareness; as in "go for the gold," the ultimate goal or success; a crowning achievement; as in the crown chakra, can indicate psychic awareness or divine communication; can refer to money or the abundance of money; may indicate great wealth and monetary or other emotional commodities such as love, respect, and the like; can refer to financial gain; can indicate positive investment or wealth used wisely; if seen negatively can indicate a shortfall or lack of financial gain; may indicate success in a venture; success in all things; can indicate optimism or an optimistic person

Gray: can indicate poor health or health concerns; as in going gray, can refer to age or growing old; can also represent something that is constant or present; alternatively, can indicate the ability to change or morph when exposed to other things; can represent neutrality, as in the middle of black and white; as in gray matter, can represent reading between the lines; can indicate the decay of something or someone; may represent a hardness as in steel; may refer to cloudy pictures or images or something being unclear; can represent a change in the weather for the worse; may suggest a darkening period or a time of confusion; can indicate efficiency or lack of personality; may suggest a need for rest; may indicate sadness or depression

Green: the fourth color of the rainbow and the fourth chakra or heart chakra; may represent the physical heart; may indicate a need for healing; alternatively, may indicate someone who is a natural healer or is in the healing profession; peaceful surroundings; as with grass, can refer to someone who is connected to nature or a need to ground oneself; can indicate a need to rest; a person who is relaxed; can indicate fertility, especially when mixed with pink and yellow; represents growth in all areas of life; may represent growth and rebirth; can indicate money or financial success, especially when combined with gold; can represent the need for or the culmination of change or transformation to facilitate growth in some way; as in the heart chakra, may represent love; the natural rhythm of things/life; as in "green with envy," may represent jealousy; alternatively, may represent forgiveness; may also represent a need to clear out clutter and confusion; a need to cleanse physically, spiritually, and emotionally

Indigo: the sixth color of the rainbow and the sixth chakra or third-eye chakra; represents spirituality; indicates clairvoyance or clairvoyant ability; can represent the ability to see things both figuratively and literally; indicates psychic ability, either known or unknown; as in "indigo children," children born psychic; may suggest a need to meditate or someone who meditates; someone who is striving for spiritual perfection or enlightenment; may indicate wisdom or knowledge; may be associated with someone who is philosophical; may represent dreams or the dream state

Ivory: similar to white (see also *White*); unclear version of white; as in "ivory tusks," something that is precious; may indicate something that is not quite right; only partial truth; someone who is not quite spiritual; as in "ivory tower," someone who is detached or apart from others, or someone who is aloof or standoffish; not 100 percent pure; in the aura can mean someone who hides their truth or their emotions or has not yet realized their truth or their emotions; can represent someone who is striving to do good but having a difficult time achieving or sustaining it

Magenta: can indicate someone with a strong personality; someone who desires to or does stand out; someone with entrepreneurial skills; may refer to overabundance; may symbolize an insatiable appetite for everything in life; in the aura can indicate someone who loves fully, but possibly has lower self-esteem or someone who is dedicated to others but not to themselves; can refer to a soothing or calming presence; a need for balance (see also *Fuchsia*)

Maroon: can refer to the base or root chakra (red chakra, see also *Red*); in the positive can indicate a sense of strength and stability; bravery; can refer to someone in power; alternatively, in the negative can indicate a shaky foundation; may represent anger or rage; when dark can indicate someone about to explode or explosive temperament

Orange: second color of the rainbow and second or sexual chakra; represents sexuality; can indicate creativity; in the aura can indicate sexuality and vitality; may refer to someone who is sensual; may indicate artistic ability; may indicate temptation or sexual temptation; in the negative can refer to a lack of sex drive or an inappropriate or out-of-balance sex drive; may indicate menstrual or reproductive issues or current menstruation; vibrant clear orange can indicate a healthy balanced appetite; can also refer to a change in residence or a new home; can indicate a need for oranges (the fruit) or vitamin C; may refer to a geographical location such as Florida or California

Pink: can refer to female energy or a young female; may indicate pregnancy or a baby; associated with new or innocent love; can represent love from the divine; as in "in the pink" or "tickled pink," can mean healthy and happy; in the aura can correspond to someone who is in love or who lives life fully in joy or is optimistic; may represent health

Purple: the outer edge of the rainbow; may suggest someone or something that is regal or noble; can indicate power and strength; dominating; in the aura can indicate someone who is of a strong or powerful or of royal lineage, can also refer to psychic ability or spiritual development; spiritual power; as with the "purple heart" can represent an earned high honor; someone who makes others happy through selfless acts; as with grapes, can refer to a need for fruit or fruit juice or vitamins A and C

Red: the first color of the rainbow and corresponding to the first, base, or root chakra; can indicate a need for stability or structure; in the negative can indicate anger, rage, or jealousy; can represent trouble; represents base desires; in the aura may present as rage or anger; often seen as insecurity or trouble with identity; life force or vitality; as in "seeing red," feeling uncontrollable anger; often present during periods of manifestation

Silver: symbolic of divine communication or a spiritual message or messenger; can represent money, as in silver coins; in the aura may indicate someone who is intuitive or psychic; as in "silver tongued," someone who has the power of persuasion, a smooth talker; as with the etheric silver cord, the line that connects the physical body with the individual and universal souls; sparkly silver can indicate the presence of fairies or fairy-like energy; as with "silver fox," may refer to a good-looking older man

Tan: may imply simplicity; back to basics (see also *Brown*); as in "tan your hide," can refer to cruel beating or punishment; tan in the aura can imply calmness or quiet; someone who keeps to themselves; someone who is trustworthy; a friend; may indicate someone who moves under the radar naturally; may refer to someone who enjoys research

Violet: the top color of the rainbow and the seventh or crown chakra; indicates divine guidance; spirituality; supreme being; psychic messages; enlightenment; as in "crowning glory," the best one can achieve; the highest self or the highest being; in the aura may represent inspiration, creativity, intuitive awareness; can be present in someone who is kind and generous; someone who is open and receptive to psychic and symbolic messages; may represent someone who channels information or messages; may represent flowers

White: pure of mind, body, and spirit; divine or divinity; hope; faith; perfection; in the aura can imply purity of mind or thought; may imply psychic ability or intuitive awareness; may suggest an inner calm or peace; can refer to a virgin or virginity; divine connection; clairvoyance and claircognizance; messenger of the divine; angelic messenger or presence; truth; clean or cleanliness or sterile environment; may refer to something that is precious

Yellow: the third color in the rainbow and the third chakra or solar plexus chakra; bright and happy; sunny disposition; associated with clairsentience; power and confidence; in the aura can refer to someone who is bright, cheerful, easygoing; can indicate intuitive awareness; in the negative can represent fear or that which we fear; may refer to a need for or the act of cleansing or clearing; can refer to the sun or the warmth of the sun

Exercise 1: Interpreting Additional Colors

Turn to a new page in your journal and write the word *Colors*. Record any additional colors that may come to mind. You can write down different hues of the basic colors listed on the preceding pages. For instance, you may wish to explore blue further and record colors such as turquoise and aqua, or you might be drawn to emerald green or forest green or even celadon green. This will be your chance to really tune in to what you feel represents the truth of these colors. It will also help you to recognize what the colors feel like to you.

Exercise 2: Create Your Own Mandala

Draw a circle on a fresh sheet of paper. You will use this circle to create your own personal mandala. Sit comfortably, take a few deep breaths, and relax. Grab a box of crayons or colored pencils and just begin allowing yourself to use whatever colors you feel and draw anything that feels right. Colors, shapes, numbers, letters, words, or whatever else you can imagine can be part of this beautiful self-portrait.

When you are done, go back and "read" your mandala. See if there is anything that jumps out at you, either something you understand or something you don't. Use the color-reference guide in this chapter and the basic symbols glossary in this book to assist you in interpreting the meanings of the various details you have drawn.

Draw a very light line vertically in the very center of the circle from top to bottom to divide your past from your future. Draw a horizontal line directly through the center to show your conscious mind (on top) and your subconscious (on the bottom).

Date your mandala, and then name it. This will be a good reference to look back on. Every few months, draw a new mandala and compare it to your old ones. Notice the ways in which your mandalas may have changed and the ways in which they are similar. Notice in what ways the mandalas relate to your physical life.

6

Chakra and Aura Symbolism

Chakras and auras are connected, though they are separate parts of the spiritual body. Most researchers agree there are seven main energy bands that compose the aura that emanates from the body, similar to the seven major chakras within. As author and healer Cyndi Dale puts it in her book *The Subtle Body: An Encyclopedia of Your Energetic Anatomy*: "The human energy field is primarily composed of the *aura*, a set of energy bands that graduate in frequency and color as they move outward from the body. Each of the auric fields opens to different energy planes and energy bodies and also partners with a chakra, thus exchanging information between worlds outside [the aura] and inside [the chakras] of the body."

Chakras, a Sanskrit word meaning "spinning wheels," are energy centers within the body, also commonly referred to as spiritual batteries. There are seven major chakras located in a metaphysical line starting from the base of the spine to the top of the head. When I see these colorful spinning wheels with my third eye, or clairvoyance, they are funnel-like, each having its own location within the physical body. Each center of spiritual power is associated with very specific colors. They also represent various physical organs within the body.

Associated with the chakras are auras. Everything living has an aura or an energy field surrounding its physical body. Auras are usually perceived as colors or sometimes white light and emanate externally out of the body. Auras vary from chakras in that they can be seen psychically *or* with the naked eye by focusing on the edge of the physical body (see the "Seeing Auras" exercise at the end of this chapter). Often the more in tune you are psychically, the more colorfully you'll begin sensing chakras and auras and the symbolic messages they express.

Chakras

Like charging stations, chakras energize us and help manage and co-ordinate how we function on the whole. In his book *Psychic Navigator*, psychic medium John Holland describes his experience with chakras as crossing the barriers between both Eastern and Western philosophies: "Human anatomy is engineered by a complex network of etheric wiring through which energy flows, and the chakras are the organizing centers for both the reception and the transmission of life energies (chi/prana), which are essential to our physical, mental, and spiritual development."

Quite often, people will clairvoyantly see symbols connected to various locations along the body. These locations may relate to a particular chakra. By understanding chakras we are able to interpret the message more clearly. For example, if you see an image of a windshield wiper in front of someone's forehead it may not have anything to do with a car. It probably means the person needs to clear out or clean their third eye or clairvoyance chakra so they can receive symbolic messages visually. Learning about chakras opens up the metaphysical connection. This helps increase intuitive awareness, which promotes the ability to recognize, and use, symbols.

Understanding the chakras' connection to colors also contributes to symbolic knowledge. For instance, seeing a hazy green or pink projecting from someone's heart may suggest a recent breakup, or a bright green can indicate a new love. You may begin to symbolically see the actual physical manifestation of chakras as well. You may look at someone and clairvoyantly see if their psychic wheels are spinning or have stopped. You may see this as an old-fashioned water wheel or you may see it symbolically represented by a bicycle wheel spinning. That same bike wheel may have the brakes applied, indicating there is something stopping that chakra from spinning. All in all, understanding chakras and the way the chakra system works can help you to interpret symbols on a much deeper, more spiritual level.

The first of the spiritual batteries or chakras is known as the root chakra. This powerful center is the color red. A warm and bright, almost blood-red color, this base chakra is at the bottom of the spine, bordered by the sexual organs and the anus, between the legs. This spinning wheel of energy is responsible for survival. The root chakra represents groundedness and support or foundation as well as feelings of security—domestic security to financial security. This beautiful red-colored chakra keeps us stable, creating the base or foundation for all seven energy centers.

This root chakra is often disrupted because of childhood trauma or abuse. This may cause a blemish in self-worth or self-esteem. If you see this chakra as muddy in someone's energy, it may mean they need to ground themselves or that they have some type of foundation issue related to self-worth. It may also mean they are having a hard time with work or even finding a job.

Notice if you feel it as more of a physical problem versus a domestic issue. If the muddy red also shows up in someone's lower joints, that person may be experiencing pain in their knees or ankles, as this chakra is connected to lower-extremity problems and arthritis. You may feel a stuck sensation when you see a dull red color in someone's first chakra representing an imbalance. This can cause weight issues, constipation, and bladder, prostrate, or elimination problems. Possibly, this out-of-kilter center is presenting physically in the lymphatic system or the adrenal glands. Interestingly, if you are seeing a symbol for a dentist as you are tuning in to the first chakra, it makes perfect sense. This base energy center is in charge of the entire skeletal system, including the teeth.

The second chakra, or sacral chakra, represents sensuality and sexuality. This energy wheel is a vivid orange in color and is located a couple of inches below the navel or belly button. This chakra is connected spiritually to the spleen and the reproductive and sexual organs. This second chakra is where you feel or sense things, the beginning of clairsentience. This is also the seat of your creativity and imagination.

If you see someone's orange chakra out of balance—perhaps a less than vivid color, or lopsided in some way—it may mean they need to tap into their creativity. Possibly it's time for them to indulge in some form of artistic expression like painting, drawing, or music. You may find that the orange color is dampened due to lack of sexual relations or if someone has had their tubes tied or has reproductive issues. Notice if the person has a muddy first chakra as well; this combination could indicate poor self-esteem leading to sexual dysfunction.

If it seems too big, or overly bright, making the other chakras pale in comparison, it may indicate a reliance on sexual relations for happiness or that the person relates sexual passion to love, confusing true love with sex. Alternatively, if they have a bright, beautiful clear second chakra, chances are they have a great balance of creativity as well as sexuality.

Yellow is the color of the third, or solar plexus, chakra. This spiritual power center also connects you to your clairsentience or your clear feeling. This solar plexus chakra is associated with the stomach and intestines, the liver, the pancreas, and even the skin. The third chakra represents your will; it is the power center, your very core. It regulates self-esteem and self-confidence and is where you "center" yourself. It is also where the phrase *gut instinct* comes from. Yellow is a very psychic color, a very intuitive color, and is where intuition sits.

If you see a beautiful yellow emanating and spinning in perfect balance, chances are that person is very intuitive as well as very confident. Notice if the yellow color blends together with the lower chakra colors, indicating strength in intuitive processes but a shaky foundation or lack of confidence.

If you see a dull or muddied yellow, that person may be experiencing digestive issues. Metaphysically, someone may be giving them a load of bull that they are having a hard time ingesting. Physically, they may be eating the wrong foods and may require a more natural diet.

If you observe that someone has a large protruding belly, it may also be possible this person is trying to psychically protect themselves. Often, adding that layer of protection or weight helps to ward off any psychic attacks or attacks on self-esteem. Unfortunately, this can lead to other physical and even spiritual issues. The best way to deal with these emotional or metaphysical attacks can be to follow a healthy diet and invoke that protective circle of white light every day. This will keep one safe on the inside and the outside.

One of the most physically demanding chakras is the heart chakra, or the fourth chakra. This chakra is located in the center of the chest and spins an amazing emerald green. This beautiful, warm chakra is responsible for love, healing, and peace. It is also connected to compassion, empathy, and forgiveness.

If the color or energy of this green center is fading or pulsing slowly, it may indicate heart or circulatory issues. Be very careful of voicing this, however; you do not want to conjure up a self-fulfilling prophecy. If the color is muddy green, almost dripping down through the torso, this can point toward problems with the lungs and chest—a possible indication of respiratory ailments. You might also notice this chest chakra color is not as vibrant if the person has issues with their immune system, as this energy center is also connected to the thymus gland. If you feel this chakra is not working properly, notice if there are any other colors or symbols or images that combine with the muddy or dirty green; if there is a hazy pink it may mean the person's love life is suffering. If there is a brown or gray color it may suggest they should have a mammogram done soon—especially if you see this in conjunction with an image of a pink ribbon, the symbol for breast cancer.

One of the hardest tasks for people is acceptance of one's own self. We cannot accept others without first truly accepting and loving ourselves. If you see black mixed into someone's green chakra, that person is probably holding on to a long-lived hurt or experiencing a very difficult emotional period in their life. If you are confronted with or know someone who is habitually grumpy, irritable, or mean, tune in to their heart chakra and see what color it is and whether you see it spinning or not. If it looks to be a mess, send them some beautiful emerald-green energy to brighten up their chakra and observe whether there is a difference in their attitude or not; sometimes they just need a little nudge in the right direction. They may simply need to accept themselves. "The most terrifying thing is to accept oneself completely," Carl Jung said. As Jung suggests, loving oneself is something we could all use a little help with.

Contrary to an unbalanced heart chakra is a beautifully clear fourth energy wheel, spinning just right. You'll recognize this in a person who is very loving, who cares for themselves and others. This person may be very involved with charity, often helping people one on one, and may be the person who is behind the scenes, not needing the recognition. This person will also live their life happily, without much drama. If this fourth chakra appears to be perfectly balanced, such a person may be experiencing a perfect harmonious relationship in their life or they may have achieved a healthy mental equilibrium between giving and receiving. More significantly, they might have discovered how to truly love themselves.

The fifth chakra is the communication chakra. Known aptly as the throat chakra, it is located in the neck and regulates the thyroid gland. This beautiful blue-colored power center is associated with clairaudience, or clear hearing.

When this chakra is rotating in a balanced spin it is indicative of someone who is a good communicator, someone who is good at sharing or teaching ideas as well as listening to and understanding others. This brilliant blue chakra is associated with the ability to be a good presenter. When combined with strong lower chakras, particularly the yellow or third chakra, a balanced fourth chakra can enable a person to be a captivating public speaker or spokesperson. It may also indicate someone with intuitive prowess. People with talented singing voices tend to have beautifully spinning blue energy centers.

An unbalanced or sluggish communication chakra can be present in someone who has a very difficult time relating to others, listening to others, or even talking with others. It may present physically as trouble with the vocal chords, the larynx, or the ears or hearing.

When the fifth energy center is unstable it causes some people to experience difficulty accepting directions, which can also contribute to attention deficit disorder. Instructions can get lost in the filtering process due to focusing issues. This out-of-kilter energy wheel may also add to a person's lack of talent when it comes to karaoke.

The sixth chakra is possibly one of the most commonly recognized and is referred to as the third-eye chakra. Located low in the forehead, centered above and in between the eyes, this chakra is responsible for clairvoyance or the ability to psychically see. This indigo-colored clairvoyant area is linked to the pituitary gland, the forehead, and the eyes.

This powerful energy center, also known as the brow chakra, is associated with the way we view or see the world. It also contributes to the ability to imagine and perceive things. A balanced sixth chakra helps us to have clear sight or clear vision both physically and psychically and to see things in a positive light.

A clear third eye also contributes to the ability to concentrate, focus, and learn. This contributes to the retention of knowledge as well as spiritual or psychic wisdom. If you come across someone who is very clairvoyant, you may notice a lot of indigo floating around their forehead area. You may also see this around people who are very visual. For example, if you see indigo as well as orange you may be in the company of a very talented artist.

A balanced sixth chakra can be associated with insight, common sense, intuition, and psychic awareness. This indigo color may be very pronounced around someone who is not only clairvoyant but also very psychic. Combined with the blue color of communication it may indicate someone who is actively making a living at holding private sessions or conducting psychic readings.

Alternatively, an out-of-balance or out-of-focus third eye can lead to an inability to see psychically or receive clairvoyant messages. If you see a hazy indigo color it can represent someone who is closed off to this natural psychic ability.

A dirty indigo color may also be symbolic of someone who is currently having or who regularly experiences headaches or migraines. It may represent some one who is physically in need of glasses or psychically in need of a "windshield washing" to clear their third eye. If you know someone who endures nightmares on a regular basis, it may be due to an unbalanced sixth chakra. Seeing negative images or pictures can be a hint to clear out the third eye. A muddied indigo third eye blending with a dirty blue communication chakra may indicate a need to develop an understanding of the psychic symbolic language. It's possible messages are coming through but aren't being recognized. Doing the exercises at the end of the chapter will help with the transmission of these communications and get those chakras spinning beautifully again.

The final chakra is the seventh, or crown, chakra. This chakra is located on the top of the head and is a tether to the universal consciousness. This amazing violet-colored chakra is associated with universal knowledge and divine wisdom. It is also symbolic of enlightenment and psychic knowing. This chakra is considered to be the connection to divine guidance, aiding in all psychic ability, intuition, and the ability to receive messages from the other side, angels, and God.

Physically this powerful energy center is associated with the brain as well as the central nervous system. When this chakra is open and spinning beautifully there will be a feeling of wellness, of wholeness within oneself as well as the community and the universe. This will also be prevalent in someone with great psychic ability, as this crown chakra is associated with claircognizance or clear knowing.

If someone has an off-balance crown chakra, which is quite common, they may have a skewed sense of right and wrong. It's possible they experience headaches or confusion. They may also have trouble connecting to others or feeling connected to anyone, giving them a sense of aloneness. In addition, they may feel like the only person experiencing what others perceive as mundane everyday occurrences in life. When out of balance, this energy center can contribute to a sense of depression or social withdrawal. If you see someone with a very dark, muddy violet chakra, it is possible they may suffer from some sort of serious mental confusion like schizophrenia. More commonly they may just be extremely opinionated or argumentative. If you come across someone who is extremely prejudiced or bigoted, it may be that their crown chakra is out of balance, filling them with negativity as opposed to positive energy. They may also be apathetic or closed off to others, often not even knowing why.

A balanced chakra system helps lead to a healthy life: physically, emotionally, and psychically. This in turn leaves you open to receive, interpret, and understand psychic symbolic messages on a regular basis.

Knowing which energy centers correlate to which psychic abilities can help you to strengthen the areas you may wish to enhance. For example, if you feel as though you don't have any ability to see psychic symbols you may want to work on your sixth chakra to open up your clairvoyance. If you have a hard time interpreting your intuition, you might want to strengthen your gut instinct chakra or your solar plexus chakra as well as your third-eye or brow chakra.

Use the exercises at the end of this chapter to help you fortify and reinforce your various psychic communication abilities. And don't forget there's a basic principle to remember: your physical and psychic bodies are temples. The stronger these bodies are, the stronger your chakras or energy centers will be for you to receive symbolic messages. This means, of course, that if you are trying to build up your solar plexus or third chakra, your belly area, don't eat more chocolate cake. "Feeding" your chakras the wrong way will just disrupt them.

Auras

Auras have often been depicted in history through art and literature as halos over the heads of saints. These are only one small part of an aura's makeup, as auras surround the entire body, but they are a very common way to convey the clairvoyant image an artist has of the subject's aura. Have you ever seen a child's drawing in which the child colored the people differently? Possibly Mommy was green, Daddy was orange, and the child's brother was blue? This is very typical. Children are more open to experiencing auras on a daily basis. Growing up, my sister was very artistic and very visual. I remember she used to refer to people as "that green person" or "the blue girl over there." The combination of visual creativity as well as open clairvoyance produced this unquestioned belief that people truly were a variety of colors.

Children continue to stay open to this until adults as well as other children shut them down. When children are told continually that everything is either black or white, they start to believe it and then begin to see on a purely physical level instead of a psychic level.

Auras change constantly, swaying in shape and morphing into a variety of colors based on mood or what is happening. As Ted Andrews puts it in his book *How to See and Read the Aura*: "Everyone has an aura. Everyone has already seen or experienced the auric field of others. The problem is that most people ignore the experience or chalk it up to something that it is not."

You may feel your body's energy or your aura changing when you walk into a room where you feel uncomfortable. You might find that you automatically "pull your energy in," protecting yourself from whatever negativity is in the room. This is your aura that you are retracting. Alternatively, you may find you are pushing out your energy or expanding your aura when you are happy, or wanting to share your excitement with others.

As you walk into that room full of people, you perhaps feel connected to somebody in particular, and start to see or feel psychic symbols. That is because you have connected to their aura and are reading them or receiving psychic information about that person. By tuning in to their aura you are opening a gateway to receiving symbols about them; you are connecting to their energy, which can produce a multitude of images or impressions.

We all have energy that surrounds us, emanating from our physical beings. This is the etheric side of energy, the subtle auric energy that helps us to see if a person is healthy or what the person is experiencing in the moment. An aura is a combination of colors that seem to stream out of each of us, not always clear to everyone, but very prevalent in psychic and intuitive work.

I was working with a student in a workshop, and we were doing an exercise with the class, learning to feel someone's energy field. I partnered up with her and we began demonstrating. Linda sat in a chair, perfectly still, and I placed my hands about two inches away from her. I could feel her energy projecting away from her body. I traveled all the way up and down her right side, and everything felt fine; her energy felt pretty constant and steady with no breaks. Then I moved to her left side. Straightaway I felt her energy had disappeared around her jaw area. I could feel it sink in next to her cheek and her neck. I told her that she possibly was having communication issues or trouble with her throat chakra. I sensed her energy was damaged in some way in that area, and I could feel that her normally blue communication chakra was blackened. I also felt the area around her root or base chakra was perforated in some way, and I saw an image of a drill.

Linda stood up, laughed, and said to the class, "I just came from the dentist. I had a root canal on one of my left teeth!"

Reading a person's aura or feeling a person's energy is very real and can also be very telling. Pay attention to those little prickly sensations on the back of your neck or the goosebumps that rise up at various times. They are your energetic way of letting you know you should be aware of what's happening in that moment or at that time.

Learning to understand the symbolic meanings of the various shapes and colors of the aura is key to understanding psychic messages about people. You may begin to look to people with an eye for color. What message does that give you about that person or what they are going through or feeling in that moment? For example, if you see blue around someone, what does that tell you?

By going through the chakra locations and colors in this chapter as well as looking at the Basic Color Reference Guide in the last chapter, you will start to understand what messages the auras have to share with you. You will also begin to associate symbolically the importance of perceiving all of the details of whatever psychic impressions you receive.

Exercise 1: Chakra Meditation

To get all of your chakras spinning in perfect harmony, imagery and meditation are a must. Begin by finding a comfortable place to sit. Make sure you are wearing loose-fitting clothing. Close your eyes and take a few deep breaths, feeling your diaphragm opening during every inhalation.

Allow your focus to travel down to your root chakra, at the base of your spine, between your legs. Imagine a beautiful red disc there, spinning brightly, at the perfect speed. Feel the warmth that this chakra gives off as it vibrates through your body. Picture any psychic debris or negativity just flying off of this red center, leaving it clean of any energy that no longer belongs there; clearing any debris that no longer belongs to you.

Envision this dark or unclear energy as it falls down into the earth to be recycled into positive energy.

Move your awareness up now, about two inches below your navel. Feel your brilliant sacral chakra spinning and opening up your reproductive area. Imagine this gorgeous orange color filling up the entire area between your hips. Clairvoyantly watch as any psychic or physical debris flies off and travels down to the earth to be recycled.

Continue further up into your solar plexus and imagine this yellow chakra spinning brightly. Feel this beautiful color expanding out throughout your whole trunk as any fragments of negativity fall away. Allow yourself to feel the warmth in your abdomen as this intuitive energy center continues to spin now, perfectly balanced. Breathe deeply and calmly as you send energy to this amazing chakra.

As you continue further up, feel the warmth of your fourth chakra with every beat of your heart. Imagine this incredible green center pulsing as it spins. With every beat see in your mind's eye any psychic or physical debris being pushed out of your body, clearing this wonderful green chakra, allowing it to spin freely.

Move your attention up to your throat chakra and breathe in deeply, filling your throat up with beautiful blue energy. Allow this communication chakra to spin brightly, sending out rays of light with every exhalation. Swallow, and allow only positive blue energy to travel through your glorious throat chakra.

On your next deep breath, bring your attention to your third-eye chakra. Relax your forehead and brow muscles, letting your third-eye space open up naturally. Imagine this clairvoyant energy center getting brighter as it spins a beautiful indigo color. Feel the change in temperature as your third eye warms your forehead and this warmth begins to spread up to your crown chakra.

Notice, as your energy continues up, how the top of your head begins to tingle as your crown chakra spins a wonderfully violet color. Feel your hair as it begins to stand up, tingling, as this psychic center opens wide, allowing divine guidance to pour in.

Sit and enjoy the energy as it spins through your body.

One by one, pull your energy back into your chakras to keep yourself free and protected from any psychic energy or debris that doesn't belong to you. You don't want to close them down completely, but you do want to be sure you are not wide open to any negativity.

Take a nice, long, deep breath and feel how calm and relaxed your body feels. Take another deep breath and open your eyes, feeling perfectly relaxed and filled with positive energy.

Use the exercises that follow to work on each individual chakra. Practice using these exercises on an as-needed or even a daily basis.

Exercise 2: First or Base or Root Chakra

Using a grounding meditation is a great way to help balance your chakras. Focus on the color red and imagine the earth's energy rising up to meet you. Visualize the brown, ruddy grounding energy as it melds together with the beautiful vibrant red energy of your first chakra. Feel your legs beginning to sink into the earth, almost as though they are reaching down to connect. Sit with this feeling until you are content and secure.

Continue this meditation for as long as it feels right, and repeat as often as you want. By grounding your energy, you are stabilizing yourself and readying yourself for any messages that may come your way.

Exercise 3: Second or Sensual Chakra

Have some fun. Go out and get an orange hula hoop. One of the best ways to stimulate your second chakra is by moving the energy around. Get that energy flowing by using a hula hoop (if you can't find orange, any color will do) and tap into your inner child at the same time. By exercising this energy center you are opening your chakra and allowing it to move without having to rely on sex or sexuality. This in turn can help you to balance your sexuality and your creativity and help to establish a confident sense of self.

Exercise 4: Third or Solar Plexus Chakra

Keeping in line with the movement used for the second chakra, try belly dancing. This is a great way to open up your solar plexus and tone not only your chakra system but your core strength as well. Use a yellow belly-dancing scarf, and you'll be on your way to understanding your body and your messages from the other side.

Exercise 5: More Solar Plexus Chakra Work

Not ready for belly dancing? Try this instead. Lie on the floor and place your hand, palm down, over your solar plexus. Now breathe a long deep breath, and focus your attention on the area directly under your hand. Take continuous short and shallow breaths, again focusing on your solar plexus area. Continue panting and allow your belly to move with every inhale and exhale. To help bring the color to your chakra, wear a yellow shirt or put yellow fabric or a yellow napkin under your hand while doing the exercise. Continue the breathing for a minute or so, but don't do it so long that you hyperventilate.

Exercise 6: Fourth or Heart Chakra

This chakra is about love, compassion, and kindness. Take the time now to stimulate those emotions within yourself. Rub your hands together, and as you do feel the warmth and energy that you create. Place your hands over your heart, transmitting the healing energy to your heart chakra. This works especially well for healers and body workers. Take this moment to love yourself.

Now it's time to give and receive love in a different way. Take a few minutes to say twenty nice things about yourself out loud. You can repeat them over and over again, but be sure to say at least twenty different things. After that, give everyone you come into contact with today a compliment. It doesn't matter how big or small the compliment, just appreciate something about them. You'll find that by appreciating them you will in turn appreciate yourself and warm up that heart chakra.

Exercise 7: Fifth or Throat Chakra

One of the easiest ways to tend to your throat chakra is to treat it to a warm cup of herbal tea. Keeping your throat moist and warm helps your voice and your hearing, which opens up your fifth chakra.

Once you've lubricated and opened your chakra, get it spinning. Go into your car and sing at the top of your lungs. Throw your favorite music in and sing wholeheartedly while you're cleaning or doing the dishes. You'll find you not only get your throat chakra in balance, but you might also enjoy cleaning!

Get together with a bunch of friends and sing from the rooftops. It doesn't matter whether you're on key; sing like you did when you were a kid and it didn't matter what you sounded like.

This will also help balance all of your other chakras.

Exercise 8: Sixth or Third-Eye Chakra

One of the best ways to open your third-eye chakra and get it spinning again is to clean it out. Relax, sit back, and enjoy the ride; you're about to drive through an obstacle course.

Get comfortable and close your eyes. Imagine sitting in a car and the windshield is your forehead. The only problem is that your windshield has a heavy coating of dust on it. Reach your hand out and turn on the windshield wipers, focusing all of your attention directly on your third eye. Visualize the wipers as they start clearing the dust and any debris off of your third eye until it feels clean. You may even notice it becoming brighter.

Hold on; life comes at you fast. There's no need to close your third eye down anymore; you can see clearly now. Watch for any obstacles or obstructions in your path, including your own doubt or denial about your abilities. Watch out for any potholes or pockets of old anger or rage, or any pitfalls or insecurities. Your sixth chakra is cleared; these obstacles no longer need to take you out. You're in control.

Exercise 9: Visualization to Strengthen the Third Eye

Now that you've cleaned your third eye of any debris, the next exercise should be easier. Close your eyes and imagine seeing someone in front of you. It can be a friend or family member or someone else you know very well. Notice every detail about this person. What color hair do they have, what color eyes? What are they wearing? How tall are they? Pay special attention to every detail. The more you exercise your third eye, the stronger and clearer it will be.

Exercise 10: Seeing Auras

Grab a friend and have some fun with auras. Find a blank wall, preferably a white one. Have your friend stand in front of the wall, about one to two inches away from it. You should stand about five to ten feet away.

Squint your eyes a bit and look directly over your friend's head. Let your gaze move up about two inches until you see a border around your friend. It may be very clear, or it may barely be there. Now, notice if you see a color. Give it a few minutes. If nothing else happens or you don't see anything else, have your friend turn around and face the wall (or face you if your friend started face in).

Repeat the process and observe if you see any auric energy at all. Have your friend envision expanding his or her energy out as far as possible, and look again. If you don't see a color, imagine you do. Sometimes, by opening your imagination to the possibility, you will actually see with your psychic eye.

Tell your friend what colors he or she is emanating and where they are on the body. Then look up the colors in the reference guide in chapter 5, and see whether they relate to what's going on in your friend's life.

Next, switch positions and see which colors your friend sees or feels around you. Does your friend's auric interpretation resonate with you? What colors do you sense around yourself?

7

Religion, Spirituality, Culture, and Symbols

Religious Symbology and Psychic Communication

The variety of symbols mentioned in this chapter barely scratches the surface of religious, spiritual, and cultural metaphysical interpretations. The ability to recognize these symbols will help you to connect to all the messages you may receive from the other side. As you will learn in chapter 9, "Personal Symbols," many of these images will hold unique meanings depending upon your own life experiences. Open your mind to the possibility that you are in control and are allowed to be receptive to symbolic impressions; the messages are always there no matter what you believe about the afterlife, no matter what religion or non-religion you follow and whatever culture you are part of. Once you understand this basic fact you can become part of a very exciting and interesting metaphysical world.

Many people worry about the consequences of being psychic or communicating with the other side. Consequently, they shut out their intuition, refusing to believe they can live a religious and extrasensory life simultaneously. However, every religion has widely recognized symbols prevalent in daily worship. These symbols have meaning and bring hope and comfort to people practicing a variety of religions.

No one should forsake their belief in a traditional church if that faith gives them hope or strength. Many people feel at home when part of an organized religion. Quite often this brings with it a sense of community, of belonging, of fitting in to society. As long as their religious beliefs aren't hurting anyone, more power to them.

Conversely, the worst thing anyone could do is to blindly follow an organization just to belong. Research it, just as you would do with any club. Understand the principles you are adhering to, and why they are in place. Know that you can connect to your "God" or universal energy anytime, directly, and that because we are all energy, we can also connect to deceased loved ones and spirit guides. This is helping to create a major shift in spiritual awareness. Knowing, in this day and age, that we can all connect, with no need of a facilitator, changes the very structure of religion and challenges our beliefs while contributing to our intuitive awareness.

I became aware a long time ago that our beliefs change with each incarnation. This continues to ring true for me. We all go through many lifetimes. Searching for God or the "universal energy" brings us together to worship in church. Manmade rituals and doctrines are used to comfort us, and give us the structure we need to feel connected. As we progress in our subsequent lives we develop a greater knowledge and understanding of the universal energy of God, which is love. We come to realize that love is all around us and that we can communicate directly to God, this universal energy. It is through this understanding that our faith in organized religion may dissipate naturally. This does not lessen our desire to trust in our sense of community; it just changes the way we pursue that community.

I did a reading for LuAnn, someone I roomed with at a workshop many years ago. I symbolically saw an image of a photograph. The picture was ripped down the middle, not totally disconnected but torn about two-thirds of the way down. On one half was LuAnn; on the other half was a large building I symbolically took to be a church. I also saw bits of the photograph almost stretching to be reattached. I conveyed to her that I knew she was having difficulty with her religious faith but that by working on it or focusing on it she would be able to reconnect to it. I continued by expressing to her that she needed to do what felt right to her in order to get the answers she needed. A year or so later she wrote to me with regard to her religious convictions. She told me she intuitively felt the need to go back to school or take a class. Then she told me what happened after she listened to her symbolic message.

> *The second thing you said to me was that I am a "spiritual person but it had been missing in my life for awhile." I am Catholic and had been struggling with the priest scandals and other things within the church so I had been estranged. I thought about what you said a thousand times over that summer and took a religion class where the instructor brought in a priest, a rabbi, and a Muslim leader to have open dialogue. I got reassuring answers to a lot of questions and wrote many papers about my struggles with my faith. I was then able to let go of most of my turmoil and once again found a spiritual home. That has really given me peace in my life. Thank you, Melanie, for your insight and for planting that seed that grew into a beautiful flower in my life!*

The psychic reading I gave LuAnn actually helped her to reconnect to her religion. It doesn't need to be *either/or*; it can be *and*. Everyone needs to find where they fit in, where they feel secure. I am confident there is more to life than this earthly body and that I won't be convicted to spend eternity in hell when I die. That to me is comforting.

We are sent messages we can relate to, and that make us feel safe. By sending religious and iconic messages, God is helping us to tune in to what feels right, instead of scaring us with symbols that feel dangerous. How you use these symbolic messages is up to you, but being aware of them is the first step. The pure essence of universal love will not ever send you messages you can't use; on the contrary, you are being given an opportunity to tap into the universal consciousness through an ideology that works for you.

Tuning in to these symbolic messages can provide insight into your life. Being open to the impressions you receive can help to firm up beliefs or philosophies you may be questioning. For example, if you are wondering whether going to a religious class will be beneficial, and you receive the image of Jesus as a symbol, you can be assured it will be.

On the other hand, receiving religious or cultural symbols is not always prefaced by questions regarding religion or culture. You are sent symbolic messages in ways that you can relate to and understand. If you meet someone and are unsure about their intentions, but you see an image of a halo hovering over them, chances are it will be positive. The universe will provide you with symbols that are familiar to you so that it is easier for you to react to them.

Duality of Symbols

Being aware of the duality of symbols allows us to be sensitive to more than one interpretation. Multiple meanings are as common in the symbolic language as they are with many words in the English language. This means that in order to truly understand each symbol we can't always take it at face value; we need to realize there is the possibility for more than one translation.

The fish, for instance, holds a general symbolic meaning of fishing, or having a fish as a pet, or eating fish. The fish is also a sign of the zodiac, Pisces, and may indicate astrology. Finally, Christians look to the fish as representative of a follower of Jesus.

There are also symbols with meanings that stretch to their polar opposites. Take, for example, the swastika. Most of the population identifies the swastika with the atrocities during Hitler's reign of terror, including the Holocaust. Present-day swastikas are usually associated with white supremacy groups, such as the Klu Klux Klan or the "skinheads." Interestingly, Buddhists and Hindus take offense to that association because *swastika* comes from the Sanskrit word *svasti*, and means "good fortune," "luck," and "well-being." Typically the swastika is shaped like a cross, with the four ends bent to the left or counterclockwise. In Hinduism the ends are bent to the right or clockwise as well as counterclockwise, with each image carrying a different meaning. Clockwise it means the sun or the god Vishnu, while counter-clockwise, somewhat like the Nazi swastika, represents Kali, a Hindu goddess representing death and destruction and magic.

As seen by the widely divergent descriptions for the swastika, you can understand the complexities of recognizing psychic symbols. That is why it is so important to remain open to different interpretations, especially with religious icons.

There are numerous other religious and spiritual emblems that carry dual meanings. For instance, the Star of David (originally Magen David) in Judaism carried the meaning of the shield of King David, or God, the protector of David. Later, through Kabbalism, the Star of David came to mean protection from evil spirits. Many people may be unaware that this six-pointed star, two equilateral triangles laid over each other in opposite directions, also represents Christianity. It is the Christian Star of Creation or the Creator's Star, and represents the belief that the world was created in six days, hence the six points. Another common Christian interpretation is it symbolizes the six characteristics of God: power, wisdom, mercy, love, justice, and majesty.

Typically, in the extrasensory world, we associate these symbols, both the swastika and the Star of David, with their most common interpretations: the swastika meaning hate, Hitler, white supremacy, and racism; and the six-pointed star representing the Star of David and Judaism.

Generally, if you see a swastika over someone's head, or if you get a flash of a swastika when walking into a building, it will normally mean that there is extreme racism or that deep anger and hatred are present. This may be a sign that you don't want to expose yourself to this person or place. It may also be a spirit communication that this person or building is not going to be friendly to you. You should listen to that message from the other side, but always consider the duality as well.

The Star of David is a positive symbol of Judaism. If this symbol appears around someone, you may feel a sensation of peace or security and know that the Star of David is surrounding that particular person with protection from evil or negative energies. This person may have a faith in God that is unwavering, or could be someone you could easily relate to on a spiritual level.

God and Jesus

It is very common to see the preconceived image of God as a symbol: the being of light, magnificent with the long flowing white gown and beard. When this image presents, many immediately feel love surrounding them or blowing over them. This is because this icon of religion and creation is symbolic of love and omnipotence. God, in the most traditional Christian monotheistic existence, is understood to be the creator of the universe, thereby the father of all living organisms. Depicted traditionally as a man, he is all-knowing, all-seeing, and everlasting.

If you see a representation of God psychically it can indicate importance in whatever matter you are discussing or whatever is occurring in your life at the moment you see him. It may also be a time for prayer, or a rekindling of your faith in God. Often the symbol of God appears as a message from the other side to let you know He is there and there is purpose to all things. It may also be a reminder to be sure you are living with integrity and are acting honorably or in the most trustworthy manner possible.

For most of the populace, receiving God as a psychic message is a symbol of everlasting love and peace, a sign that all is working the way it's supposed to and that there is help readily available. Associating God in the negative usually represents that God knows everything that is happening in your life and that it is time to straighten out; there are no excuses for bad behavior.

The iconic visualization of Jesus denotes a white, sometimes tattered robe, with brown beard and hair. Jesus shows up metaphysically when we need to be reminded that we are worthy of being loved; we belong here on the physical earth. We also see him in times of crisis, to let us know he is helping us or there is help available. Conventionally, as taught in the Christian religion, it's believed that Jesus, the son of God, died for our sins so that we may live.

Receiving this symbol may mean it's time to look at our lives, and revisit whether we are living peacefully and virtuously. It can also be an indication, once again, that it's time to reunite any Christian bonds through prayer or church. This archetypal symbol may also represent that a period of suffering is coming to an end.

Characteristically, seeing either God or Jesus clairvoyantly can also represent that someone's physical life is coming to an end. If you see this around someone, note whether or not the person has been ill or is nearing the natural end of their years. Pay attention to how you feel when you see the symbol around that person. Frequently, that can be just as important as the symbol itself. Seeing or interpreting God or Jesus symbolically can also convey a simple message: trust in the infinite spirit, the continuation of the soul, and the understanding that life is eternal.

Crosses

Another psychic symbol frequently seen is the cross. The cross as symbol has existed for thousands of years. When receiving it as a psychic message we may immediately think of religion, specifically the Christian faith. If, for example, you were asking for guidance and you saw a cross, it may suggest that connecting to your religion can provide you with comfort or help. For some, the cross also represents suffering or rebirth, humiliation, agony, death, punishment, or a "cross to bear." If you are not practicing a religion it may simply be a sign to "have faith"; have faith that everything will be all right, or have faith that you will overcome whatever obstacle has been set before you, or have faith that God will only give you what you can handle. It may also suggest you ask God for help.

The Celtic cross is another symbol that is regularly received from the other side. If you receive this symbol, it may refer to the blending of Christianity and ancient Celtic traditions. Traditionally rooted in Ireland, this cross is from the pre-Christian era. The Celtic knots on the cross symbolize the constant merging and interlacing of the physical and spiritual paths in our lives. It is also symbolic of eternity, and God's eternal love. The Celtic cross also represents the number four, for its four arms. Taken even further, it represents the four directions of the compass (north, east, south, and west), the four elements (earth, air, fire, and water), as well as the four parts of humanity (mind, body, heart, and soul). Many believe the ancient Druids created this mystical cross when they clairvoyantly foresaw the coming of Christianity.

If you receive this symbol psychically, this may be a time in your life when you need to combine both your physical and spiritual paths. It might be a good idea to get outside and walk barefoot through the grass, connecting you to your earthly spirit. If you see this symbol in relation to another person, it may represent their Celtic history; they may be of Irish, Scottish, or Welsh descent.

Another type of cross is the Egyptian ankh. This is similar to the traditional Christian cross, but has a lasso-type oval as the top leg. This "god staff" is commonly seen buried with pharaohs and is believed to promise everlasting life or life after death. It can also be referred to as the symbol for future life or the continuation of life after physical death. If this icon appears around someone, it could easily represent their mortality or spiritual immortality in that life goes on in a spiritual plane of existence. It may signify fertility, pregnancy, or the sexual union between male and female. The ankh may also suggest someone with a zest for life. Alternatively, this staff may indicate someone from Egypt or travel to or from Egypt.

Angels as Symbols

One of the most frequent extrasensory symbols is the angel. People have dedicated their lives to studying angels, through writing, communications, pictures, and even angelic oracle cards. Angels are prevalent in spiritual communication. Look at the circumstances surrounding the presence of the angel. Ask yourself: Was I or someone else in danger? Did I need help?

When an angel appears, usually it is a message from the other side. If we receive an angel as a psychic symbol it can be interpreted in a variety of ways. Angels represent heavenly help. If we see an angel during periods of stress or distress, it is usually a psychic message meaning there is assistance available from the other side, or that God is watching over us.

When working with psychic symbols, and in this case angels, pay attention to the feeling you get when you see or sense the specific symbol. For example, happiness when you see an angel at a certain location can mean that your angel is guiding you to a place that will be very comforting or even exciting to you. It's the same for people. If you see an angel when you think of a specific person or if you are with someone and get a psychic flash of an angel, note the feeling you get as well. Do you feel happy? Do you feel sad? Does it feel positive or negative? Are you experiencing any joy or alternatively any discomfort? This is very important in determining the psychic message that has been brought to you.

If the person you are with is ill, you may feel negativity attached to having this angel appear. It may be an indication of the "angel of death" giving you the opportunity to say goodbye. At the same time you may feel a peacefulness coming over you knowing that the person you love or care for is soon going to be reconnected on the other side to their loved ones and angels.

Now and then you may see an angel in a psychic flash when you are all by yourself, with no one or nothing else connected to this vision. At that point you should also pay attention to how your body reacts. Although you shouldn't be scared if you are "given" an angel, you should be aware of your feelings in that moment. Do you feel afraid in some way? Is that angel trying to warn you of some threat in the near future? Is the angel there to try and guide you to safety in some way? Heed their unspoken warning by being cautious. Do not be afraid, as they typically are there to help you.

If you see an angel and don't feel any emotion in particular, other than possible awe at seeing this glorious flash, it may simply be to let you know you are connected spiritually. Or it may be a message that you are opening up more to spiritual communication. In addition, it could possibly be a strong sign of peace and well-being for the future.

One of the greatest lessons I have learned as a psychic has been to ask what the message means. If, for instance, you see an angel and have absolutely no idea what message the angel is trying to send to you, *ask*. You can literally say, "What are you trying to tell me? Please send me another message to clarify."

More often than not you will receive another symbol or sign to help you understand what it is the angel wants you to know. Don't ever feel like you can't ask for additional help when receiving messages from the other side. After all, these communications are being sent to help you; we all need clarification sometimes. As these symbols become more pronounced and begin to occur more often, you will find that their meanings become clearer, especially if you receive the same visions, feelings, or sounds more than once.

Praying Hands

Often seen with rosary beads threaded around them, praying hands are a sign of strength, prayer, and devotion to God. Most frequently linked to Christianity, the praying hands are very emblematic with many religions and denominations. Using symbolic language, these hands may represent the need for prayer or to connect with God or spirit in worship. When this image appears with rosary beads draped around the praying hands, it may be a more distinct symbol directing you toward the Catholic faith or to go to church to pray or worship with others. The praying hands may also show up when there is a need to "repent," as in the Catholic practice of confession, to repent your sins or to ask forgiveness in some way from God or the church. If you have a feeling of guilt when you receive a vision of these hands, that usually means it is time to admit you have done something you know wasn't fair or just or that you have intentionally done harm. It may also have to do with the commonly known Catholic guilt, leading you back to the confessional.

There may be other times that you feel your hands moving together in prayer. This can be a psychic message as well, received claircognizantly or clairsentiently, giving you that feeling of knowing or believing it is time to pray or worship. This psychic message can also be viewed as a direction to commune with God. Consider it an open invitation to start a conversation about your desires and your needs as well as your misfortunes and your misgivings. If you experience this symbol around someone else, that person may need your prayers. Such a person may be going through a personal crisis or illness and need your support. It's also possible that this person needs help opening up and connecting to their own spirituality.

The praying hands can also be closely linked to yoga. Many poses utilize prayer hands for balance. The normal conclusion to a yoga session is to wish your instructor, "Namaste," meaning "I bow to you," or "The light within me is also inside you." Connected as well to Mudra positions or "hand yoga," it can be a direction to meditate or to open up spiritually to send prayer and receive guidance through meditation.

No matter what the specific intention, receiving "praying hands" as a psychic symbol from the other side is a clear message to reconnect to your spirituality. This can be done specifically through prayer or meditation, which can be a tool to worship or connect with God.

Dove

The dove and olive branch symbol is widely recognized as a sign of peace. In the biblical story, after a catastrophic flood Noah sent out a dove from his Ark to find if there was any land. The dove flew back with the olive branch in its mouth, symbolizing the receding waters of the great deluge. This also symbolized peace, as Noah then knew they would once again be grounded. Now, many Western religions view this symbol to mean peace and security.

As with Noah and the Ark, this image can be interpreted to mean that better or more stable ground lies ahead, figuratively or literally. This may also mean someone will present you with a token gesture to forgive you or ask for your forgiveness for something. If you receive the symbol psychically, it can mean peace is on the way. It may also represent that there is a need to offer a truce or make an offering of peace through apology. Also, if you see the dove you may expect a change in the air for the better. It may represent better, more positive things to come.

Places of Worship and Prayer

Another common religious symbol is that of a church or an abbey. It may be a very simple building or a grand one. Images of a church can mean it is time to find your faith again. It can denote a simple message to open to God. It may also be a way of letting you know that your sacred or spiritual side is relevant and it is important that you be aware of that. If you see a church around someone it may mean they are connected to clergy in some way; you might find they are a priest, a nun, a pastor, or even a church choir director. This may symbolize that the person needs to reconnect to their faith.

A further way to view this image is to understand the importance of prayer and worship with others, in a congregation, in order to feel whole and feel like a part of something. If you receive this as a psychic symbol repeatedly, it may be a way to nudge you toward going to or going back to church on a regular basis. It may also signify the need or desire to be folded into the protection of God, surrounding yourself with the protective walls of the church itself.

For some, this structure may represent a different belief, a belief that the church is controlling or unforgiving. It may represent a fear that one will not be accepted. Pay attention to what feelings go along with the symbol of the church in order to determine whether it is a good or positive symbol or if it has a negative connotation.

Having a temple appear before you may also be a common occurrence. Typically, receiving this symbol psychically can refer to worship or prayer, similar to the Christian church. Temples are prevalent in many religions. This may be a signal for you to tap into a different area of spirituality. If you see this image and you are part of a religion, you may find it's time to reunite with your beliefs. This may also indicate a need to meditate in solitude or give yourself over to prayer in the style of Buddhist monks.

Clerics, Saints, and Halos

Similar to the church or abbey symbol is the priest or nun. What thoughts immediately come to mind? When I think of a priest I see their traditional black clerical attire with the white collar; the same goes for the nun ... the typical black clothing. If you hear the words *priest* or *nun* or see an image of either, it may mean something very personal for you based on your own religious experiences or it may be something more generic.

Psychically the priest or nun may represent a spiritual presence, spiritual matters, spiritual guidance, or safety. They can also represent authority to members of Christian churches. It could be a simple reference to church. Having a flash of a priest psychically may mean specifically that you are in need of spiritual advice or mentoring or even spiritual cleansing.

Having a psychic vision of a nun may imply someone who has removed themselves from the general population in search of spirituality or God or their total devotion to God. Alternatively, some may conclude this has to do with Catholic school and the historical "ruler across the knuckles" associated with disciplining the students.

Another significant symbol in the religious realm is the halo. Traditionally depicted through history around the heads of saints, it can represent saintly tendencies or pious attributes. If you see a halo around someone it may mean that person is very spiritual, possesses an affinity for pure kindness, or is "good" in general. It could also mean the person is very psychic. It is easy to confuse or associate the halo with the aura. An aura is the projection of energy emanating around every living being. (See chapters 5 and 6 for more on auras.)

Aureoles are similar to halos, but halos surround the head while aureoles surround the whole body. Generally, these almond-shaped rings of light represent energy, a higher spiritual awareness, or enlightenment.

Buddha

Buddha appears regularly to people who are traveling on a spiritual path. The original Buddha, Siddhartha Gautama Buddha, is believed to have lived around 500 to 400 BCE. This enlightenment began Buddhism about 2,500 years ago in India. Buddha is the "enlightened one," the ascended master who has gained all the knowledge of the world.

He is the epitome of spiritual awakening. As the website Aboutbuddha .org phrases it, "In general, 'Buddha' means 'Awakened One,' someone who has awakened from the sleep of ignorance and sees things as they really are."

Buddha is also very symbolic of peace, tranquility, and happiness. If you see or hear Buddha it might be time to begin a period of prayer for all that is good. It may signify a need to meditate or do some relaxation techniques. It may also be a time of recognizing your own immortality and to appreciate that life goes on after death. This is also a reminder of karma, or the determination of your future lives based on the life you are currently living. In other words, do unto others as you would have done unto you.

Experiencing Buddha may be a reminder that all living creatures have souls, and that we need to respect everyone and everything around us. As the Buddhist monks do, it may be time for you to devote yourself to solitude, or to contemplate life and peace. Whether the Buddha symbol is there to encourage solitude or respect, it is showing up in your life to promote happiness. This is why there are so many images and statues of the "laughing Buddha"; he became enlightened and lived in sheer joy. On a lighter note, having Buddha show up symbolically may indicate a need to curb your appetite. You may be developing a "Buddha belly"!

Buddhism

In line with the Buddhist and Hindu beliefs comes the beautiful lotus flower. Typically, in Buddhism, the lotus flower represents a blossoming of spirit. Buddhists believe growth of the soul is expressed through the growth of the lotus flower. Coming from the mud, the roots of the lotus signify earthly life and materialism. The stem, reaching up through the water, connotes the experience gained as it grows. And finally, it flowers into the bright sunlight, which represents enlightenment.

The lotus flower is known as the most emotional or poignant of the "Eight Auspicious Symbols" of Buddhism, the others being the parasol, golden fishes, treasure vase, conch shell, endless knot, victory banner, and wheel. Depending on the color, this beautiful flower rep-

resents different things. The pink lotus is recognized as being the supreme lotus; this is an honor attributed to the original "Great Buddha."
The white lotus represents purity of thought and spiritual perfection.
The red lotus represents love, compassion, and passion. The blue lotus
represents victory over the senses, wisdom, and knowledge.

It is most common to receive the image of a white lotus as a psychic
message from the other side. If you see this beautiful flower, know that
you are headed in the right direction spiritually; you are either on, or
about to embark on, a spiritual journey that will take you in the direction that you need to go. If you see a lotus around or connected to
someone else it may be their time to travel on the path of spirituality.
This might indicate a person who meditates or chants or prays on a
regular basis. This can also be a message from the other side to let you
know that this person is of the Buddhist faith.

The parasol, the second of the auspicious symbols, represents protection, royalty, honor, and respect. Similar to the protection an umbrella provides from the rain, the parasol provides protection from the
sun, and represents covering or encompassing something that deserves
protection or needs protection because of social status. If the parasol is
given to you symbolically, know that you are special and are protected.

Another of the auspicious symbols is the wheel, which represents
the rapid spiritual changes stimulated by the teachings of Buddha.
Known also as the *Dharmachakra*, it is the wheel of law and wheel of
transformation and is one of the most important of the Buddhist symbols. The wheel is also the perfect spiritual circle, and can represent
a mandala or drawing of the soul. It has eight spokes that symbolize
the Noble Eightfold Path, which consists of (1) right beliefs, (2) right
aspirations, (3) right speech, (4) right conduct, (5) right livelihood, (6)
right effort, (7) right mindfulness, and (8) right concentration. Getting
the Buddhist wheel can indicate you are going through, or are about to
go through, spiritual change in a positive way.

The endless knot represents the wisdom and compassion of Buddha, and again is one of the eight auspicious symbols. It also symbolizes
both full, balanced harmony and ultimate simplicity. It is a continuous
knot, with no end and no beginning, which is the fundamental basis of

all existence. If you receive this design as a psychic symbol, know that karma will be responsible for future positive events.

The golden fishes are another auspicious symbol and represent freedom and happiness and living in fearlessness. They also signify fidelity and unity or the coming together of two people in a committed relationship. This symbol can also represent water or the sacred rivers of India, the Yamuna and the Ganges. If you receive this symbol psychically it may suggest that coming together in marriage or a committed relationship will create emotional freedom and contentment. If you have asked whether or not to marry someone and you receive this symbolic message in response, go for it! You will be happy together.

In Buddhism, the conch shell is representative of authority and power. As one of the auspicious symbols it also signifies the ability to ward off evil: spirits, natural disasters, and poisonous creatures. The conch shell signifies the melodious and far-reaching teachings of the Dharma laws or Buddhist teachings. Symbolically, if you see this image it may represent a need to be positive, stay honest and true, and leave negativity behind. Remember, however, as with any symbols, there may not be a connection to the eight auspicious symbols in Buddhism, but instead it could represent something else; the conch shell may simply signify a visit to the beach or a vacation or a trip to an island.

Buddha is symbolic of never-ending spiritual abundance. The treasure vase symbolizes this, as it represents infinite treasures and inexhaustible material desires. This Buddhist symbol represents storage and can indicate wealth, prosperity, and long life. If you receive the vase, know there will be an abundance of whatever it is you need, or waiting in storage are all of your desires to be released.

Finally, the victory banner signifies just that: victory. It represents ignorance being beaten by knowledge, or triumph over negativity such as emotional defilement, passion, fear of death, and lust. If you psychically see a victory banner flying, know that you will prevail, or that as long as you are intelligent or coming from a place of wisdom, you will triumph over ignorance.

Another symbol of Buddhism is the Buddha eyes, also known as wisdom eyes, which are often drawn on shrines in Nepal and Tibet.

They represent the omniscience of the Buddha, the all-knowing and all-seeing eyes. If you see this symbol psychically, it may be a reminder to keep your eyes open to humanity. It may signify a need to open your eyes spiritually or to look to Buddhism as a practical and loving religion. Additionally, this symbol can represent your clairvoyance opening up in a spiritual, karmic way.

Yin and Yang

Widely recognized in Chinese philosophy and spirituality is the *yin-yang symbol*. This Taoist diagram symbolizes how naturally opposing yet connected forces or energies are dependent upon each other to flourish and create equilibrium. When received psychically, this symbol, more properly called a *taijitu* ("diagram of the supreme ultimate"), usually indicates a balance in all things. Traditionally, the yin, or the dark portion of this circular picture, represents the feminine, passive, tranquil, and relaxed energies. The white portion, or yang, is the counterpart, representing the male energies: fast, active, and aggressive. Yin yang is the epitome of duality—two sides, balancing each other out, having opposing qualities, and each coexisting because the other exists.

When you get this symbol as a message from the other side you may be living an unbalanced life. Possibly you are ignoring your spiritual needs and instead are paying more attention to your material desires. You may be having a hard time being a parent and working full time. You may feel tired and sluggish, eat an unbalanced diet, lack exercise, and live a sedentary existence.

Classic Western interpretation perceives yin yang as polar opposites: good and bad, rich and poor, kind and mean, heaven and hell. It may be nature's way of telling you to call in your masculine energies to balance your feminine energies (or vice versa). Seeing this symbol when trying to make a decision about something in life may indicate you need to be sure you are being fair to all involved. It may also show up during times of stress, reminding you to balance the good with bad, allowing you some freedom to enjoy life rather than living each day like it is a chore. While the archetypal yin-yang symbol represents balance, it is important to remember that both too much and too little of something can throw a person off-kilter: too much going out versus too little going out, too much meditation versus too little meditation, living too much in your spiritual realm versus being grounded and present on earth.

If you receive this yin-yang symbol psychically, notice when it happens. Is it a time when you are overindulging? Do you see it when you are trying to help someone with a problem? Does it show up at work? At home? When you are socializing? Pay special attention to where and when you receive this symbol so you can understand what it is that you need to balance.

In its purest form, if you experience this icon, know that it represents spiritual peace and balance. Take a moment to tap into your intuition, your inner guidance, and ask, "What do I need in order to balance my life right now?" The answer may come immediately or it may show up in the form of a sign. Whatever way the answer is presented, listen to it. This is a significant psychic symbol; realizing the essence of the yin-yang principle can help advance you to the next level in your intuitive life.

Pentagram

Another common psychic symbol is the pentagram. The pentagram holds many different meanings and has been part of many different religions throughout history. Traditionally linked to Paganism as well as Wicca, this basic upright five-pointed star is surrounded by a circle. On the one hand, the pentagram represents the five elements of nature: spirit being the top point, and air, fire, water, and earth being the others. On the other hand it is connected to the Wiccan religion, involving nature worship as well as witchcraft.

Classically, this symbol is protection from evil and has been known to be worn over the heart or chest to keep evil away. Quite regularly, though, this symbol is psychically perceived upside down with the point aimed toward an assumed hell rather than heaven. Many attribute this shape to Satan and link it to devil worship. If you receive this symbol in this way it may be a warning of danger or that evil energies are present. It may also be an extrasensory notification that serious or severe problems may arise if you continue traveling the path you are on.

Exercise 1: Defining Your Religious and Spiritual Symbols

Open your journal to a fresh page. On the top of the page, write *Religious and Spiritual Symbols*.

Sit down and get comfortable. Inhale and imagine white light around you, protecting you. Take a few more deep breaths and close your eyes.

Allow your mind to begin thinking of religious or spiritual icons from this chapter or your own personal recollections. Put your pen to the paper and, when you are ready, open your eyes. Write down any symbols that come to mind. Note any thoughts, feelings, images, or sounds that come to you while you are recording each religious or spiritual item.

Take another deep breath, close your eyes, and notice what other religious or spiritual symbols make themselves known to you. Repeat the process of recording whatever meanings come until you are all done or no additional symbols come to you.

Go back and read what you have written. Is there anything else you need to write down? Is there anything that doesn't make sense? Have you written down anything that surprises you? Have you recorded anything that is different from the traditional or typical meanings or descriptions listed in this chapter?

Keep some space open after your entries so you can go back at any time to record any additional religious or spiritual icons that come to you.

Exercise 2: Expanding on Existing Symbols

Choose a symbol from this chapter. Open your journal to the next fresh page and get comfortable. Write the symbol on the top of the page and then record the basic meaning that is listed in this book. Don't stop there; take it one step further. Continue writing whatever comes to you about that symbol until there is nothing left to write or nothing comes.

Go back and read your entry. Does it make sense? Does it hold meaning in your life right now? Is it relevant in some way? If so, record your connection. If not, repeat the exercise using a different symbol from the book.

8

Tarot Symbols

The mere mention of tarot cards may be enough to intimidate anyone, psychic or not. There is a very distinct belief, inherent in most people, that in order to "read" tarot cards you have to be a trained expert. Nothing says symbolism more than tarot cards. From as early as the fifteenth century, tarot cards have represented fortunetelling through colorful archetypal images. Professional intuitives use tarot cards to help conduct readings. You don't have to hang out your psychic shingle to use tarot cards; you can translate the pictures now for your own intuitive guidance every day.

I will never forget the time about ten years ago when I was at a mind/body/spirit expo. I had just finished teaching a class on developing intuition. Coming out of the conference room, I saw the foot traffic in the main hall had slowed down, and I needed a break from being the leader. I decided to take advantage of the lull. I left up the notice I had put on display in my rented vendor space saying "Be back shortly," and I headed over to the psychic tables.

I perused the different readers who were working. As is typical, some of them definitely looked the part, adorned in lots of jewelry and flowing scarves. You could tell they had been doing it for quite some time and were very comfortable. Then I noticed a young woman, probably early to mid-twenties, advertising tarot readings. She looked pretty normal, with one simple decorative cloth draped over her table. She also looked a little anxious. It seemed to me she was waiting for customers. I felt drawn to her so I decided to get a reading.

When I sat down, she was very polite, very nice, and very accommodating. She introduced herself, "Hi, I'm Charlotte."

She immediately asked me what kind of reading I was looking for and if I'd had another reading that day or if I had just gotten there. I answered by telling her I hadn't had a reading yet that day and left it at that.

"What questions do you have?" Charlotte asked.

"I'm interested in finding out if I'm going to advance or expand my career. I feel it's kind of stagnant right now," I told her and waited to see what she would do.

Now, it's not that I was testing Charlotte; I just had a feeling about her. Intuitively I could tell that she was very gifted, but she just didn't trust her instincts strongly enough, yet. I was excited to hear what she would say.

"Okay. Let's see. I'm going to use tarot cards," she replied and began shuffling them.

She spread them out, and instinctively I started to read them, silently, to myself.

"The first card is the Two of Pentacles," she said, and then she pulled out her book to look it up. She explained or, more precisely, she read directly from the book what the card meant.

Then she pulled another one and flipped it over. "Ace of Swords," and again opened her book and read verbatim what the description was.

I couldn't help myself; I wasn't going to let her continue this way. "You know what, Charlotte? You're really good, but you could be even better. Instead of using the book, just go with your gut. What is the card telling you? Look at the picture, the colors, even the numbers. What does it mean to you?"

She looked at me with her jaw on the floor and replied, "Oh, but it is a new deck, and I just wanted to make sure I got it right…"

"I know, and I'm not trying to be obnoxious or mean, but just trust yourself. You know what the cards mean. Do me a favor and for my reading can you please just go with your feelings? Don't use the book anymore. It's too technical anyway, and it's not going to tell you what the cards mean when they are next to each other."

Now, perhaps I was still in teaching mode, but I couldn't let her persist the way she was. In addition to the feeling I had that she was good enough to not need the book, I know how skeptical people can be. I knew that if she pulled out the book with someone else, someone who had come to the expo specifically to get a reading, her credibility would have gone down the drain the second she referred to her tarot guide. It really is only "acceptable" to refer to a guide when you need additional clarification for very specific questions; you can't use a book to conduct the entire reading.

"Okay," she said, "I'll try," and she actually seemed excited to get started.

The reading continued, and was more relaxed and more interpretive than before. Charlotte even gave me some insight that I hadn't picked up when I read the cards to myself, which of course was why I wanted a reading in the first place. We thanked each other and I went back to doing my own thing.

After that expo I didn't see her or even really think about her. Then, the following year, I did another expo. While I was doing a reading at my vendor table, I glanced up and saw someone patiently waiting. She looked vaguely familiar, but I couldn't quite place her. She came over to me when I was done with my client.

"Hi, Melanie," she said with total confidence.

"Hello," I smiled, still not recognizing her, but I could tell she knew me.

"I don't know if you remember me or not, but I gave you a reading last year. You told me to stop using the book to look up the meanings, but to interpret them using my intuition instead," she went on.

Oh, boy, I thought to myself, *I'm in big trouble.*

She continued, "I just wanted to say thank you. My readings have gotten so much better since I took your advice. Thanks again."

"Oh, that's great." I replied, now remembering who she was.

"Okay, well, I'll see you later," she added, and turned and walked to her table.

I *had* overstepped my boundaries a bit by telling her how to do her readings. Luckily, in doing so I had really helped Charlotte to enhance her already strong abilities. She was able to use her own psychic filing cabinet to aid her in interpreting the cards. The same holds true for everyone, professionals and amateurs alike. Just as with anything else, the more you practice, the better you'll get.

Professional tarot readers study the archetypal meanings for years, learning and exploring the deep meanings each card holds. Becoming a skilled tarot-card reader takes time and an appreciation of the interpretations that professionals like Rachel Pollack and Mary K. Greer have put together in books such as *The Complete Illustrated Guide to Tarot* (Pollack) and *Tarot for Your Self* (Greer). Another book I've found that is helpful and simple enough to understand for beginners is Anthony Louis's *Tarot Plain and Simple*.

Knowing the archetypal definitions for the tarot decks is beneficial; it gives you a fantastic jumping-off point and is in fact a great way to study emblematic meanings. However, there is absolutely nothing wrong with viewing each card individually, and tuning in to the symbols with your intuition. For instance, when you see a woman on a card, you may automatically feel a softer, feminine energy as opposed to a louder masculine energy. Or, when you see pentacles, you may immediately know it has to do with material possessions, money, physical body, and so on.

Studying the tarot deck, looking specifically at the colors and the pictures, will help you determine the meanings that each card holds for you. It doesn't matter whether it is the historical interpretation or not; it is your interpretation. This symbolic wisdom can then be applied to all other psychic symbols as well.

Rachel Pollack says in one of her many books, *Seventy-Eight Degrees of Wisdom*: "Tarot readings help us develop confidence in our own perceptions. Partly this comes from the knowledge gained, and partly from the need to make choices and stick by them.... As we read more we find ourselves starting to sense the answers to ... questions. As a result we gain more trust in our understanding and intuition."

Rachel, a very accomplished tarot reader and teacher, uses the cards to tell stories to people about their lives. She doesn't just reference the traditional meanings; she creates meaning by looking at the individual card's pictures and colors.

I studied with Rachel at the Omega Institute for Holistic Studies, in New York State, where she conducts a variety of tarot classes with another world-renowned author and teacher, Mary K. Greer. Not only did we have an enjoyable time learning about the cards, but we had an amusing time playing with them as well. We used the cards to play Texas hold 'em poker. What was interesting about that game, and others to follow, was we found it very difficult to mentally assign value to the cards. With a normal playing-card deck, there is a hierarchy: the two is the lowest, moving all the way up to the ace. Generally, with tarot cards, no card has more value than another, especially after removing the twenty-two major arcana cards. (Some people hold the belief that the major arcana are more important or more powerful than the fifty-six minor arcana cards.) We found that we bet on a personal favorite card, or bluffed a hand, when we had nothing but a good "reading."

The symbolic meaning is there, on every card; we just have to look for it. Mary K. Greer writes about major symbols or thematic groups in her book *21 Ways to Read a Tarot Card*: "The focus here is on shared concepts and variations on a theme. In no way should the significance of any symbol be limited to what appears here or in any book. For instance, if a querent sees the Ace of Wands as a carrot on a stick used to lure him back into a relationship, it will be far more significant than traditional meanings like 'a new idea.'" In other words, Mary is saying to read the cards with regard to your own personal experiences in order to get the most out of each reading.

In order to truly begin to understand tarot decks you need to know what their components are. To do a reading you can look at six simple factors. In a typical deck, such as the most common Rider-Waite deck, you will have twenty-two major arcana cards and fifty-six minor arcana cards. Separating the minor arcana are four suits, similar to a regular deck of playing cards. Each card has a corresponding number: the four suits are from Ace through King, and the major arcana are numbered one through twenty-two. Each card is illustrated in its own way. Lastly, each card has an overall color theme or variety of colors.

The twenty-two major arcana or trump cards tell a story. As Anthony Louis puts it in his book *Tarot Plain and Simple*: "Many Tarot experts believe that the series of situations depicted in the Major Trumps represent an archetypal story of human development—the journey traveled by the Fool (Trump 0)." The basic gist of the story is "The Fool" starts out, brand new, with everything he needs in his pack, and travels through life, changing, meeting, and morphing into new aspects and new situations as he goes, as shown by the various major arcana cards. Finally, ending with "The World" card, we see "The Fool" having great things to come, fulfilled by his travels and the wisdom he has gained, taking a break at the end of the cycle before a new cycle can begin. The following is a basic explanation of the traditional major arcana cards.

Zero, The Fool: Beginning of a journey; crossroads on a journey; discovering one's own destiny; fulfillment of wishes; infinite possibilities; possessing everything needed for a new journey

One, The Magician: Represents motive; a search for knowledge; a quest to understand all things; combining one's resources; tapping into talents and abilities without holding back; receiving guidance through intuition; extracting knowledge from all sources

Two, The High Priestess: Represents intuition; introspective or serene period; refers to love, wisdom, and inspiration; can indicate contemplation of things; may suggest a connection to a mystical authority

Three, The Empress: Fruitful accomplishments or successes to come; personal growth; abundance; motherly; nurturing caregiver; loving; beauty

Four, The Emperor: Taking practical or reasonable action; power and stability; structural basis; knowledge and desire to lead or rule surroundings

Five, The Hierophant: Suggests being open to new interpretations or outlooks; looking for knowledge or truth; being open to direction or change; may indicate papal advice or indicate a belief system or religion

Six, The Lovers: Can represent a need to make a choice, either romantically or otherwise; can indicate partnership, pleasure, desire, passion

Seven, The Chariot: May represent moving forward in conquest or success; can suggest a need for self-discipline or restraint; may suggest having the will for victory; self-confidence; may indicate a need to proceed forward while keeping an open mind

Eight, Strength: Fortitude; can indicate personal control; responsible and compassionate; possessing stability and perseverance; able to overcome obstacles; actual strength

Nine, The Hermit: Withdrawing inward; a time of introspection; needing to align with higher guidance or power; needing to look within, in solace, for answers

Ten, The Wheel of Fortune: Making wise decisions now will lead to desired or better future; may suggest a change for the better; can suggest a turning point or an opportunity; may suggest a sudden change or event

Eleven, Justice: May indicate logic and reason; can suggest a need to trust oneself; weighing opinions of others; can indicate impartiality and intellect; may suggest a need for fairness; can refer to the legal system

Twelve, The Hanged Man: Suggests connecting or tapping into higher power or higher levels of spirituality and wisdom; feeling trapped but there of your own accord; needing to transcend everyday thoughts

Thirteen, Death: Indicates a need for something to end or cease to exist before something new can begin; rebirth or transformation; change; an end of a cycle

Fourteen, Temperance: May indicate a need for patience or harmony; slowing down or finding a balance; blending emotions with spirituality and practicality; a need for moderation; may suggest synthesis; can refer to health

Fifteen, The Devil: Represents overindulgence; suggests focusing too much on material or external things; suggests it's time to overcome addictions

Sixteen, The Tower: Can indicate a need to rebuild after inevitable change; represents a need to move forward or let go of the past; can suggest chaos or crisis with the possibility of a positive outcome

Seventeen, The Star: Acknowledgement of success and accomplishments; rewards; help from higher power or higher self; flowing love and tranquility; psychic

Eighteen, The Moon: Can suggest a need for caution; possibility for change; can indicate intuitive abilities; may refer to hidden enemies or need to caution against the unknown; possible displeasure; deceit, fear, or being metaphorically or figuratively stabbed in the back

Nineteen, The Sun: Warmth and fulfillment; opportunities; memories of childhood; optimism and happiness; unlimited possibilities; childhood freedom

Twenty, Judgement: Can indicate a need to be objective; can indicate the acceptance of past actions; renewal and redemption

Twenty-one, The World: Represents completion, accomplishment, fulfillment of activities; end of cycle and beginning a new cycle; ability to start fresh; the world is yours

The four suits in the minor arcana are typically known as *wands*, *cups*, *swords*, and *pentacles*. Each suit carries with it a basic symbolic significance. In other words, a Two of Wands means something different from a Two of Pentacles. They may share traits like balance, union, or a need to juggle two different areas of life because they are both "twos." However, a Two of Wands is more about opportunity or playing the waiting game during new stages of development, while the Two of Pentacles often signifies the need to juggle finances or come up with creative ways to cover financial obligations.

Wands typically represent fire or the spark that drives everything in life: creativity, sexuality, new ideas. They may refer to someone who is enthusiastic or who takes action. They may suggest someone who can fight for what they want. Wands may also point to new projects or risk-taking or business entrepreneurs.

Cups represent emotions: how we feel or relate to something or someone. Cups are about our reaction to things or how we process things emotionally. They refer to empathic abilities as well as psychic abilities. Cups relate to family and nurturance and emotional support of others.

Swords are more about intellect and cutting through obstacles to get to the heart of the matter. They relate to critical analysis and strategies. Swords can point to someone who is quick-witted but often emotionally unfulfilled. While swords are good at problem-solving, they can be quick to argue, positively and negatively.

And finally, pentacles relate to material possessions, money, physical attributes, or the actualization or manifestation of physical or material gains. Pentacles refer to successes and results, as well as self-esteem. Often, pentacles point to business acumen or success, possibly through a more service-oriented or sensible position.

The first ten minor arcana cards are generally associated with our own personalities or characteristics. They represent our own feelings or the way we meander through our daily routines. As with the example above showing how both "twos" carry different meanings when they are of different suits, cards of the same suit carry different meanings depending on their number. The following is a generalized list of what the numbers mean.

Ace (also known as one): the basic element or quality, the root or seed of the matter, beginning

Two: union or partnership, duality, balance, manifestation

Three: elemental expression, creation, amalgamation, fertilization

Four: foundation, structure, stability, security

Five: conflict, upsetting the structure, loss, discomfort

Six: communication or re-communication, rebuilding harmony, concord, success

Seven: victory and upset, perfection and limitation, the good and the bad

Eight: movement, progression, mastery, independence, acknowledgement

Nine: almost complete, struggle, compromise, fulfillment

Ten: completion of a cycle, need to review and move forward to new cycle, transition, final ending

Beyond the ten base numbers are the court cards. These generally include the Pages, the Knights, the Queens, and the Kings. As with the rest of the minor arcana, these cards represent our sense of identity as well as characteristics or personality traits. They can also refer to actual people, events, or circumstances coming into or occurring in our lives.

Pages: young men and women, adolescents through early twenties, messages or messengers, news, communication

Knights: young men, late teens through mid-thirties, new people or experiences, movement, drive, energy, quest for knowledge, quest

Queens: women, authoritative or mother figures, love, creativity, understanding, personal power, maturity

Kings: men, authoritative or father figures, will, public honor or recognition, leadership, maturity, action

To get down to what each card really means, you need to look at the pictures. The card number and suit will mean next to nothing if you don't remember what the general translations mean—which makes it so much more important to look at the pictures and the colors on the card. For instance, if I were to pull the Five of Wands I could see by the picture that there is some kind of struggle occurring. There are five people, all holding wands in a circular mock battle, with a multitude of colors. I may take that to mean that there is some kind of inner conflict, chaos, or competition. Without even knowing what the suit of wands or the five means, I am able to discern what the card is telling me. Taking it one step further, I may be able to apply the meaning of that card to a particular question or instance in my life.

Pay attention to all of the aspects of each card. Each card will have numerous artistic displays; each picture will be different from the next and will convey a separate meaning. The following is a general list of the pictures that you may come across:

Activities
Animals
Banners
Beasts
Bowls
Celestial or star patterns or shapes
Clothing
Clouds
Colors
Containers
Cups
Directions
Earth/Ground
Emotions
Flags
Food
Furniture
Instruments
Landscape
Liquid
Numbers
Patterns
People

Portals

Shapes

Structures

Supernatural beings

Tools

Various objects

Vegetation and trees

Vessels

Water

Weapons

Using only common sense, you can translate each card by just looking for these pictorial clues. Is there any vegetation (vines, blossoms, grass, trees, moss, etc.)? Are there any flowers or fruits (apples, lilies, pomegranates, roses, seeds, sunflowers, and so on)? Are there any people (female, male, children, peasants, royalty, cleric, craftsman, dancers)? Are there any structures (castle, building, hut, church, cave, home, and so on)? Are there any animals or beasts or supernatural beings (lion, dog, wolf, horse, fish, snake, angel, devil, etc.)? Are there any other objects (cup, plate, table, chair, chariot, book, boat, precipitation, weather, and so forth)? You can take it further by translating the images metaphorically. For example, vegetation may indicate potential, growth, healing, life force, opportunities, and the like.

Look at each part of the illustration separately, and then as a whole. You will be amazed by what you find you already know. And remember: although two tarot readers may express similarities when reading the same cards for the same person, they will each have their own take or opinion. Reading the tarot is very personal, and every individual has great reader potential. Mary K. Greer suggests offering tarot readings all day, straight through; by the time you have gone a few hours, you no longer worry whether you are right—you just call it as you see it. That's what tarot reading is all about: understanding that you let go of the outcome and read with integrity and truth.

Sample Reading (note that the best questions are not Yes / No questions)

Question: How can I best fulfill my desire to expand my practice?

    Card 1: Situation/Self

    Card 2: Obstacles/Advice

    Card 3: Possible/Probable Outcome

The Emperor	Eight of Wands	Six of Wands

Card 1: The Emperor. Depicts a strong leader, someone who is in control of the situation. It talks about using rational thought and organizational skills to create stability. This is someone who has the ability and just needs to move forward.

Card 2: Eight of Wands. Shows eight wands moving forward. Planning and moving quickly are beneficial here. Keeping on the straight and narrow will get the job done. There is a need to clarify goals and move swiftly.

Card 3: Six of Wands. Success! Hard work will result in positive self-esteem and rewards. Public recognition and victory are headed your way.

    This sample three-card reading is one of many different spreads, but it is commonly utilized because it answers questions in a simple yet direct fashion.

    Looking at the pictures, numbers, and colors, we can easily translate the overall meaning of each card, creating an accurate and clear reading. There are no wrong answers as long as you read from the heart.

You may find that you are drawn to one tarot deck over another. Last year, on her birthday, I gave my friend Becky a deck called "The Housewives Tarot." The cards are entirely different from any traditional decks and portray 1950s housewives in their day-to-day activities. This has become one of our favorite decks to play with.

The message is still the same no matter which deck you use. The pictures are still telling us a story to help us live our lives to the fullest. Start experimenting, and you'll find that you will be drawn to certain decks for their pictures or their feel. That may change over time as your interests develop. What's important is reading from the soul; that's the best you can ever hope for!

Exercise 1: Defining Your Tarot Symbols

Open to a fresh page in your symbols journal. On the top of that page, write *Tarot Symbols*.

Get a tarot card deck. (If you don't have a tarot deck or you don't have access to a tarot deck, you can look up each individual tarot card online to create your own deck.) Shuffle the cards, and without looking at them pull one out.

Look at the picture on the card. In your journal, begin recording the colors. List the most prevalent color first with the color that appears the least last. Record a brief description of what the color means. You can do this intuitively, by memory, or you can look up the color in chapter 5 of this book.

Once you have recorded all of the colors on the card, and all of their meanings, go back and re-read your entries and notice whether there are any recurring themes with the colors.

Next, notice whether the card is a major arcana or a minor arcana card. Remember: in most decks the first twenty-two cards are major, and the last fifty-six are minor. If the card is a minor arcana card, write down the suit of the card and then record what that suit means. Again, you can do this by memory, or you can look up the meaning in this chapter.

If it is a major arcana card, write down the name of the card, and anything that comes to mind or that you remember from the chapter. Next, write down the card number. For example, "The Fool" card is 0; "The World" card is 22; and the Three of Swords would obviously be 3. Record what the number means. Now it's time to analyze the actual pictures. For instance, if you're using a Rider-Waite deck and you've pulled the Three of Swords, there are three swords piercing a bright red heart. Write down what a heart signifies. Then record your interpretation of the swords cutting through the heart.

After you are all done recording everything you can think of for all of the pictures on the card—the colors, the numbers, the wording, etc.—go back and re-read what you have written and see if you can summarize what you think the card means. Most tarot decks come with a miniature book that gives meanings for each card. You may own a different tarot book, or you can also look up meanings for each card online.

Compare your summary with the meaning(s) in the book(s) or online. Are they similar? Does your summary make sense? Keep in mind that a good tarot-card reader will analyze each card individually, on his or her own, only referring to someone else's description when needing additional information or clarification. Your synopsis of the card will not be wrong. It is how *you* read the card, similar to how you interpret your own personal symbols.

Now that you've gotten the hang of it, do it again. With seventy-eight cards in a basic tarot deck, you'll have plenty of material to practice with.

Exercise 2: Using Symbolism to Practice a Tarot Reading

It's time to do a reading. Grab a friend and have them sit with you for a tarot-card reading. Remind your friend this is a very basic reading, and everything you tell them should be taken with a grain of salt! Have your friend ask you a question, and shuffle the deck while your friend thinks of a question. When they are done, take the cards and lay out three cards facing you. For now, don't worry about reading cards in reverse. Instead, turn the cards so that all three are right side up to you.

The card on the left is in the "Situation/Self" position. The card in the middle is the "Obstacles/Advice" card, and the card on the right is the "Possible/Probable Outcome" card. Look at the situation card. Begin to read all of the clues on the card, including the number, the colors, the pictures, and the summary of everything together. Does this match up to your friend's question? Does it make sense?

Do this with each card, being sure to give details and descriptions of everything you "get" from reading the symbolic messages. Wait until you are done describing everything to your friend before listening to their response. Have your friend tell you what makes sense or what works with the reading versus anything that didn't seem to fit.

When you are done, take stock of how you did. Did it feel comfortable? Did your description of each card match up with the descriptions in your tarot books or in this chapter? If so, how close? If not, how different?

Practice this on any of your friends or family members who are willing to be guinea pigs. You may find that you become a better reader the more you practice. Do it again! And again, and again, and again. Read until you no longer worry about whether you are right. That's when it will get really good.

9

Personal Symbols

When you are done with this book, you will have your very own symbols journal. This journal will contain symbols and meanings that are relevant to you personally, in your own life. This is important because not everyone views things the same way. Personal symbols hold power for each person. What is powerful for me may not hold the same weight for you and vice versa.

Take a moment to imagine your childhood home. First, you might see the overall shape or design. Then, maybe the color. You might also jump right into specific rooms. The main idea here is that it's your house, not mine or someone else's. Because of this you are able to conjure up the image from your memory. This image then may become your personal symbol for a house, or it may be your new symbol for childhood.

Alternatively, if you see algae floating at the bottom of what appears to be an ocean, it may represent one of the millions of different types of marine flora that exist. To me and most other people, it just looks like plain old algae, because we don't have a million different species stored in our databank.

Years ago, I was in a remote-viewing class at one of my favorite schools, the Omega Institute for Holistic Studies, and we were doing an exercise. Coordinate remote viewing was started many years ago by the United States government as a top-secret, psychic espionage program designed to determine the validity of psychic ability. David Morehouse was one of the government officers recruited into this program, which was called "Stargate." In his book *Psychic Warrior*, Morehouse quotes the program's director as saying, "What we do here is train selected personnel to transcend time and space, to view persons, places, or things remote in time and space ... and to gather intelligence information on the same."

In order to do *our* assignment at Omega, we needed to transcend time and space, and see, hear, and feel everything we could at a specific location that we were given random coordinates to view psychically.

As we worked throughout the week, I psychically saw many things, but one that stood out to me was a man's foot in a sandal. Now, you might think that's pretty obvious; it is a symbol for a shoe. At first that's what I thought, too, but the real answer wasn't so obvious. In fact, it threw me off for the rest of the session.

My mind shot off in a million different directions. "A shoe, what could it mean? It's a sandal; what could that represent? But, there's a foot inside the sandal. Let me move up a bit. I see a bare leg. It's a foot. I'm also seeing sandy dirt under the shoe. There's a bit of white fabric, like a toga. Well, the foot is prevalent so it's got to have something to do with the foot. I've got it; it has to be soccer. Wait, what's that image now ... I'm seeing an old stadium, maybe in Greece. That's got to be it. It's an old Greek stadium, and it's a man with a bare leg and foot in what has to be a Grecian sandal. That's it!"

Well, that wasn't it. I wasn't too far off, though. What I was seeing definitely was a sandal. And, I even interpreted the stadium part right. But it wasn't in Greece; it was in Rome. It was the Roman Coliseum. The assignment was to "psychically" view the location in present time, which meant what I was seeing was not literal. It was a representation of what I now know was a Roman gladiator, and it was my new symbol for Roman gladiators and the Roman Coliseum. Granted, there probably won't be too many times that will come up, but hey, you never know. Luckily for me, it has also developed into a general symbol for Rome.

Obviously, that is a very personal pictogram. You might find the Leaning Tower of Pisa is your symbol for Italy, or you may see the "boot" shape of Italy as your symbol for Rome. You might even find that the image of a foot in a Greek or Roman sandal represents soccer for you now that the thought is in your mind. That's what is so amazing about having personal symbols; it's where your mind goes when you think of something, calling up memories from your own individual databank. This databank is ever changing as well. Your symbol for the game of football may currently be a uniformed athlete on the New York Giants' roster, but two years from now you might see a football instead.

Some time ago I was teaching basic remote viewing in my office. I gave the students in my class coordinates for a sample target. When I asked them to share their locations, each person discounted their information because it was different from the person who shared before them. One of them saw a windshield with wipers sweeping against rain. Another felt sick and nauseated, as though she was a passenger in a car. The next person saw bright lights coming at her fast and passing her. The person after her kept remembering turning into the parking lot for my office building, and another heard beeping and honking. This type of feedback continued until everyone had explained what they received.

The target I had given them was a very busy road, Route 7, which my building was located on. Amazingly, every one of the students interpreted specific information about the road, but they all received it differently. Even more interesting to me was that every one of the students felt as though their interpretation was incorrect specifically because it was different from the others. However, they were all right! They were seeing or feeling or even hearing their symbolic information according to what was most prevalent in their personal databank. They were each able to get to the same place using different symbols to complete their journey.

Creating your own symbols journal allows you to keep reference information for each impression you receive. This will help you recall your own translation if you're given the same symbol a year or two down the road. You will have a date when you first received or recorded your interpretation, which can be of great importance when that symbol appears again. For instance, if you receive an image of a specific book it may not just refer to the book. Instead, it may refer to the time in your life when you originally received that symbol—what you were doing, who you were with, what was important to you.

Interpreting symbols becomes even more personal when more than one symbol appears at a time. For example, a baby carriage may indicate an upcoming birth, but a baby carriage combined with a speeding car can tell you there is danger ahead or possibly that you may have to rescue a baby before it gets hurt. On a positive note, if your symbol for legal difficulties is a contract, when you view this contract together with a pile of shiny gold coins it may indicate some kind of financial windfall coming your way. Many common symbols are often seen together, such as ice cream and children, or a pencil and paper, or sunshine and a swimming pool. There are also combination symbols that tend to indicate the same things, such as a policeman and a jail cell, or a roulette wheel and a deck of cards.

Once you begin to understand basic symbols and what they mean, it will be easier to understand what the combinations mean and easier still to understand your own personal symbols. Your personal symbols can be similar to, or extremely different from, the examples in the basic symbols glossary in this book. One of the best ways to develop your own translations is to write them down in a symbols journal. How fortuitous that you have your journal all ready!

Exercise 1: Defining Your Personal Symbols

Listed on the following two pages are a variety of words. Write them down, one at a time, in your journal. Immediately begin recording whatever comes to mind when you read each individual word or term. Continue writing until your mind is blank. You may find that all you have is one word, or you may fill a whole page to help you define what thoughts are provoked when thinking of each word, term, or object. If you discover you are writing extensively for each topic, you can break up the list: do some now, some later, and even finish the list tomorrow.

Remember: there are no wrong answers. Don't discount your thoughts, and try not to be critical. Also, refrain from going back and re-reading your answers until your list is complete. This will help limit judgment.

Car	Dog	Hand	Coin
Cupcake	Sneaker	Leaves	Spaghetti
Cat	Christmas tree	Eye(s)	Paper clip
Pink	Watch	Stars	Wolf
Truck	Paper	Man	Shirt
Cross	Piece of wood	Book	Square
Bicycle	Computer	Jungle gym	Television
Necklace	Rose	Paper towel	Glass
Earrings	Umbrella	Angel	Pants
Log	Chair	Rock	Pen
Glasses	Quartz crystal	Foot	Tree
Garbage can	School	Dollar bill	Wheels
Dove	Baby	Jell-O	Fire
Woman	Turkey	Sun	Garage
Shorts	Wire	Spider	Mouse
Tulip	Clothes	Grass	Pool
Saw	Backpack	Hair	Radio
Net	Fish	Glue	Slide
House	Yellow jacket	Scooter	Ring
Bumblebee	Church	Bus	Water
Bird	Present	Ladder	Scooby-Doo
Heaven	Lounge chair	Cactus	Mouth
Spider web	Delivery man	Telephone	Scarf
Dark	Trampoline	Rainbow	Nose
Swing	Praying hands	Money	Tractor

Shed	Amethyst	Mouth	Bed
World	Electrical plug	Moon	Silver
Diamond ring	Fence	Birthday cake	Garbage
Jesus	Mickey Mouse	Tattoo	Light
Bra	Bathing suit	Child	Ears
Seat cushion	Venus	Hammock	

After you are done with all of the words, review your entries. Notice if you have any definitions that are similar. You may find the images that flashed into your mind or the descriptions you heard or the way your body felt for groups of words were exactly the same. On the other hand, you might have different entries for every single word. Remember: this is your symbolic directory; there are no incorrect answers.

Have fun with it. Review your list and randomly pick out two of the words above and write down what they mean to you when you see them together. You may find they have similar meanings when translated individually, or you may find that together they mean something entirely different.

If, over time, you find that your symbolic references change for you, feel free to edit your directory and adjust or add to the descriptions. Life experiences contribute memories to your mental filing cabinet, giving you additional interpretations to use in the future.

Exercise 2: Tracking New Personal Symbols

Begin today writing down any impressions or symbolic sights, thoughts, or feelings you receive from now on and what you think they mean. Turn to a fresh page in your journal. Write *Date* in the top left corner, *Symbol Received* in the center, and *Interpretation* in the right-hand corner.

Next, challenge your memory to go back to the last symbolic moment you can recall.

Write down the estimated date; the symbol; whether you saw, felt, or heard the impression; and record what it meant to you.

Continue by scribing any psychic symbols that come to you in the future.

You may find there are times the symbols repeat. Notice whether their meanings seem to be the same or different from when you interpreted the symbol initially.

10

Symbolic Dreams

Falling into a deep REM (rapid eye movement) sleep allows our conscious mind to move out of the way and rest while our subconscious takes over. Without the filter of consciousness to sift the information coming in, it is easier to receive messages from the other side. Don't be confused, though. Not every dream is a psychic communication; sometimes it's just that piece of chocolate cake you ate before bed talking to you.

We dream for many reasons: to process the events of the day, to work through a problem in life, to foretell future events, to address something we have been avoiding, or possibly to receive communication from the other side. My husband thinks we dream to "keep our minds open, like a portal. Our dreams let us access other worlds and otherworldly knowledge." According to Sigmund Freud, "The interpretation of dreams is the royal road to knowledge of the unconscious activities of the mind."

As Freud said, dreams take place in the subconscious or unconscious part of the mind. People have a tendency to get so overwhelmed in everyday life that it becomes difficult to decipher everything consciously. Dreaming, then, becomes one of the easiest ways to comprehend life and life's questions and challenges. As Carl Jung put it in his book *Man and His Symbols*, "The general function of dreams is to try to restore our psychological balance by producing dream material that re-establishes, in a subtle way, the total psychic equilibrium."

Symbols play an important part in dreams. As with waking messages, of this reality and from the other side, symbols make it easier to communicate. Think about watching a good movie or television show. You can tell the "B"-rate or lower-quality movies and shows because the acting and the scenery may not be so good. The same holds true for dreams. The clearer the information is presented or the better it is depicted, the easier it will be for you to understand what you are getting.

Often, literal translation is not necessary for dreams. It is therefore essential to become familiar with symbols and their messages. For example, if you were to dream about a roller coaster ride where you were throwing up, though you know that in your waking state you would love to be on a roller coaster, it may require a symbolic translation. The roller coaster may indicate life's ups and downs, and the vomiting could mean you are going through a hard time and you need to release all of the negativity, but that there are many twists and turns to life and sometimes it's okay to be a little down before you are up, but don't give in because the trauma or drama will soon be over.

On the other hand, if you are planning a trip to Disney World next week, maybe you should look at it as a premonitory dream; the roller coasters might make you sick to your stomach. A premonitory dream or a dreaming premonition is when you psychically see, hear, or feel (or all of the above) what will happen in the future. Frequently, this is how many people receive their psychic symbols.

Imagine you had a dream about your uncle, someone you haven't seen in quite a while. In the dream, you saw your uncle taking a walk and having ice cream in a park. When you wake up you have no idea why you dreamt of your uncle, considering the lack of communication you've had with him for so long—until he knocks on your door later that afternoon. Now, it's all making sense. It was a premonition of him coming to visit.

Imagine dreaming of that same uncle, but this time he is running through the park, looking panicked, dropping his ice cream as he goes. This can definitely be a premonitory dream of something bad happening to him. It could also indicate the bad event is totally unexpected because of the ice cream cone; he wouldn't have gotten an ice cream cone if he anticipated trouble. The mere act of dropping the cone means he was probably having a leisurely day in the park, enjoying his ice cream, and then some unforeseen attacker or antagonist gave pursuit.

In the first example, the ice cream does not necessarily play a pivotal role in the dream. It may simply imply it will be a happy, possibly indulgent visit. But in the second one it is important, because it helps us understand that this is some random unexpected event, something that we can let him know about to possibly prevent him from being in the situation. With dreams, as with all symbolic communication, we have to be ready, open, and willing to read and interpret the information, weeding out what's relevant versus what seems superfluous.

Dreams can also represent visits from the other side. These visitors usually come to let you know they are around you, that they haven't forgotten about you. Other times they have messages for you, either to answer questions you may have or to help guide and direct you.

One of my clients, Lola, was convinced she had been deceived; her boyfriend, Derrick, with whom she had cohabitated, had died while she was out of town visiting old friends. She believed he disappeared, that he hadn't died, and that she had been lied to. Lola was sure he found out she was with his former best friend, who happened to be her ex-boyfriend, and that this was why he left. She carried this feeling of distrust around with her for twenty years, until one night, recently, she had an amazing dream.

In the dream she was shown many symbolic impressions. Derrick appeared to her, but told her his name was Michael Roberts. He then showed her a map that highlighted Florida. After that, she dreamt she was logging in to Facebook.

When she woke up the next morning, she felt as if she'd been through the wringer. She didn't think it was an ordinary dream, and she felt that all of the emotional turbulence she had gone through twenty years ago had just been reignited. Though she felt warmed by the dream, she was even more incensed. She believed the dream was telling her that her so-called "deceased" boyfriend had indeed taken off, changed his name, and was hiding out in Florida.

That day, she was on her computer, checking her own messages on her Facebook account, and she decided to look up Michael Roberts. (I've changed his real name here for privacy reasons.) What she found shocked her. A man named Michael Roberts was alive and well and living in Florida. She sent him a private message, and it turned out Michael was indeed connected to Derrick; astoundingly, Michael is Derrick's brother. Michael and Derrick's mother had remarried shortly after Derrick died, changing Michael's last name. Because Lola and Derrick lived in a different state twenty years ago, she had never met Michael, so hadn't recognized him as Derrick's brother.

What Lola realized, thanks to all of the symbolic messages her dream visitation presented her with, was that her boyfriend had in fact died twenty years ago. By visiting her from the other side, he helped her reconnect to the other person that meant so much to him while he was still living. Lola and Michael are now in touch and are scheduling a time when they can meet each other. If Lola had ignored the symbolic messages she was given in her dream visitation she wouldn't have gotten closure; she would still be unsure whether or not Derrick had faked his death; and she never would have met Derrick's brother. Though it took her a long time, she is now able to grieve the death of her old boyfriend because she followed the symbolic information she was sent in her dream.

Lola was given very distinctive and specific information while she slept. Sometimes, the only way to get us to trust the symbolism we get is to receive it while we are sleeping. This is when our doubtfulness is quiet, and the truth is able to penetrate past the conscious barrier we create when awake. Usually, this is accomplished by someone visiting from the other side.

Dream visits are actually quite common. They are those dreams that leave you with extreme goosebumps when you wake up. They feel real, as opposed to regular dreams that seem similar to watching a made-up story on television. These visitations are similar to all dreams in that there is a necessity for interpretation. By recognizing different symbols it becomes easier to understand what the dreams are. Whether they are psychic messages foretelling the future or memories from your past, every dream has a story to tell.

Another client of mine, Stephanie, came in looking to understand what was going on in her life. She didn't feel passionate about anything and seemed to go through these periods a few times a year. She couldn't understand what was happening, but knew she wanted to feel better. I tuned in and saw a symbolic image of a silhouette of a person with *Zzzzs* in a cloud bubble above her head. I knew then there was a connection to sleeping or dreaming, so I asked her.

She described a recurring dream she'd had for years. In this dream, she saw a chubby baby in a puffy cloth diaper sitting on the floor at the bottom of a basement staircase. There was a rug in front of the baby. She described everything as being kind of hazy and dusty. She saw a lump underneath the rug moving toward the baby. As the lump moved closer, the baby slowly lifted the corner of the rug. What came out was a huge, hairy tarantula. Instead of being afraid of the spider, the baby grabbed it and put it in her mouth. Stephanie described seeing the image of the furry spider legs hanging out of the baby's smiling mouth.

Stephanie didn't recognize the baby or the house. She told me she'd had this dream about two or three times a year for the past couple of years. Stephanie was having this dream when she was feeling bored or experiencing a lack of enthusiasm in her life. Taking her statements into account helped to cement further the meaning I was associating with the dream.

When I tuned in to my intuition and looked at each symbol, I was able to put together an explanation or reason for the recurring dream. Stephanie needed to go back to her childhood, to a time when things were simple. She needed to tap into the appetite children have for everyday life. She needed to open her creativity. Her foundation, or base chakra, as well as her second or sensual chakras, were off. She no longer felt secure; she felt like there were too many things penetrating her once-protected foundation and causing ripples in her stability. She knew, though, that she could swallow whatever life was throwing her way, as long as she was able to enjoy it.

Because she was so detailed with the symbolic images in the dream, we were able to take it apart and figure out what was going on. The basement was her foundation, her root or base chakra, and represented her feeling of stability. Her foundation had been stable and protected earlier in life, the puffy diaper. The dusty, hazy basement indicated something that hadn't been attended to in quite a while. The baby represented new beginnings, and the need to revert to childlike innocence. The spider indicated that although there were fearful thoughts and feelings, she could create a web of security. Swallowing the spider was about conquering the fears she had about moving out of the old foundation or structure, and the stairs symbolized moving toward the new. The baby smiling while eating the spider suggested happily transitioning to a fearless state in her life.

Translating the dream symbols helped Stephanie move to the next phase of her existence. It helped her realize she would be happy if she tapped into her imagination again, and allowed herself to enjoy the childlike energy she had when she was creative. She was able to take the symbolic message to heart and start living and enjoying life again by making sure she included something creative every day. As always, Stephanie was able to choose whether to follow the advice of her dream; luckily for her, she did.

My client Nikki had a dream in which she was with her children and a couple she was close with. She remembered experiencing the nurturing feeling of motherhood. They were on a beach, complete with sand and water. The beach was also strangely industrial with kind of a "yucky" feeling, according to Nikki. All of a sudden, there was a huge tidal wave coming in toward them. They turned to run, but were hit with a tidal wave in all directions except a small opening on the right-hand side.

Initially, she thought it was an unfounded fear of tidal waves, but that didn't make sense to her so she called me. By analyzing each piece of the dream we were able to determine the true meaning of the dream.

She was overwhelmed with emotions (tidal waves) and trapped by her situation (tidal waves in almost all directions). I felt part of it was due to a loss of her mother (mother feeling). She confirmed she had recently lost her mom. Her children understood her feelings and felt the same way, which is why they were there in the dream. Her friends who were with her had also experienced the loss of their parents.

She was also not happy with her job (yucky industrial feeling) and was very stressed (tidal waves, chaos), but again was feeling trapped (tidal waves). There was only one way out (small opening on right), but she wasn't able to quite make it there, yet. The opening was on the right because we generally receive information from the left and put it to use or externalize it on the right. Therefore, the opening on the right refers to the future. She will eventually be able to leave her position; she could see the opening, but it was too far away and far away in time. Her husband was not with her in the dream because he had not experienced or did not share the same experience of both losing a parent and wanting to quit a job.

After I interpreted the dream with her, she was amazed by the accuracy of the analysis. She was also shocked by the differences in the symbolic meanings versus the imagery she experienced during the dream. Nikki decided not to make any changes based on her dream examination. Instead, she chose to wait it out and let the changes come slowly.

As with many dreams or dream messages, there may be literal translations. More often than not though, they are symbolically based. This means if we take each dream apart and translate every individual object using the symbolic meanings, we can interpret the dream in an entirely different way. As with Nikki's dream, the symbolic message may be totally unlike the actual dream.

Taking it one step further you could analyze not only the objects or subjects in the dream, but also investigate the colors of the dream. This may lead to an even more in-depth translation of the dream's message. One of the easiest ways to remember dreams is to write them down immediately upon waking. Once you are fully awake and in your conscious mind you will find that your subconscious or unconscious mind gets pushed to the background, and takes a lot more coaxing to recall. The sooner you record the images, thoughts, and feelings from your sleep, the more you'll remember.

Often, dreams seem very mixed up and disjointed, almost as if there's too much going on. This may be because you are remembering more than one dream when you wake or are working on more than one issue in your sleep. These dreams are usually the events processing in your mind from the day. Regardless of the type of dream, symbols will be present to help you comprehend the meaning.

Spirit leaving the physical body is also a possibility during a dream state. The spirit can stay close to home and simply float above the bed, or can travel as far as another galaxy. This is called *astral travel* or *astral projection* and has been documented during surgeries and near-death experiences as well.

Imagine traveling to a foreign country and understanding the language, but not knowing how or why. Something similar can occur during astral travel. Symbols also play a role during this dream state, because chances are when you awaken you will no longer understand the foreign language, but you will bring back to your consciousness memories of persons, places, or things that were present there. For example, if you traveled to Australia, maybe you see an image of an Aborigine. This could become your new symbol for Australia. Possibly you travel to a pharmacy and see medicine being disbursed. If you are able to clearly see the label on the drug bottle it may be a symbol to let you know this medicine may be beneficial for you in some way.

One night while I was sleeping I woke up, because I felt a presence around me. When I looked to my left I saw, in the moonlight streaming in through the windows, my husband sitting up on the bed looking at me. I have to admit, I was a little freaked out; it was disturbing that he was staring at me and I didn't know why. I asked him what he was doing. No answer. I repeated my question, asking him what he was doing. Again, there was no response. He wasn't answering me.

I became a bit agitated, still feeling something was wrong, and I sat up. Again I said, "What are you doing?" this time a bit louder.

Suddenly he turned and looked up at me, startled. He then asked what *I* was doing. He was never sitting up; he was lying down, sound asleep. It was his spirit that had been sitting up, observing, and that's why it felt so off to me. Though I was a little disconcerted when it originally happened, I've come to understand that symbolically translated, it was his spirit wanting to protect me, and keep me safe by watching over me.

Regardless of the type of dream (processing from the day's events or a difficult situation, visit from the other side, astral travel, intuitive message, or precognitive), there will always be symbolic information to decipher in the conscious state. Knowing how to interpret this symbolic information is key to translating the true meaning behind any dream. Writing down the dream, with as much detail as possible, will help you remember the symbols you received.

For example, let's say I had a dream where I was bicycling down a country road that was paved on the side of a mountain. I was heading downward, and I was being followed by bears on tricycles. On the surface it would just seem a bit disjointed, and maybe even circus-related. But in order to decode my dream I'd write it down. I'd start by adding a heading in my journal: *IMPORTANT SYMBOLS*. My journal entries would look something like this:

Me: thinner version of me; wearing big, flowy straw hat; flowing white and pink flowery dress; white sneakers with short white socks

Bicycle: red, kind of like a '70s bike, with wide rounded bars

Big giant hill, blocking out anything else, covered in tall grass, wildflowers, dirt, and small trees; the shape resembling a banana

Ground: road rough-paved, with crackled dirt edges, ditches traveling along the length of the road, kind of dusty and dirty

Direction: traveling downward, slow decline, circular road around hill, viewing descent from left to right

Bears: like the monkeys in "The Wizard of Oz," wearing capes and caps, riding tricycles, look of determination on their faces, two of them

Tricycles: glowing, fluorescent yellow, smaller than the bears, like something you'd see in a circus performance

By recording these sorts of details logically, it helps us to remember the other aspects of dreams. I'd continue with this by breaking it down into more detailed categories. Underneath the basic description, leaving a few blank lines for anything else I may remember, I'd write *SOUNDS* and record what I'd heard:

The evil witch's song from "The Wizard of Oz"

I'd continue with *EMOTIONS AND FEELINGS*:

Me: exhilarated, a bit anxious

Bears: focused, exhilarated, driven

Next, I'd summarize it as though I was describing the dream to someone else. This helps access the storytelling part of your brain, as opposed to just remembering the basic facts. By looking at it from different perspectives you are allowing your mind to process your memories differently, possibly pulling forth more information or more details. I'd write *DESCRIPTION OF DREAM* and record in sentence format what was happening:

I was bicycling down a country road that was paved, but on the side of mountain, and heading down, and I was being followed by bears on tricycles. It was very much like watching TV, as I was watching everything happen rather than being part of everything that was happening. However, somehow I still knew I had to get away; the bears wanted something from me and I didn't want to give it to them. I was very determined, but they stayed the same distance from me and I couldn't pull away no matter how hard I tried.

As always, reviewing the description of the dream to see if there is anything else you've just recalled that is "symbolic" that you haven't already recorded under symbols will assist you even further in decoding the meaning behind the dream itself. For instance, I wrote *TV*, which is something that I didn't have under my initial *IMPORTANT SYMBOLS* heading. I would go ahead and record any of these additional symbols.

Finally, I'd go back to each of the symbols under *IMPORTANT SYMBOLS* and dissect them. In my example, I list "Me," but I go on to describe various things or symbols about "Me" such as a flowing, flowery dress.

By "re-listing" all the symbols, one by one, I'm able to look up their meanings in the basic symbols glossary in this book, as well as in other chapters (such as chapter 5, on color symbolism), and in other resources.

For example:

The "Me" symbol: by looking up *Oneself* in the glossary, I'd see that I may need to take a look at my life presently, where I'm going, and what I'm doing.

Then, also regarding the symbols I noted under "Me," I would look up, in chapter 5, what *white* and *pink* mean, and I'd check the glossary for the meaning of *flowers*.

Continue recording the meanings for all the different things you noticed in your dream. Be sure to use all of the references in the book, including the various chapters on religious and spiritual symbols as well as basic symbols, personal symbols, tarot symbols, and the rest. When you are all done looking up the meanings for all of the different aspects of your dream, put them together. The example dream can mean something like this:

I was running from an issue, not wanting to look in the mirror at what I was doing, and the bicycle was showing me that I am in charge of my own journey/destiny. The big hill symbolizes a big obstacle in my life. The bears represented the challenge that was going on, that the spotlight was on me (circus) and I was having a hard time openly loving (pink/white/circus) myself.

It is time now for me to face up to the challenges I have with losing weight (skinnier version) and to stop being so protective of myself (as my mother was: bear) to the point of making excuses or running from the issue or even being in denial.

This dream has even more to say, once we dive deeper into the various meanings, but as you can see it is not simply a bike ride down the mountain. Accessing your dreams can be this simple as well. What you may find is you've known the answers all along; they make sense to you now that you know how to interpret the symbolic information you are able to extract from the dreams. By following the example above you'll be able to begin working on the exercises below. You may not remember all of your dreams, but usually you'll remember the ones of significance. By recording them, you'll be able to look back at them and feel, intuitively, whether they held truth in your life or in your future. Deciphering them may also help you to process something you've been having trouble with.

Exercise 1: Interpreting Your Dreams Using Symbols

Turn to a new section in your journal and write *DREAMS* in big giant letters. You can use a Post-it note to create a divider page, or if you have built-in dividers add *DREAMS* to the tab.

On the next page, write *DATE OF DREAM* in the left-hand corner of the top line. Then write *DATE* in the right-hand corner on the top line, followed by today's date. You may note you haven't filled in the date of dream. That is because you are going to use a dream that you can remember from your past, but chances are you won't remember the date. If you can, write down the time period, like the year. If you can only remember a more recent dream, it is perfectly fine to use that one.

Skip a couple of lines and write *IMPORTANT SYMBOLS*. Underneath this, record, line by line, every important aspect of the dream you are journaling. Continue, by following the example in this chapter. Write the headings *SOUNDS, EMOTIONS AND FEELINGS*, and *DESCRIPTION OF DREAM*. Remember: all of the sections except the description section will be in list format or logical format. The description will be as though you are telling someone a story.

Go back and see if during your description you've listed any other symbols. Also, did it feel more like you were actually there and were traveling on the astral plane? If so, why does it feel that way?

Now, summarize the dream as you have recorded it. What is it telling you? Check out your dream as you have deciphered it. Does the dream make sense? Does it fit with your life or any problems or issues you need to look at or resolve? Notice any questions you may have had around the time you had the dream and check the dream meaning to see if there are any answers.

You may find that something that had been or is still on your mind has presented itself with answers through your dream. Alternatively, you may notice that there is something showing up in your dream state that you have been avoiding in your life. Leave a page so you can add any other details that may prove important, that you might recall at a later time.

Remember: this is your dream. Whatever you've recorded is what you needed to record. Never worry about whether or not it's 100 percent accurate or whether you've done everything right. What's more important is understanding the symbolic message behind your dream. Some of the minutiae may become lost, and you may or may not recall it. That's all right; again, it's your dream and your choice to use the symbolic messages as you wish!

Exercise 2: Analyzing Your Dreams From Now On

First thing in the morning, write down your dream from the previous night. While you are just waking up it will be fresh in your mind. Record it the way you did in the first exercise and analyze it in the same way. Notice whether or not it is a dream for your current life, a future or prophetic dream, or whether it was merely that late-night snack.

Share your dream with a friend, and have your friend analyze the dream without using this book as a guide. Then, have that friend analyze it using this book. See what similarities there are and also what differences there are.

Repeat this process every morning that you remember your dreams from the night before. You may find your nighttime symbols repeat themselves in different dreams or in different ways during different dreams.

11

Recognizing Symbolic Synchronicities Every Day

"What does *that* mean?" Deana, a new client, asked me as we sat in my office during her reading.

"I'm not sure, but I know it will be significant in some way," I answered. "All I know is it's an orange 'Y' on a white T-shirt; it could mean anything. Do you or your husband have a T-shirt from the YMCA? Maybe it's Leonardo da Vinci's Vitruvian Man. All I know is when you see this big orange 'Y' on a white T-shirt, you will know all will be right."

This was the last conversation I had with Deana until about two weeks later, when I received a phone call from her.

"You're not going to believe this, but I was in the city last week on an interview and realized I was lost. Then, to top it off, I'd forgotten to bring my wallet. I didn't know what to do. I was starting to panic until I looked over and saw a man with a sign that said he was raising money for a homeless shelter. When I saw what he was selling I almost fell over: white T-shirts with a big orange 'Y'! Apparently, someone donated the shirts and he was selling them for a couple of dollars each. Right away I felt myself relax. I looked in my purse again, thinking I could donate at least a couple of quarters and found pushed up against the side was a twenty-dollar bill that I hadn't seen before. Well, all I can say is, Wow! I don't know how or why, but I know that was a sign."

"Signs are everywhere. We just need to recognize them," I told her, and I smiled, content in the knowledge that this amazing symbolic language had helped another person.

Signs *are* everywhere. We just need to read them. Similar to symbols, signs are useful in their own right; symbols are representations we psychically perceive, whereas signs are symbolic messages we can see or hear with our physical senses. Recognizing signs opens us to synchronicities and can help us to be aware of the significance of coincidence.

They are the little things in life that show up when we are ready to recognize them. They are there to let us know we are on the right track or, alternatively, that we are going in the wrong direction. They also appear to help us receive messages from our deceased loved ones or guides. They become visible when we need answers, and most importantly, they can help direct us toward success.

The universe gives us what we can handle or use. This is a pretty generic statement but one that is very significant. Everything that is put in our path is there to help us to continue in the direction we are going or to come up with a new plan. There are helpers to push those signs our way. According to Adrian Calabrese, PhD, in her book *Sacred Signs: Hear, See & Believe Messages from the Universe*, a sign "…is a direct manifestation from the spirit world in material form."

Driving to the pediatrician with my crying one-year-old introduced me to a whole new way to look for signs: request one. So, I asked for a sign. My daughter's doctor wanted to operate and put tubes in her ears because she was continually getting ear infections. I didn't want her to have the surgery, and I had a feeling if I kept her off dairy she would be fine. However, this was my daughter, and was I willing to risk her health based on my intuition?

So, I asked for a sign as I was driving toward the doctor's office. "God and the angels, if you really are out there I need some help. Please tell me what to do. Should I follow my intuition, my divine guidance, or should I trust the doctor?"

I didn't hear any heavenly music, and I didn't see the hand of God coming down holding a message board with answers. What I did see was a red light coming up, and I was second in line to stop. As I did I noticed the small white car in front of me had a bumper sticker. It read, "Angels are everywhere. Listen to their message."

I knew then that I needed to follow my intuition, and I never had the tubes surgically implanted in my daughter's ears. Instead I eliminated dairy from her diet throughout her toddler years. She is almost nine now, and, thankfully, her ears are just fine.

A sign is only useful if it is recognized. That means that you have to be open to understanding synchronicities, a term coined by Carl Jung to describe seemingly random yet related occurrences. There is a widespread belief that there is no such thing as coincidence. I believe all coincidences are synchronistic, and therefore I understand coincidence as being real. My work has taught me that by recognizing coincidental events, they become synchronicities. As I sit here writing there is a television playing a police show in the background, a show that is totally unrelated to anything psychic or supernatural. Yet, believe it or not, an actor on television just said, "There are no coincidences!" Talk about synchronicity!

A coincidence is an accidental occurrence that happens without planning, often more than one thing happening at the same time or place without planning ahead. Instead of being coincidental, most of these occurrences are synchronistic events. Essentially, this means that everything happens for a reason or everything happens as it is supposed to; the universe is not just filled with random events. Think of the times you start to pick up the phone to call someone at the precise moment the phone rings with the person you were going to call on the other end. Or the times when you're late for an event, but by getting there late you score the front-row tickets just released for sale. Those are synchronicities.

Synchronicity is also sometimes precognizance disguising itself as coincidence, such as the time you noticed a specific street, one you've never paid any attention to before. Then, your daughter calls you and asks if she can spend the night at her friend's house.

"Sure," you say, and you ask her the address of the friend, and it turns out to be that same exact street, the one that never held any value or interest to you before.

The main difference between coincidence and synchronicity is that you become aware that for some reason it was significant that there was a coincidence. Does that mean it has to be a major event or theme? No, absolutely not. Sometimes the simplest ideas or items of note lead to the most amazing *Aha!* moments.

I brought my daughter Samantha to her friend's house to play. While the friend's mother, Laurie, and I were chatting, the subject of middle names came up. We turned it into an impromptu guessing game. After guessing all the middle names of everyone currently at the house, the kids wanted to guess my older daughter, Molly's, middle name. At the exact moment Laurie was about to try and guess Molly's middle name, an actor on the television said "Miranda," clear as day. I chuckled to myself, thinking of how "coincidental" this was and told Laurie they had just said it on TV. Now, this television had been playing the whole time, quietly in the other room, with no one paying any attention to it. Immediately Laurie answered, "Is it Miranda?" She looked at me then and said, "Oh my God, this is crazy. This happens to me all the time, and I don't believe in coincidence."

"Great," I told her, "because neither do I!" and went on to explain all about synchronicities.

Recognizing synchronicities for yourself becomes extremely productive when tuning in to your own intuitive awareness. The mere act of connecting one event or thought of significance to another becomes its own synchronicity.

A client of mine, Ro, described a coincidence that she recognized a few months previously. She had been driving along, going nowhere of real relevance, and she passed a gas truck. Not a gasoline truck but a propane delivery truck. She knew it was propane because she saw a local propane company's name on the truck. For no reason she could think of, she wondered what would happen if one of the gas lines in the town were to explode. She immediately thought of the devastation that would be caused, and also thought about how the impact could possibly be contained by quick action.

The very next day, there was an explosion. A town work crew that was digging up a road in town to repave it struck an underground gas line, and it ignited, causing immense, voluminous billows of black smoke to rise up above the entire southern end of town. The houses closest to the blast were impacted; their vinyl siding melted, literally dripping down the exterior walls. The paint inside the nearest house blistered and cracked. But, luckily, no one was hurt. The crew acted immediately, calling 911, and the fires were contained within minutes, both coming out of the gas pipe and attacking the houses. The firefighters were able to shut down the gas lines and tap into fire hydrants very near by. "Coincidentally," the fire station was right down the street from the explosion.

This accidental event has had lasting effects on Ro. She realizes of course that there was no unplanned coincidence that day. She had what is known as a premonition. Imagine how many lives could be saved by tapping into that precognizant state before an earthquake or a flood or tsunami or any other natural disaster happens. And, what about being able to detect terrorist attacks before they occurred? The possibilities are endless.

Understanding premonitions and synchronicities seems to be one of the hardest tasks we as a population have. Sometimes we are able to accept them for synchronistic events immediately. Other times we are not able to discern the connection because we have forgotten or we have mistaken an original impression we received, or we choose to ignore it. Sometimes, as I said earlier, the original part of the connection is immediately followed by the identifying synchronistic part. There are also those times when you recognize the synchronicity but don't understand the significance of the actual event.

The more aware you become of the probability of synchronicity, the more you will identify occurrences. This will lead to a fuller understanding of why things are happening in your own life as well as in the lives of those around you.

Exercise: Creating a Synchronicities Journal

There is a way, however, to tap into your synchronistic events, every single day. Create for yourself your own special "Synchronicities Journal." This will be a journal for you, and you alone, to help you distinguish and notice things that seem to happen or come to you for no apparent reason.

Get a new journal or a pad of paper, different from the one you've been using, and go through the act of actually committing this to be your "Synchronicities Journal" by writing this title on the cover or the inside of the first page. Differentiating this book from others you are creating signals the intention of actually following through and using it for this very special purpose.

Next, write down events or occurrences or thoughts that you have had in the past when you were able to recognize the synchronicities, whether you called them synchronicities or coincidences. Be sure to include your thoughts and feelings about the initial event or circumstance as well as where you were, the date if you remember it, what you were doing, and the time of day.

Then record the subsequent event, thought, or occurrence that allowed you to connect the two as synchronistic. Again, write down the thoughts and feelings surrounding this second event. Record your location, the date and time, and what you were doing when you recognized the "coincidence."

Also, write down whether this premonition involved just you or other people. If it involved just you, write down how you initially saw yourself in your vision or what you perceived about yourself initially, and in the subsequent event or occurrence. If other people were part of your event, be sure to note any details you can remember about how you felt about the other people or how you envisioned them to be or any similarities or differences between the initial and subsequent experiences.

Then, most importantly, write down your first thoughts after you realized this was a coincidence or a synchronistic event. It could be something as general as "Everything happens for a reason" or as specific as "Now that's why that happened."

Analyze in the recording of your past experiences whether there is any kind of theme or pattern to your personal synchronicities. You may notice that you are more "susceptible" in the early morning hours or the late evening, when your body is drowsily going into or coming out of the hypnagogic (or dreamlike) state. Perhaps you tend to be more open to your intuitive coincidences during or after a workout. Maybe you seem to sense things more in the shower, or at work. Pay attention to these subtleties.

You may realize that whenever you think about someone you haven't seen in a while, they just happen to appear to you soon after. You may notice that you have premonitions that something is going to happen to yourself or someone else, and then it does. Write all these connections or themes down in your journal.

After you have finished writing all of your past synchronistic occurrences, turn to a fresh new page and carry your journal with you. Any time you have a random thought or see something that makes you remember someone or something, or evokes a feeling or precognitive-like idea, write it down. Remember to list where you were, the time of day, who you were with, what you were doing, and if you had any other thoughts at the same time, or about that particular thought or event. And then leave room in your journal. Leaving the space to fill in the subsequent event allows that intention to float out into the universe, creating the expectation that it will become a synchronistic event or occurrence.

"How do I recognize the possible initial events in order to write them down in the first place?" This is a great question. The answer is simple. You don't always. But keep your mind open to anything that seems to happen or appear out of the ordinary. Notice any stray information or thoughts that come at you, totally unexpectedly. These are the times when you will have a coinciding subsequent event. These are the times that will stand out. And if you don't remember to write down or you didn't recognize the initial event, record it when the synchronistic event happens. There is no wrong way to do this. This is your very own special intuitive journal.

Again, notice any themes or commonalities among your content. Does it mean anything to you? Do you notice similarities or differences? Notice if there are any learning undertones. Are there lessons you keep revisiting? Are there any associations to be made among people or circumstances? Are there any familiarities to be aware of concerning work or children?

The more you journal, the more you will begin to recognize and understand all the correlations between the synchronistic events in your life, and you will be able to appreciate all the meaning buried within all of these occurrences. The more you comprehend the significance of these commonalities, the better you will understand your life's path.

Remember, as clichéd as it is, *everything happens for a reason* ... even if the reason is not always initially apparent.

12

Using Symbols to Manifest Your Desires

By now, almost everyone has heard of the book *The Secret*, by Rhonda Byrne. In a nutshell the book is all about manifesting and holding on to what you want. What is manifestation? It is the act of creating something or "making something evident by showing or demonstrating it very clearly," as the *Encarta Dictionary* phrases it. Spiritually, we all have the ability to manifest what we want in life. We have been taught, however, that the only way to get anything is through hard work, suffering, or luck. While we still need to put forth an effort to contribute to our own well-being, we can also create what we desire. By combining symbols with desires we can visualize and bring into reality everything we want.

In their book *Angelspeake: How to Talk with Your Angels,* Barbara Mark and Trudy Griswold call it "A.B.L.T." They define that acronym thusly: "The way to success is to Ask for what you want, Believe it will be given, Let the process work, and say Thank You."

After I became a Certified Angelspeake Facilitator back in the 1990s, I tried this and it worked almost immediately.

I still owned my children's consignment store at the time. I wanted to sell it. My needs were very simple: I wanted a fair price, to sell before my lease ran out, and I wanted my store to be owned by someone who would love and nurture it the way I had. Creating it from scratch, I'd put a lot of blood, sweat, and tears into it. It was time to sell. I was done.

To do this, I combined A.B.L.T. with images. I visualized symbols to represent what I needed to receive in order to sell my store. Taking it one symbol at a time, I started with the fair price. I envisioned a banded amount of dollar bills with a smiley face on it. I created a fair deal symbol, by imagining two silhouetted people shaking hands, smiling. Next, I saw a symbolic calendar with the day before my lease was to run out highlighted. Finally, I symbolically pictured a silhouette of a smiling person with a heart symbol over them, sun shining around them, standing in my store with their arms open wide.

After I symbolically pictured everything I wanted, it was time to let it go, but I wasn't quite ready to give it over to the universe. I decided I still had to do something that would let people know the store was available, so I made one flyer and hung it in my store window. When I received a few phone calls from prospective buyers, my employees couldn't understand why I wasn't returning those phone calls. I knew, claircognizantly, they were not the people who would purchase my store, even without talking to them. What happened next was amazing.

I got a phone call from the mother of an old friend of mine; I hadn't spoken either to her or her daughter, my old friend, in years.

"Are you still selling your store?" she asked.

"Yes, I am. How did you hear about it?" I replied, thinking one of her kids had been by when I wasn't there and had seen the flyer.

"George [another mutual friend] mentioned a couple of years ago you had spoken of possibly selling at some point in the future. It's always been a dream of mine and my sister to open a consignment boutique."

Done. The flyer I'd put in the window hadn't even been necessary. Everything happened so smoothly: fair price, in the right amount of time, and they love it like I did and still run it to this day.

Creating or using existing symbolic clues to help you manifest is one of the easiest ways to generate what you want. By imagining what it is you really desire, and by being specific by visualizing symbols, you are more likely to fulfill your wishes. Pay attention to the details that compose what it is you want to achieve or receive; employing the symbols will help you fully understand what it is you are *really* hoping to manifest.

My sister Tammy has always had an almost uncanny ability to manifest things in her life: money, friends, clients, etc. Her problem with manifestation never came from the capacity to initiate; rather, it occurred because she wasn't concise with exactly what she wanted.

Many years ago, before her psychotherapy practice thrived, she needed to bring more money in. So, she imagined having more clients, reasonably believing this would create an abundance of cash. The problem was Tammy wasn't using symbols to manifest. Because of this she was able to attract the clients, but they brought with them issues instead of money. She was getting new clients who couldn't pay her and clients who were bouncing checks.

What happened with Tammy was not unique; it is actually a regular occurrence. Tammy and I learned that you need to concentrate on what it is you truly want. This is easily accomplished by utilizing symbols that represent what you crave. These images, thoughts, feelings, and so on can be taken from the symbols glossary or the personal symbols you've created, or they may be brand new, depending on what comes to you as you imagine what it is you desire.

One of the simplest ways to manifest your desires is by focusing on a symbolic image of what you want; this will bring it into the forefront of your mind. By concentrating, you supply energy to the object, experience, or occasion you are hoping to have in your life. Be specific, and decide exactly what it is you wish for so you can accurately visualize it coming to you. You want to make sure you get what you actually want and in the way you want it. Just like the old adage "Be careful what you wish for, you just might get it," you need to understand exactly what you are hoping for.

The young daughter of one of my clients decided she wanted a new animal for her birthday. She decided she wanted one, and that was that. Without learning how, she naturally began telling her mom she was going to get a new animal for her birthday. A week later, her birthday arrived and she ran downstairs hoping for a new puppy. Though her parents had warned her she wasn't getting a new puppy, she hadn't believed them. She knew she was getting a new animal for her birthday, and she wasn't going to let anyone tell her differently.

While at the bus stop that morning with her mom, her neighbor asked if they wanted a hamster. Friends of theirs had one that had babies, and there was one left that needed a good home right away. At that point, there was no way the mom could say no. The little girl got her birthday animal; it just happened to be a hamster instead of a puppy. She knew she could wish for it and it would happen; she just hadn't learned yet how to symbolically visualize what it was she truly wanted. The universe works in mysterious ways, however, and although she thought she wanted a puppy, she was ecstatic to get a hamster. Her mother was happy, too!

When we create a life we love, we not only need material possessions such as money and, yes, hamsters, but we need loving relationships as well. Finding a partner is one of the most common applications of manifestation. Again, the key to finding someone who meets all of your requirements and desires is to be very specific.

Think about how the Internet plays such an integral part in matchmaking these days. If you sign up for eHarmony or Match.com, you have to answer numerous detailed questions. This is so the computer program and the employees can create the best possible relationships based on your responses. It is the same way with manifesting. The more detailed you are, the better. If you want someone who is 6'2", with dark wavy hair and a healthy muscular build, visualize him! See him symbolically in your mind. Imagine the muscles stretching tightly under his skin. Feel your fingers running through his hair as you reach up to kiss him.

Or, if you want someone who is petite, five feet tall with blond hair, blue eyes, and fit, see her. Feel yourself bending down and wrapping your arms around her as you gaze into her loving stare. The better you can visualize the symbolic pictures, the more accurate the universe can be when it delivers your partner to you!

It is imperative that you are aware of everything you are looking for in a mate, however. Manifesting a partner, solely on looks or appearance, superficial as it is, can cause you to create a relationship with someone who has no personality. While visualizing the person's appearance, include also their demeanor. How would someone carry themselves if they were confident and secure? I imagine someone standing strong with a slight lean to their stance. What if they were enjoyable, funny, or fun-loving? I see an image of someone actually laughing. There are many other personality traits that may take precedence or at least be an important factor in an ideal mate. The impressions you imagined when thinking of other traits that are important to you can now be used to help you manifest a new relationship. Be sure, however, also to include details like "single." You wouldn't want to have all this go to waste because the person you've manifested is already married or partnered.

We crave attention from people as well. This attention can be attracted the same way, through manifestation. We don't always require full-on relationships; occasionally we just need something special or personal from someone.

I was in a workshop years ago with author and teacher Doreen Virtue, a famous "angel" reader with numerous books and cards about fairies and angels. During her three-day workshop, I, along with the rest of an audience of a couple hundred of my new "closest friends," listened to her lecture from her chair up on stage, leading us in an occasional exercise.

As Doreen is a world-renowned reader, I was secretly hoping for an individual session, but she told us she was no longer offering private reading sessions; instead she was referring them out to her angel therapy practitioners. I love getting a good reading almost as much as I love giving one, and I am always excited at the prospect of sitting with someone who is so well-respected. I was disappointed.

So, during the next exercise when Doreen said it was time to "ask your angels for what you want," I decided I wanted a reading from her. I challenged my angels as well as hers to get her to give me a reading right there and then. I figured it would never happen; first of all you should never "challenge" your angels, and second of all it was very selfish, but I did it anyway.

I focused on her standing by me, symbolically seeing her talking to me, sharing energy with me. I focused on the transfer of auric colors symbolically flowing between us. I imagined seeing a symbolic sign that said "Reading in Progress" hanging next to us.

After our meditative exercise Doreen resumed talking, asking people to share their experience and what they requested from their angels, and suddenly she stopped. She looked through the audience to where I was sitting about three-quarters of the way toward the back of the room. Down she came, flowing like a goddess with her statuesque figure and long blond hair, all the way down the aisle until she was directly in front of me. When she put her hand on my shoulder and asked me to stand up I did, but my jaw remained firmly planted on the floor.

I have never doubted my ability to manifest my desires, my wants, or my needs; I've just been confused about how much one could actually ask for. This was huge, and I'd thought it was too great and too selfish. But it was in that moment that I knew with absolute certainty that the power of manifestation is real on every level. It is more than real, it is deliberate and specific. I had said I want a reading from Doreen Virtue. I may have gotten one at some point in the future, but I wanted one now. And that's exactly what I got, for about five full minutes.

What made it even more defining for me was the fact that she stared at me almost dazed, and it was very clear she had no idea why she had come down to read me. She knew her angels and mine had coerced her, but beyond that it was apparent she was baffled as to why she was there. For me, Doreen Virtue lived up to her reputation that day. She is genuine, of that I have no doubt. It will always be a workshop to remember.

I believe, though I originally thought it was a selfish manifestation request, that the universe encouraged Doreen so she could help me on my career path by validating my psychic and intuitive abilities during her reading. Manifesting desires carries responsibilities. You should not whimsically pursue the manifestation of anything out of pure greed or selfishness. These wishes may or may not come true, but know that if you are indeed able to realize the goal of your manifestation, it will probably come with negative consequences. There is a natural law with manifestation; leave your ego out of it. As with other symbolic concerns, putting your ego in charge will only hinder your spiritual progress and will more often than not carry with it negativity.

This is not to say that you can't wish for more money or abundance just because you are not currently destitute. Simply, it means appreciate what you do have, and ask for what will make your life better, in a positive manner, with gratitude. It is similar to winning the lottery. People always question why, if we receive symbolic messages, we can't see winning lottery numbers. As much as I'd like to win a lot of money, I understand that symbolic messages are gifts, just like the power to manifest is a gift. When we try to bring abundance to ourselves out of ego, or so we can brag about distinctive wealth, we are acting in a very self-centered way. Coming from a place of love, for yourself and others, is the only real justification you need to manifest your desires.

If you find yourself believing there is a kind of natural "limit" to what you should ask for, or you feel you'd be in some way exploiting the ability to manifest, take baby steps. If receiving one hundred dollars by the end of the week will help you pay your phone bill, start there. Allow the universe to work for you, guilt free. Next time go for something bigger! Remember that the sky truly is the limit. You can manifest whatever you need, and if it's for your greater good, you'll probably get it. Don't let fear hold you back; you deserve abundance.

Fear keeps us from manifesting because it makes us afraid to realize what we want. Being fearful of the outcome of fulfilling what we wish for can cancel the wish altogether. Imagine trying to manifest money. You go through all the steps, visualizing the money coming to you, seeing the symbolic pile of gold. But after you are all done going through the process of seeing the symbols, you can't help but think the only way you will receive the money you are trying to manifest is through inheritance, which means someone you love would have to die. Now, instead of visualizing the pile of gold, you are seeing a coffin, your symbol for death. That fear of losing someone is keeping you from being able to actualize what it is you are trying to manifest. The fear is getting in the way of making your dream come to fruition.

Trying to manifest in fear is like running in circles; you're just going to keep spinning your wheels. In her book *Wishing: How to Fulfill Your Heart's Desires*, teacher and healer Elizabeth Harper writes, "You can make as many wishes as you like, but your fear will block you like a sixty-foot wall and prevent you from receiving something that is so ready to be yours." Essentially, the universe is ready to provide you with abundance, but you have to get out of your own way to receive it. What's holding you back?

There is a joke about a spiritual man who is in the middle of a flood. He climbs out his window and onto his roof and prays to God to save him.

A person comes by in a rowboat. "Hurry, hop in! The tide is rising," he says to the spiritual man.

"No, God will save me," the man replies from his perch on the roof, and the boat rows away.

Seemingly out of nowhere a helicopter flies over the man's house and drops a ladder to him as the water rises. "Hurry, jump on! The water is rising!" the helicopter pilot shouts down.

"No, God will save me," the man tells the pilot with conviction, even though the flood continues up the sides of the man's house onto the roof.

Finally the roof is consumed by the flood waters, and the man drowns. When he arrives in heaven he asks God, "God, why didn't you save me? Why have you forsaken me?"

God replies, "I tried! What did you think the rowboat and the helicopter were for?"

Although this is a joke, it is of great relevance when we think of manifestation. Often the changes we desire will manifest through various signs, steps, or directions in our lives. We have to recognize those signs in order to allow or help our wishes to come to fruition. Be cognizant of what's happening around you or in your life and try not to discount opportunities that may present themselves to you. We have to be active participants in our own lives.

Essentially, manifestation is the changing of your circumstances to allow what you want into your life. When we use symbolic manifestation we create the optimum or ideal situations to increase our chances or our propensity to attain our desires. This means when we journey through a money manifestation or we focus on bringing more money in, it doesn't just fall from heaven; we open ourselves to the possibilities that allow money to come to us. So, essentially, when we use symbolic visualization we are picturing or imagining the outcome rather than the process. This is crucial to achieving whatever goal we have set, because it permits the universe to make it happen however it is achievable.

When I sold my store I focused on the outcome, not the means to the end. Never in a million years would I have guessed the sale would have gone down the way it did. By leaving it open, I allowed the energy to permeate into the universe and create the reality I wanted.

You can create a life you love. By using symbols, you can easily visualize the outcome you want and open the manifestation process. There is no limit to what you can create when you set your mind to it! You need only to remember to do it. I always seem to forget that the simplest way to get what I want or to achieve my goals is to ask for it. If it is for my greater good or something that will help me, I know I will obtain it. Practicing manifestation helps to make it a more natural process and a regular part of your life. Use the exercise below to help you manifest your true desires!

Exercise: Using Symbols to Manifest Your Desires

Think of something that you really want. Keeping it simple will help you practice the act of manifestation. Make it realistic; you don't need ten million dollars tomorrow! Now, think of what you want with regard to outcome. What is the end result you are looking for?

Think of five different symbolic images that you can relate to whatever it is you want to manifest. For example, if it's money, you can start with actual cash, stacks of money. Next, you might visualize a specific dollar amount listed as a deposit on your bank statement. Possibly, next, you could visualize all your family, friends, and loved ones gathered together laughing and enjoying themselves, no one missing and no one hurt in any way. This can help to reiterate that you want to receive this money only with no harm to yourself or anyone else.

You can also picture what you want the money for; is it to purchase particular items, to help someone, or to pay your bills? Imagining the symbols for what you want the money for can help to create the wherewithal to receive what it is you desire.

Take this time now to record your five different symbolic images in your journal, under the new heading *Manifestation*.

Begin focusing on your first symbol. Visualize that symbolic image for at least one minute in your mind, directing all your energy to any details you attribute to the image. Be sure all the imagery is positive. If it's not, change it, make it so. You want to manifest positivity, not negativity.

Continue, one at a time, until you are finished with all five symbols. Now, go back to the top of the page and write down a realistic date by which you'd like to have your desires manifested. Visualize a calendar with that same date highlighted in some way, with color or with a money sign or a star on that day.

Now, and this one is hard, let it go! You've done all you can. Let go of the process and allow the universe to work its magic! If at any time in the future you think about what it is you are manifesting, just visualize those images again, quickly this time. You don't want to put too much of your energy into it, as that could cause negativity or a negative obsession, which in turn could cause what you originally wanted not to be manifested.

After your first desire has manifested, do it again! You may find that the more you do this, the more natural it becomes. Just remember that you have to recognize the signs to help manifest what you want. For example, if you asked for more money, don't ignore calls from new clients or don't turn down that offer of a side job. Don't forget: you never know how your desires will manifest themselves!

Conclusion: Living Symbolically!

How do you decide which method to use to tune in to your intuition symbolically? That's easy. Whatever works! Seriously, whatever feels right, intuitively. I know, this sounds like a cop-out, right? Not really. It's simply that as you've been practicing all the different ways to tune in, you've probably noticed one modality felt more comfortable or more natural than another.

This is very normal. This is exactly what intuition is all about. You may find that you have a propensity for clairvoyance or you may feel things with more discernment. We all have one or two intuitive senses that are more focused. The more we develop these particular senses the stronger they will become.

One of the most important considerations is recognizing what is "fun" for you. It is quite possible that if you begin to feel aggravated or frustrated or even angry when using automatic writing, then it is not suited to you. Notice what method you enjoy employing the most and run with it. Chances are many of the other techniques will begin to work their way in, becoming easier each time. In other words, if it doesn't feel good, don't do it! Developing your symbolic awareness should be an enjoyable experience.

Having said that doesn't mean it's all fun and games. Expanding your awareness is hard work. Digging in and really trying will give you a greater understanding of your own intuitive nature. You have to make a commitment to yourself and make an effort to practice daily. This is also when it becomes the most fun.

Determining which approach to use when also depends on what task you have at hand. If you are trying to find a missing bracelet, you can ask your guides to help you by showing you clairvoyantly where it is, clairaudiently telling you where to look, or telling you symbolically. On the other hand, you might use a procedural or mapped-out process to locate a missing person. Remote viewing may be more appropriate in this matter, and there are numerous books out there to get you started.

Don't be afraid to mix it up a little. During readings, I frequently utilize many different techniques to tune in. I did readings for two women yesterday in my office. I actually gave them each gift certificates for half-hour tarot-card readings for Christmas and they finally used them. I brought out my tarot deck, expecting that I would have to begin by tuning in to their energy through the cards. Regularly, when reading for people I know, it can be more difficult to discern what I'm receiving psychically from my normal everyday impressions of them. I was pleasantly surprised when, instead, deceased friends and family members of my clients immediately started lining up from the other side and began to give evidence they were there! I heard names clairaudiently and was able to tune in clairsentiently and claircognizantly, getting information that truly helped these two clients with real-life crises they were experiencing. By allowing all of these symbolic and intuitive tools to work naturally, I was able to give these two women the solace they needed to make it through the next day.

The bottom line is this: with practice you'll know what fits when, and, yes, you'll know it intuitively!

Now that you've learned how to tune in and understand your psychic symbols you will probably observe other changes in your life. These changes may appear insignificant at first, but just wait. Psychically tuning in to the other side will increase these changes considerably over time.

You may find that you trust your instincts much more now, possibly even using them to guide you through daily life. How wonderful to have this sensitivity. You can now listen to your intuition to determine which route to take driving home. You may find yourself having the ability to tap into your symbolic filing cabinet to find out whether your next date is worth going on. You'll find your confidence will also improve, and you'll no longer need to rely on other people's opinions to make decisions.

More confidence will bring a greater balance to your life. I'm not talking about the kind of false confidence that comes from the ego. That's different. That's using the intuitive gifts you've tapped into as a kind of parlor trick or expecting people to put you on a pedestal. What I'm referring to is real confidence: the self-esteem-building kind that comes with psychic and intuitive knowledge.

Throughout your symbolic journey with this book, you've no doubt felt a push or a pull, as though your intuition was reaching out to you, or even a little tug of war on occasion as you've tried each exercise, maybe more than once. This can have a tendency to throw you off-kilter a bit. Digest all of this new information; acquaint yourself with your feelings about all of the psychic symbolic methods you've practiced. Eventually you will experience a feeling of balance. This balance is essential to living as a sentient being and will induce calmness and serenity, which will carry through into your everyday life.

You may also find that once you begin living an intuitive life you won't be able to easily go back. This doesn't mean that you will always remember to check in with your intuition, but it does mean you will use it and recognize the symbolic clues with greater frequency. The more you use it, the more comfortable you will be.

Pay attention to which colors you feel for yourself and other people. Start noticing if you feel a tingle in any of your chakra centers. Embark on a new symbolic journey while manifesting your destiny.

Take one or two symbolic images from your personal symbols journal entries or from the basic symbols glossary and really tune in to them each day. Once you start focusing on them, you'll observe these same signs appearing more and more often in your life.

You are an intuitive being. Celebrate!

Glossary: Basic Symbols— Your Psychic Reference

Everyone receives symbolic messages, and we are all able to connect to the other side through this intuitive communication. Melita Denning and Osborne Phillips write, in their book *Practical Guide to Psychic Powers*, "Psychic powers are part of your rightful heritage, and their development will bring you enjoyment and satisfaction, as well as many practical and spiritual benefits." Learning the meaning of archetypal symbols will help you to tap into your "rightful heritage." Remember that we are all intuitive beings.

During my years of professional intuitive work, I've learned by doing. What I mean is, like everyone else, I don't always know what the symbolic impressions mean that come through as messages. It has taken me a lot of time and conscious effort to understand and mentally catalog the symbols I've been presented with, and I can honestly say that I continue to receive new impressions with every reading.

As with the stories from the beginning of the book about the house in Arizona and the eggs dropping to the floor, I am able to store in my memory the different images, feelings, sounds, tastes, and smells that are representative symbols rather than literal translations, answers, or intuitive messages in my psychic filing cabinet. It is quite probable that I will receive the same impression more than once, during readings for different people. This helps reinforce the validity of the symbolic information I am receiving.

For example, I was doing a reading for my friend Chrissy on a house she wanted to buy, and I psychically saw an image of a dark and wet corner in a basement; I could see the cement blocks making up two walls and the concrete floor. By receiving this symbolic image I knew there were water issues in the house. Initially, I received this image many years ago, for my client Julie, so I knew this was my symbol for a damp basement. Neither one of these basements had looked the way the image in my mind looked; it was a symbolic interpretation rather than a literal one. What was interesting about this specific symbol was in both cases I saw the dampness on the concrete floor recede to dryness. This told me the infringing water was not permanent and was not going to cause mold.

Along the way, I have been able to reference many books when I've had questions about the various messages I've been given—about intuitive abilities, psychic awareness, psychic symbols, people who are psychic, and dreams. This has helped me to integrate and understand many of the symbolic messages I've received. Another way I have developed my comprehension of symbols has been, and will continue to be, by going to psychic events. Whether I am teaching, participating, or merely watching an intuitive perform, I find there are so many psychic symbolic impressions to walk away with. Being aware of the presence of symbols contributes to the capacity to recall the meanings to the psychic language.

In creating the following glossary of basic psychic symbols, I've utilized my own personal experiences, memories, and impressions to decipher and discern all of the meanings I have listed. I've drawn on interpretations I have been exposed to through the thousands of readings I've conducted, the psychic circles I've hosted, and the intuitive development classes I've taught and attended. Whenever I had questions about any symbolic images, thoughts, feelings, or sounds I've heard, I took advantage of the ability to research my impressions on the Internet and in books. Dream interpretation books and even dictionaries can help decode psychic symbols. One book I've utilized on various occasions is an all-encompassing, comprehensive guide called *The Encyclopedia of Symbolism*, by Kevin J. Todeschi. Essentially, whatever feels right or resonates with you can help you interpret symbolic messages.

The glossary I've put together is a basic representation of the most common psychic symbols received by professionals and laypeople alike. When looking up specific words, do not negate any interpretations of your own that you may intuitively have. Instead, integrate the meanings based on what rings true to you.

Knowing how and when to apply these symbolic messages depends on how and when you receive them. If you are asking a question and receive a symbol in response, look up that symbol and you will better understand the answer that has been sent to you. If you happen to get a symbolic message when you haven't been asking for one and you don't know why you've gotten it or what it means, again, look up the symbol in the glossary. It's possibly a symbolic warning of something coming up, or a nudge to contact someone in your life whom you may have thought of when you received the intuitive message. It can also suggest, based on whatever symbol you received, that you need to review that something or possibly that part of your life to see if what's happening or what's involved is for your better good.

You may be getting this symbolic information as a congratulatory or celebratory message for an upcoming event or accomplishment. Symbols sent from the other side may be meant to steer or guide you in the next step or direction to go in your life, generally or specifically. Alternatively, it may indicate what you need to stay away from or rid yourself of. Also, as always, you may simply be receiving messages from the other side to let you know your deceased loved ones are around you and are still there for you. What you do with this information you are presented with is up to you; it is your choice to act on it or ignore it.

Use this back-to-basics, easy-to-understand reference section of the psychic language to help you interpret metaphysical messages. Keep in mind that all of the symbolic words and terms listed on the following pages may also hold very rudimentary meanings. It is possible you are being given a specific symbol that doesn't need an interpretive translation. For example, you may see a bicycle. Normally, you might think this symbol is about exercise or taking a personal journey, but it might just refer to an actual bicycle. Tapping into your intuition to determine what type of symbol it is will assist you. This basic psychic symbols glossary will help guide you.

Glossary

Abacus: expect a change, an addition or subtraction to your life; what do you need to add to your life?; what do you need to get rid of?; calculating the worth of something in your life; you can count on something to happen; putting forth a calculated effort will help you get what you want; count on or look to ancient Chinese wisdom or methods to help you achieve; calculated ideas; could be a business opportunity possibility connected to Asia

Abbey: *See* Chapter 7: "Religion, Spirituality, Culture, and Symbols"

Adam and Eve: the creation of all; the ultimate partnership; a relationship based on temptation; sexual temptation; the need for balance—male and female; representing sexuality; number one or the first; the beginning of a new partnership or creating a partnership from nothing; duality needed to mutually coexist

Africa: could imply foreign travel is possible; could relate to slavery or a feeling of being enslaved; as with all foreign countries, may represent the unknown; if from Africa, could indicate a need or desire to go back to your roots; may represent a visitor or someone from Africa; *See also* CONTINENT/COUNTRY

Air conditioner: it's time to cool off, cool down; it's too hot or the heat is on; it's time for a breath of fresh air; may need to check your breathing, your lungs, or your pulmonary system; may represent summer or summertime; can indicate a warm geographical location

Airplane: travel is in the air; it's time to take a journey; you will go a great distance; it's time to spread your wings and fly; as associated with 9/11, can indicate severe fear; depending upon point of view, can be a physical body; crashing may represent fear or the end of an idea in a disastrous way; if grounded, may suggest an idea not taking off; if taking off, can indicate the beginning of a new project, idea, or venture; idea coming from somewhere else; if departing, may represent the end of a relationship; if incoming, may represent a new relationship on its way. *See also* FLYING, JET

Akashic records: metaphysical storehouse where every universal event, person, place, and detail of the existence of humanity is stored; place where interplanetary information is kept and can be retrieved; "God's filing cabinets"; place where all knowledge of every instant and every occurrence is stored; may represent a need to research or get answers from the past

Alarm clock: this is your wake-up call; it's time to pay attention; a sudden jolt back to reality; wake up!; it's time to stop sleeping and become aware; may indicate something needs your attention; surprise

Alcohol: the message or your thinking is unclear or diluted; may suggest you're looking for an easy out or a way to avoid reality; can represent a party or partying; may represent or indicate an alcoholic or substance abuse

Alien: may represent the unknown; some idea or person that is different or foreign to you; may indicate a foreign visitor or travel to a foreign land; may indicate messages from an unknown source; may indicate presence of, or belief in, other planetary or spiritual beings; *See also* FLYING SAUCER/UFO

Alligator: may be associated with words: big mouth, harsh, or dangerous words; something that you are afraid of or a subconscious fear; being fearful of harsh words; having a tough demeanor or rough exterior; someone or something is untrustworthy; an unpleasant surprise

Ambulance: there's an emergency; it's critical that you move fast now; it's time to save your life (metaphorically); be careful; keep watch for accidents; an accident may occur; injury, or someone is emotionally injured; help is needed or help is on the way; move with caution; *See also* DOCTOR, EMERGENCY ROOM, HOSPITAL, NURSE

Amethysts: a positive stone, possessing positive spiritual qualities; representing the higher self; an energy-clearing or cleansing stone; may suggest calmness; *See also* JEWELS/GEMSTONES

Anchor: feeling secure or having a secure hold on something; as in "anchor around the neck," tethered; feeling weighed down, heavy with problems or issues; feeling uncomfortable with settling down in a partnership or family; feeling stuck in situation or problem; lifting an anchor-weight off your shoulders or a problem resolved

Angel: God's helper; message from God; divine messenger; help is there for you; you're in the presence of divine helpers; all you need to do is ask for help; peace, love, and divine guidance is here for you; feeling the presence of a birth or death coming; birth or death of a new idea; *See also* Chapter 2: "Where Symbolic Messages Come From" and Chapter 7: "Religion, Spirituality, Culture, and Symbols"

Angelfish: may indicate the presence of angels or angelic messages; *See also* FISH

Animals: natural instinct or instinctive decisions; feeling like an animal; *See also* BEAR, BIRD, CAT, COW, DEER, DOG, DOLPHIN, FISH, FROG, GIRAFFE, GOAT, GOPHER, GORILLA, HORSE, JUNGLE, KANGAROO, LAMB, LION, MONKEY, MOUSE, OCTOPUS, PIG, POSSUM, RABBIT, RAT, SKUNK, SQUIRREL, TIGER, TURTLE, WHALE, ZEBRA, ZOO

Ankh: *See* Chapter 7: "Religion, Spirituality, Culture, and Symbols"

Apple: need for vitamins; as in "an apple a day keeps the doctor away," represents health or the need for healthy eating; as in the Bible's Adam and Eve, the forbidden fruit, something that is tempting and dangerous; as in Sleeping Beauty, that which is poisoned; *See also* FOOD, FRUIT

Aquarius (born January 20–February 18): the eleventh sign in the zodiac, ruled by the eleventh house of friends and society; usually denotes intelligence, with many thoughts and new ideas; visionaries who want to make the world better; very giving, sympathetic, and compassionate, but on their own terms; very friendly, but don't like to share feelings; as in "dawning of the age of Aquarius," time of peace, love, and happiness; *See also* ZODIAC/ASTROLOGICAL SIGN

Arc: as in electrical, a shock to your system; shocking news or shocking story; a spark of interest; an intuitive spark; a flash of intuition to pay attention to; a welder; as in geometry, someone throwing you a curve; going around a problem or situation instead of straight through it; what goes up must come down

Aries (born March 21–April 19): the sign of the ram and the first sign in the zodiac, ruled by the first house of self; usually is someone who is very headstrong or stubborn; a self-ordained leader; generally impulsive, starting new projects before finishing old ones; usually blunt and to the point; not always honest with their beliefs. *See also* ZODIAC/ASTROLOGICAL SIGN

Ark: as in the biblical reference of Noah, duality and balance; heading to new land; moving your place of residence; going on a journey; starting a new path with balance; beginning of a new direction with a new partner; large ship; may refer to a veterinarian or suggest someone who helps animals; *See also* Chapter 7: "Religion, Spirituality, Culture, and Symbols"

Arrow: shooting forward; moving ahead swiftly; proceeding in a rapid manner; heading straight for the bull's-eye; shooting for the target or goal; taking aim and going for it; moving on the straight and narrow; receiving a direct message; meaning something intentional and direct; can indicate Native American guides; message from Native American guide; *See also* INDIAN (NATIVE AMERICAN)

Asian writing: may suggest a need or desire to explore the Asian methods; look to Buddhism for help; may be associated with travel to or a traveler coming from Asia; important scroll information; can represent a tattoo or a desire for a tattoo

Astrological sign: See ZODIAC/ASTROLOGICAL SIGN or entry for specific astrological sign

Athlete: corresponds to need to be agile, flexible, and in shape; someone who is physically fit, healthy, and strong; can represent a specific sport or sports team; needing to play the game of life; training and dedication; focus; *See also* FOOTBALL, SNEAKERS, SPORT SOCKS

Attic: the highest power, highest consciousness; representing the crown chakra; representing the brain, wisdom, and the mind; memory; may be time to dust off old ideas; *See also* HOUSE

Aura: energy surrounding and emanating from every living thing; *See also* Chapter 6: "Chakra and Aura Symbolism"

Aureoles: See Chapter 7: "Religion, Spirituality, Culture, and Symbols"

Automobile: See CAR/AUTOMOBILE

Ax: destructive or creative and useful tool; representing a need to split apart or split something up; destructive or abusive power; may represent an aggressive male; a need to cut something or someone off; *See also* KNIFE, SWORD

Baby: need to explore childhood; you or someone around you may be pregnant or expecting a baby; need to care for your inner child; stop acting like a baby; something new; new idea or birth of a new idea; if the baby is crawling, new idea taking off; if baby is falling, idea or new endeavor is falling apart; need to nurture your creative side in order to construct a new concept; representing the beginning of life; *See also* BOY, GIRL, PERSON

Bag/Baggage: may represent that which holds your thoughts or emotions; can represent life experiences, responsibilities, or burdens we carry; type of bag may suggest how we deal with or associate our past or our emotions; may represent material possessions we cannot live without; past experiences brought forward; *See also* LUGGAGE/SUITCASE, PURSE/POCKETBOOK

Ball: can represent sports; may represent children or a need to address your inner child; can indicate a period of relaxation or recreation; may represent spiritual wholeness or oneness; well-rounded or well-thought-out idea; as in "let's play ball," can imply the beginning of a working relationship; as in "don't drop the ball," a warning not to fail; as in "eyes on the ball," pay attention to what you are doing or what is important; *See also* FOOTBALL

Banana: may suggest the need for fruit; need for vitamins, specifically potassium; can indicate a need to open up your third or yellow chakra; may refer to a male or male sexuality, phallus symbol; as in the "big banana," can imply the boss; *See also* FOOD, FRUIT

Bandage: may indicate a fresh wound that needs healing; can indicate the time to heal old wounds is now; may suggest a relationship you're in may need attention or need to be fixed; can suggest a need to remove a protective covering to reveal the healing beneath

Basement: representing the root or base chakra; starting at the bottom; beginning on the ground floor; can indicate working your way to the top; dirty and dusty basement meaning unbalanced first chakra; holding a storage of wisdom or information; your base desires, such as sexuality; representing the subconscious or unconscious mind; stuffing your emotions down into your root chakra; *See also* DUNGEON, HOUSE

Bath/Bathtub: can point toward a need to cleanse spiritually; may represent baptism; may suggest water, which in turn may be a sign of emotions; if the tub is full or empty, suggesting state of emotion: overly emotional or emotionless; may point to a need to pour out emotions; can represent feeling emotionally drained; *See also* BATHROOM

Bathroom: may represent a need to cleanse physically, spiritually, emotionally; need to eliminate what is no longer useful to you; a place of privacy; a real need to eliminate waste from your life; release of physical, emotional, or mental discomfort; may suggest a problem with the digestive system; *See also* BATH/BATHTUB, HOUSE, SHOWER, SINK, TOILET

Battery: it may be time to recharge your inner battery; time to get rest and rejuvenate; a store of energy to apply to your situation; needing a jump start currently in your life; corresponding to the heart chakra; may indicate power or a power source; can represent a portable or emergency energy source

Beach: may represent vacation; feeling at peace; time to reflect on the balance of physical (sand), emotional and spiritual (water) parts of yourself and the overlapping or blending of the two; *See also* SAND, WATER

Bear: possibly being overprotective or possessive; as in "bearish," grumpy or cranky; having both a playful fun side as well as a grumpy overprotective side; can represent the need to hibernate and meditate or rest; can be "bearing" the brunt of a problem or issue or situation; can indicate a camping trip or a return to nature; incredible strength; *See also* ANIMALS

Bed: time to rest, lie down, and sleep; associated with sex or sexual relations; desire; relating to the second chakra or sexual chakra; if bed is unmade, suggests sloppy habits or tending toward not being neat; if bed is extremely neat, tendency to control life, especially with base desires or sexuality; "you've made your bed and now you need to sleep in it" suggests you create your own environment or situation; *See also* BEDROOM

Bedroom: represents a place to tap into second or sexual chakra; sexuality and sexual relations; place to feel safe or secure; representing private matters or privacy; can represent partnership, marriage; may refer to intimacy between two people, connecting on a physical, mental, and spiritual level; *See also* BED, HOUSE

Bee: as in "busy as a bee," industrious and hard-working; busy work; may suggest someone who delivers zingers or stinging words; being on the receiving end of stinging words; sharp-witted; sharp pain; can represent the need for local honey to help with healing and building up immunities; *See also* BUG/INSECT

Bible: may suggest a time for religion; reviewing God's word as told by men; dealing with your faith; look to God for answers; possibly feeling the need to connect to Jesus; a belief in miracles; need for spiritual wisdom or sacred wisdom; looking for spiritual guidance; stories of faith; needing a holy experience; *See also* Chapter 7: "Religion, Spirituality, Culture, and Symbols"

Bicycle: learning to balance; beginning an exercise program; need to begin exercising; movement, motion, spinning; journey by yourself; in control of your own destiny or journey; can indicate needing cardiovascular exercise to fend off illness or heart attack or disease

Bird: time to spread your wings and fly; able to go a long way; representing flying through life; taking a journey; as in "bird brain," small intellect, simple; as in "birds of a feather flock together," like people travel with like people or cliques; freedom; *See also* BLACKBIRD, CANARY, CARDINAL, CHICK, CHICKEN, CROW, DOVE, DUCK, EAGLE, FALCON, GOOSE, HAWK, HEN, OWL, ROBIN, ROOSTER, SPARROW, STORK

Birthday cake: can represent birthday wishes; a message of happy birthday from the other side; may represent your special day or someone's special day around you; you're getting older; act your age; appreciate and celebrate yourself; it's celebration time; *See also* CAKE, FOOD

Blackbird: being void of color or mixed of all colors; can indicate danger or bad or evil energy; there is a hidden side to be seen; as in "blackbirds baked in a pie," representing fairy tales; *See also* BIRD, CROW

Bluefish: relaxation on the ocean; spiritual communication; may refer to a boat trip or a picnic; *See also* FISH

Blueprint: can suggest that the direction you need to go in life is already laid out for you; may indicate there is a distinct path ahead; may suggest a need to follow the plans to receive the most benefits; may correspond to your life's destiny

Boat: may suggest a literal boat ride or vacation or cruise; can indicate making your way through your emotions; can represent one's path or journey through life; may suggest opening a spiritual route or exploring the unconscious; may be associated with the ferryboat ride to physical death; as in "don't rock the boat," don't make it difficult; as in "your ship's come in," good fortune for you; as in "we're in the same boat," we're in the same situation; as in "missed the boat," a missed opportunity; depending on type of boat suggests how you cope emotionally with life; *See also* HARBOR

Body parts: *See* BONES, EARS, EYES, FACE, FINGER(S), FOOT/ FEET, FOREHEAD, GONADS, HAND, HAIR, HEAD, HEADLESS PERSON, HEART, HEEL, JAW, KNEES, LEG, LIPS, LUNGS, NOSE, THROAT, TOES, TOOTH/TEETH

Bones: relating to the first chakra, which is connected to the skeletal system; as in "skull and crossbones," death; depending on bone could represent ancient bones or fossils; hard exterior; soft interior; if broken, may indicate you or someone has a broken bone; may represent structure; depending on type of bone, may indicate specific animal

Book: depending on the book, can mean you need to research something or look something up; wisdom or information at your fingertips; can represent knowledge and education; if you see the book, it may mean going to school or back to school to increase your knowledge and education; if you see a specific book, pay attention to what it is; may suggest a need to read between the lines; it may also refer to a teacher or teaching; *See also* LIBRARY, MAGAZINE

Box: keeping things boxed up; as in "thinking outside the box," coming up with new or different ideas; may represent contained emotions; feeling hemmed in or boxed in; having walls up; as in "Pandora's box," don't open or get into something you may not be prepared to handle; could be a gift from the other side or a physical gift

Boy: representing one's inner child; feeling the masculine side of your energy; could mean a time to tap into your childish ways or stop being childish; could refer to sports; pay attention to how the boy is dressed, as the symbol may indicate something specific about the boy; may be a visit from a deceased boy; *See also* GONADS, KIDS/ CHILDREN, PERSON

Bracelet: as with the hands, may suggest some type of service; often represents ownership of something; may indicate being held; *See also* JEWELRY

Bridge: feeling the need to connect; connecting to the other side; can indicate crossing over; bridging the distance between two people or two areas; taking a journey to another place; a new adventure; crossing a bridge to your past life; a means to get to the other side of a situation or problem; connecting your conscious mind to your subconscious

Buddha: See Chapter 7: "Religion, Spirituality, Culture, and Symbols"

Bug/Insect: annoying or an annoyance; something that bothers you; feeling unprotected from exterior sources; industrious like ants, always working/moving; feeling small and insignificant; something that creeps up on you; irritating; *See also* BUTTERFLY, CATERPILLAR, DRAGONFLY, FLY, MAGGOT, MOSQUITO, SPIDER

Business card: may indicate business meeting coming up; could mean new business proposal or venture; may refer to someone with a business; could indicate new business for you or someone significant to you; new business idea; professional; connecting with or working with professionals; salesperson; may indicate offer of a job; pay attention to type of business for relevance

Butterfly: associated with spirituality; may represent beauty or freedom; transformation and change; can indicate rebirth; also, note colors as in chakra system; formation of something beautiful out of something ordinary; often associated or viewed as a sign from a deceased loved one; *See also* BUG/INSECT, CATERPILLAR

Cake: as in "you can't have your cake and eat it too," means you can't have it all; something sweet, indicating the sweet side or sweet tooth; depending on cake, could be message of congratulations or happy wishes; indulgence; as in "piece of cake," something easy; as in "that takes the cake," may be sarcastic or serious, meaning "that's really something"; as in "icing on the cake," getting something even better than expected; *See also* BIRTHDAY CAKE, CUPCAKE, FOOD

Canada: may refer to visiting, or visitor from, Canada; can refer to northern location; may suggest snow or a cold area; may represent maple leaves or maple syrup; can refer to ice hockey; *See also* COUNTRY/CONTINENT

Canary: yellow, solar plexus chakra; intuitive message; singing messenger; listen to the message you are getting; chatty; happy or sunny mood; *See also* BIRD and Chapter 6: "Chakra and Aura Symbolism"

Cancer (astrological sign; born June 21–July 22): the sign of the crab and the fourth sign in the zodiac, ruled by the fourth house of home and family; all about home and home life; Cancers are known for their very hard exterior and soft mushy interior: they show themselves as tough on the outside but are very sensitive on the inside; greatly protective of family; can be very emotional and very moody and crabby; need to prove something; *See also* ZODIAC/ASTROLOGICAL SIGN

Cancer (disease): may indicate illness or disease; something eating away at you or someone else; something you feel powerless over; something negatively taking control; something that takes a lot of work to possibly overcome; may point to death of spirit or literal death

Candle/candle flame: as in "burning the candle at both ends," could indicate tiredness or exhaustion from not getting enough downtime; could indicate the light inside of you; could suggest a need to meditate; spirit light or lights from spirit; if the flame is wavering, may indicate the presence of someone who is in spirit or who has crossed over; lighting up the way; as in "light of your life," may point to the love of your life; the beginning of a fire or new project/endeavor; *See also* CANDLE HOLDER, FIRE

Candle holder: that which holds the light inside of you; may represent a need to protect yourself or your light/energy; may represent protection in a new project; can indicate a need to meditate; *See also* CANDLE/CANDLE FLAME; FIRE

Capricorn (born December 22–January 19): the sign of the goat and the tenth sign in the zodiac, ruled by the tenth house of career; ambitious and hard-working; diligent and organized; patient and can wait until they work their way to the top; can be unforgiving toward people who don't work as hard or are not as ambitious as they are; need to appreciate what they have instead of always wanting more or never being satisfied; can be judgmental; *See also* ZODIAC/ASTROLOGICAL SIGN

Car/Automobile: moving forward; can indicate travel; traveling on a journey or path of life; can indicate someone getting a new car; if vision is of a police car, can indicate caution; propelling through life quickly; can refer to racing through life, a need to slow down; can be a metaphor for self; type of car explains your physical or outer self, e.g.: flashy car, flashy person; or an old beat-up car may indicate a need to take care of yourself; *See also* ENGINE, HOSE, MOTOR-CYCLE

Cardinal: red, root chakra, foundation; as in "cardinal sin," sinner; strong and proud; somewhat stoic; may represent Catholicism; may suggest a warning or caution needed; may indicate continuing love and hope through bleak circumstances; *See also* BIRD

Cards: pertaining to playing cards, card games; as in "card shark," someone not to be trusted; trip to a casino; can refer to Las Vegas; can indicate gambling, a gambler, or a gambling problem; may suggest you are involved in a game of chance; as in tarot cards, may indicate fortunetelling; *See also* BUSINESS CARD, LAS VEGAS, ROULETTE WHEEL, SLOT MACHINE, and Chapter 8: "Tarot Symbols"

Carnival: can suggest a period of fun; childlike fun without a care; multicolored as in the chakra system; can suggest going for a ride; taking a ride to nowhere or going nowhere fast; may suggest specific festive events or locations, such as Carnival in Brazil, Mardi Gras in New Orleans, the Santa Monica Pier in California, the Atlantic City Boardwalk in New Jersey, etc. (notice if there are any recognizable markers); suggests large outlay of money for a very short-lived reward; can mean you or someone around you is playing games; *See also* CAROUSEL

Carousel: life is going in circles; can suggest a need for patience because sometimes life goes slower than you'd like; going around and around a situation; riding a safe horse, or a safe journey; circus or carnival or fair; can suggest specific location with carousel; may indicate journey through life's cycles; may represent childhood or childlike innocence; *See also* CARNIVAL

Carpet/Rug: can refer to your foundation, or base; may represent what's beneath you; color or design may represent what is holding you or supporting you; as in "magic carpet," can suggest transporting or traveling to another time or place magically or metaphorically; as in "got the rug pulled out from under him," being tricked or fooled or having everything fall apart; as in "swept under the rug," can suggest something hidden; as in "called to the carpet," may refer to someone being called out for something they did or being punished

Casket: can indicate a literal death; may suggest the end of a cycle; may indicate your life situation is making you feel claustrophobic; as in "dead to you," can suggest something or someone you've shut out of your life; can suggest it's time to examine your life and make some changes; may indicate it's time to let something go so you can make way for something new; can refer to a visit from a deceased loved one or friend; *See also* DEAD PERSON/DEATH, FUNERAL/FUNERAL PROCESSION, HEARSE

Castle: suggestive of royalty; feeling like a king or queen; can indicate a messenger from a different time; can represent a strong or fortified psyche; protection from adversaries or enemies; may represent a need for structure or stability; may indicate stability; *See also* DUNGEON, HOUSE

Cat: moving stealthily; as in "sex kitten," can be sexy; can indicate someone who is curious; as in "catty," gossipy or churlish; as in "cat and mouse games," can refer to someone who is malicious or cruel; as in "nine lives," may represent a need for caution; *See also* ANIMALS, LION

Catfish: bottom-feeder, not yet spiritually enlightened; always searching; *See also* FISH

Caterpillar: Indicates something that has not fully transformed; someone or something on the verge of transformation; something or someone bursting with kindness and beauty; an idea or person getting ready to transform into something great; *See also* BUG/IN-SECT, BUTTERFLY

Cave: hiding from reality; entering into a dark, scary, or unknown area; opening up to a message from the unknown; needing to delve into something; the subconscious; feeling hollow or shallow, or the situation is hollow; may refer to female sexual anatomy

CD (compact disc): music of your life; advanced messages; listen to the music; need to open your clairaudience and listen; replaying situation or needing to hear something over and over to understand; as in a computer CD-ROM, a storehouse or wealth of information; that which makes processing things easier; may refer to technology; storage of ideas; *See also* COMPUTER, RADIO

Celtic cross: *See* Chapter 7: "Religion, Spirituality, Culture, and Symbols"

Celtic knots: *See* KNOT and Chapter 7: "Religion, Spirituality, Culture, and Symbols"

Centaur: feeling like an incomplete person; needing the freedom, power, or strength of the horse; representing animal and man together, baser animal instincts; feeling the upper and lower realms; higher and lower aspects of self coming together

Chain: feeling stuck; feeling confined or restricted; chain as in necklace, choking your throat chakra; cutting off communication; feeling stuck in a belief or pattern

Chair: need to focus on the seat of your intuition; your root or base chakra, foundation, or belief system needs attention; note style of chair: throne representing ego, electric chair representing punishment, living room chair representing domestic security and relaxation, dining room or kitchen chair representing nutrition or sustenance, classroom chair may indicate going back to school or there is more that needs to be learned, steno chair representing office or office work, dentist chair representing person who is a dentist, works in a dentist office, needs to visit a dentist, or has a planned dental visit, and so on; *See also* FURNITURE, HIGHCHAIR, HOUSE

Cheerleader: receiving encouragement; cheering for you, your idea, your project; receiving appreciation or rewards or need to appreciate or reward someone else; someone is rooting for you; you have a good idea; could indicate sports

Chick: as in "don't count your chickens before they're hatched," don't count on something until it becomes reality; birth of an idea; may refer to a young girl; *See also* BIRD, CHICK, FARM, GIRL, ROOSTER

Chicken: scared; being afraid of dealing with someone or something; avoiding an issue; as in "running around like a chicken with your head cut off," going in all different directions; *See also* BIRD, CHICK, FARM, ROOSTER

Children: See BOY, GIRL, KIDS/CHILDREN, PERSON

China: can indicate travel to, or traveler from, China; may need to review or apply Eastern philosophies; can be associated with Chinese food, ancient beliefs, or wisdom; *See also* CONTINENT/COUNTRY

Christ, Jesus: See Chapter 7: "Religion, Spirituality, Culture, and Symbols"

Christmas lights: the Christmas holiday; the birth of Jesus Christ; commercialism; twinkling lights representing angels; happiness and joy; memories of Christmases past; *See also* CHRISTMAS TREE

Christmas tree: the Christmas holiday; tree representing growth; green, healing-heart chakra; traditions; fun and enjoyment; get together with family and friends; may indicate winter months; *See also* CHRISTMAS LIGHTS

Church: See Chapter 7: "Religion, Spirituality, Culture, and Symbols"

Cigarette: may represent something that is smelly or dirty; may suggest a need to get a physical; may refer to an illness or disease like cancer or emphysema; can indicate an extension of oneself; may represent an addiction to something or an addiction to something or someone that is not healthy; *See also* PIPE (SMOKING)

Circle: come full circle; wholeness; eternity, without beginning or end; completion of a cycle; container for one's inner self and spirituality; as in ring, marriage, or partnership

Circus: being the center of attention; putting on a show; being wild or clown-like in public; can represent the variety of parts necessary to create a unified integrated whole; entertainment; representing need to tap into joy of your inner child; *See also* CAROUSEL, CARNIVAL

Cliff: about to begin something in a whole new direction; do or die time; can suggest obstacle or difficult or dangerous situation; as in "leap of faith," may indicate the need to overcome or address a fear; being "on edge" or "on the edge" emotionally or physically or psychically

Closet: being shut or put away; shut out from others; hiding something or parts or yourself from others; hiding the chaos of your life behind closed doors; as in "coming out of the closet," sharing a private part of yourself, sharing with others that you are gay; *See also* HOUSE

Cloud: can indicate being filled with stored-up emotion; a dark cloud can suggest a negative situation or negative emotion hovering around or over you; a light cloud can suggest happiness or positive emotion; a hazy cloud can indicate being unable to process thoughts or emotions; as with religion, can indicate God or God's word; as in "every cloud has a silver lining," out of every bad situation something good can be found

Coat: See JACKET/COAT

Compact disc: See CD (COMPACT DISC), COMPUTER

Computer: having all the world's knowledge available to you; may represent technology or technological advances; may represent your lifeline or way to communicate; can indicate incoming messages; may refer to logic-based calculations or reasoning; *See also* CD (COMPACT DISC), KEYBOARD

Conch shell: See SHELL and Chapter 7: "Religion, Spirituality, Culture, and Symbols"

Continent/Country: can refer to a specific location; can indicate travel to a foreign land; may suggest a visit from someone overseas; can suggest someone or something that stands proud; can suggest a huge population or mass of people; may indicate moving to another continent/country; can suggest having the support of many; *See also* AFRICA, CANADA, CHINA, FRANCE, GERMANY, ITALY, JAPAN, UNITED STATES OF AMERICA

Costume: may be associated with Halloween; can represent a desire or need to disguise yourself or pretend to be something other than what you are; may represent expressing a side of yourself or what you've hidden from the world; may indicate hiding from the world; *See also* HALLOWEEN (PARTY)

Cow: fertile, nurturing, earthy feminine side; associated in India with the sacred source of life; as in "she's a real cow," referring to someone (female) in a derogatory way, as unappealing; may indicate farm, farming, or farm life; may refer to dairy or dairy allergy; may refer to someone who is docile; *See also* ANIMALS, FARM

Crab: having a hard exterior to cover a soft inside; indicates astrological sign of Cancer; representative of putting on a tough show to hide insecurities; being crabby, cranky, or possessing a bad temper; moving sideways in life instead of forward; may indicate a lateral transition; *See also* FISH, LOBSTER

Cross: See Chapter 7: "Religion, Spirituality, Culture, and Symbols"

Crow: black, synonymous with bad omen; possibly a death; evil; message of bad news; as in "eat crow," owning up to what you've done; may indicate someone who feeds on the spoils of death or destruction; as in "a murder of crows," death of an idea or actual murder; may suggest intelligence; can refer to adaptability and change; *See also* BIRD, BLACKBIRD

Crucifix: See Chapter 7: "Religion, Spirituality, Culture, and Symbols"

Crystal: need for clarity or possessing clarity; purity; cleansing; spiritual insight; everything is crystal clear; receiving clear messages; can relate to clairvoyance and clear seeing; often associated with psychic or spiritual communications; *See also* CRYSTAL BALL, JEWELS/ GEMSTONES

Crystal ball: indicating the ability to see into the future; representing fortunetelling or fortunetellers; referring to gypsy fortunetelling or clairvoyant people; keep an eye open for messages of the future; looking ahead; a need for answers or looking for answers; could refer to a "witch" or even Halloween; *See also* CRYSTAL, GYPSY

Cup: being presented with a mission or challenge; taking command or taking charge; being given the task of taking a journey; can relate to the Bible or Jesus and the Holy Grail; holding your portion or what's given to you; as in "half full or half empty," indicating optimism or pessimism; depending on type of cup can indicate position in life or disposition in life: broken old cup, champagne flute, Styrofoam cup, and so on.

Cupcake: may represent having a little; may indicate a small congratulations or little celebration; can indicate needing a little bit of sweetness; may indicate a need for portion control; *See also* CAKE, FOOD

Cymbals: may represent warning or something that needs your attention; could refer to marching or receiving your "marching orders"; depending on imagery, may represent music and harmony; *See also* DRUM(S), INSTRUMENT, MUSIC

Dead bodies: feeling lifeless; having no "life left in you"; end of unwanted or useless ideas; as in "dead weight," a need to rid yourself of something or someone in order to progress; could indicate a need to visit the cemetery; may indicate messages from the other side; something that needs to be buried or disposed of properly; may be a message to have a physical; could suggest feeling overwhelmed; *See also* DEAD PERSON/DEATH, PERSON

Dead person/Death: may indicate a visit from a deceased relative; may suggest a message or spirit communication; may represent advice from beyond the grave; may represent a warning for someone; can indicate concern for a difficult situation someone is facing; *See also* CASKET, DEAD BODIES, GHOST, PERSON

Deer: quiet, peaceful independence; as in "deer in the headlights," sometimes feeling frozen, unable to act; as in "buck and doe (dough)" can represent money; *See also* ANIMALS

Desk: possibly referring to your own work; can indicate your thoughts; look at appearance of desk symbol: if messy, as in "scatterbrained"; if organized, your thoughts are organized and well tended to; may suggest a need to get busy working; *See also* FURNITURE

Devil: representing the evil side; something evil is present; a person who is habitually mean or grumpy; associated with temptation or addiction; as in "poor devil," someone who is unlucky in life or unwell; as in "give the devil his due," recognizing both good and evil in someone; a fallen angel; going against God; something to be feared or something that is dangerous; tempted or tempting

Diamonds: may indicate wealth; can suggest a relationship or union or partnership; may be associated with marriage; may represent strength; can represent triumph over tragedy; may suggest transformation; *See also* JEWELS/GEMSTONES

Dining room: a gathering of friends and family; as in having too much or too little "on your plate," taking on too great a task or not shouldering enough of a burden; feeding your soul or mind; can indicate a need to review your nutritional needs or a need to initiate dietary changes; *See also* HOUSE

Diploma: a literal graduation; can indicate a desire or a need to go back to school; indicates higher education; learning lessons or learning life's lessons; successful accomplishments; may signify completion; *See also* SCHOOL

Dirt/Earth: a need to ground yourself or ground your energy; nature; feeling a need to cleanse yourself from feeling dirty; as in "the dirt on someone," gossiping about someone; a need to clean up something or someone

Doctor: something or someone needs healing; you need to pay attention to your body or attend to yourself physically; may indicate you are a healer; may represent someone professional, educated, trained;

may represent something's wrong; *See also* AMBULANCE, EMER-GENCY ROOM, HOSPITAL, NURSE

Dog: someone who is loyal and faithful; if seen as a growling dog, can indicate aggressiveness; as in "man's best friend," indicates a true best friend; someone who can be trusted; as in "let sleeping dogs lie," letting something go, not bringing something up again; as in "dog eat dog world," competition and aggressiveness; as in "every dog has his day," everyone has an opportunity or chance; *See also* ANIMALS

Dolphin: a spiritual messenger or message from the other side; playful but able to be serious; *See also* FISH

Door: See DOOR (BACK), DOOR (CLOSED), DOOR (LOCKED), DOOR (OPEN), DOOR (SCREEN DOOR), DOOR (TRAP DOOR), HOUSE

Door (back): need or desire to "go out the back door"; hide, retreat, escape; need to sneak away; something not entirely honest; sexually, may represent anal intercourse

Door (closed): the opportunity has expired or passed; no help is available; forward progression has stopped; no longer having a new direction; feeling blocked from someone or something; not reaching that level of attainment yet; if you are shutting door, it may be you are trying to keep safe from the outside, blocking out any future developments, or closing yourself off temporarily

Door (locked): not able to continue on your path; journey halted; not wanting to deal with your issues or situation; unable to deal with or confront obstacles; forcibly blocking out future occurrences or developments; if you are locking door, can represent closing self off from outside world

Door (open): opportunity for advancing; an open invitation from someone or to do what you are being guided to do; doorway to your soul; new opportunity is presenting itself; time to take advantage of what's being offered to you; could indicate a doorway to your past or past-life exploration; could indicate a doorway to "heaven" and the afterlife; can represent easy access; may indicate necessary direction for answers

Door *(screen door)*: not seeing things clearly; having a small obstacle in the way of forward progress; screening your options and opportunities; may represent being somewhat open to new ideas; may represent a need for clarity; sorting out what's wanted

Door *(trap door)*: falling or having pitfalls; unpleasant surprise; surprise opportunity; potential obstacle in the situation or life; may represent feeling manipulated or trapped into something

Dove: white; purity and peace; universal symbol for peace and spirituality; love as in two turtle doves, partnership; holy; *See also* BIRD and Chapter 7: "Religion, Spirituality, Culture, and Symbols"

Dragon: feeling powerful and larger than life; feeling the heat of the moment; magical or metaphysical; representative of good, conquering evil presence; something bigger than you having more power

Dragonfly: may suggest spirituality; can indicate a connection to spirit or a message from spirit; can suggest ancient wisdom; may indicate a visit from a deceased loved one or friend; may suggest the answers to your questions are there for the taking; can correspond to peace and tranquility; may suggest adaptability and transformation are necessary now; *See also* BUG/INSECT, FLY

Drum(s): may refer to a heartbeat; may suggest state of emotion; can indicate needing attention or trying to get someone's attention; can suggest a drumming circle or Native American ceremony; as in "move to the beat of your own drum," doing whatever you want or what feels right to you; as in "drum up interest," get others interested in something; *See also* CYMBALS, INSTRUMENT, MUSIC

Duck: chatty; vocal; associated with throat chakra; receiving communication from family; traveling or hanging out with a "flock" (e.g., a group or family); a follower; as in "ducking the issue," avoiding situations or problems; as in "letting the water run off a duck's back," letting go of problems; *See also* BIRD

Dungeon: subconscious part of the mind; base or root chakra needs attending; scary part of yourself; feeling jailed or trapped; baser or lower energy part of yourself; may indicate feeling less than adequate to handle something; can indicate being "put down"; *See also* BASEMENT, CASTLE

Eagle: majestic and magnificent; larger than life; soaring through life; may suggest freedom; representing clairvoyance as in eagle eye; seeing what needs to be seen; looking for the meaning or purpose to something; keeping a watchful eye; representing the United States of America; can refer to a bald person; can indicate an ability to focus on minute details; *See also* BIRD

Earrings: can represent a need or an ability to hear things clearly; may suggest messages or communication; may be associated with the fifth or communication chakra; *See also* JEWELRY

Ears: representing clairaudience; a need for you to listen; someone is trying to send you a message, and you need to listen; time to hear what you don't want to hear; open up to messages from the other side

Eel: something slippery; something or someone not to be totally trusted; liar; as in an electric eel, can indicate something or someone with jolting or overwhelming energy; *See also* FISH

Elevator: going up and down; moving constantly; life has many ups and downs; you have to deal with some pitfalls to feel the upswings as well; be sure of your footing before you step into anything; can suggest claustrophobia; travel north or south

Emeralds: may suggest healing or a healer; higher awareness or enlightenment; may indicate growth or rebirth; may represent love; *See also* JEWELS/GEMSTONES

Emergency room: you need attending to; you are hurting; you have been injured or need to be cautious so that you are not injured; it is critical you pay attention to what is happening; may indicate someone in the medical profession or a paramedic or EMT (emergency medical technician); *See also* AMBULANCE, DOCTOR, HOSPITAL, NURSE

Empire State Building: huge monumental issue; as in *King Kong*, climbing or mounting your obstacles to reach the top; huge phallic symbol representing male presence; New York, New York City; travel to New York or visitor from New York

Endless knot: *See* KNOT and Chapter 7: "Religion, Spirituality, Culture, and Symbols"

Engagement: *See* RING

Engine: that which drives you; needing to feed yourself with the right fuels; the driving force behind you; if running well, you are heading in the right direction, doing the right thing; if not able to run, you are stalled in life, needing to re-think what you are doing; if running rough, may indicate rough road ahead; can indicate a new car; a need to service your engine; may need to maintain physical self; may represent the heart; *See also* CAR/AUTOMOBILE

Envelope: as in "pushing the envelope," taking something to the extreme; receiving a message from someone; need to communicate or connect to someone; receiving long-distance communication from someone; an important message; a reminder to be sure to check your mail or pay your bills

Eraser: need to be rid of something; may indicate a need to clear something up; remove something or someone from your life; can refer to deleting or erasing a memory; may indicate a need to "wipe the slate clean" and start fresh

Eyes: associated with clairvoyance and the third eye; may refer to a need to see what you are doing, what is happening, or what you are getting into; the windows to the soul; your subconscious mind; wisdom through sight; as in "seeing is believing," belief, proof, or truth; *See also* THIRD EYE

Face: may be a literal symbol for someone you recognize; can represent either male or female; may be time to look at who you are talking to or in business with; depending on the face, can represent emotion: someone is grumpy, happy, sad, bored, angry, content, etc.; can represent subconscious needing to be heard; may symbolize spirit guides or deceased loved ones; someone bringing you a message

Factory: may be time to look at the production in your life; what are you working so hard at?; can literally represent the products or the working life in a factory; can represent the workings of the mind or the need to process something; may indicate teamwork or the need to work together to achieve a common goal; may represent menial tasks necessary for the whole to run smoothly

Fairy/faeries: may indicate a belief in magic; may refer to the four elements: air, fire, water, and earth; known as elementals or elemental energy vortexes; happy, lovable, and childlike; can indicate a message from the other side; may represent the part of you that is unpredictable; as in Tinkerbell, may be associated with children, fairytales, or even Walt Disney or Disney World; as in "he's a fairy," derogatory statement meaning "he's gay."

Falcon: fast or swift travel; hunter, searching for prey, as in bird of prey; hunting for what you want; quickly finding answers; capturing what you need to survive; majestic; *See also* BIRD

Family: can indicate a need to connect to or revisit the family or family values; can represent a visit from a family member; may indicate family is there for you, or your family or a family member needs help; may suggest a need to check up on a specific family member; may indicate a relationship or need to heal a relationship; may relate to standing by your family in times of trouble or dissension; can be associated with all the different aspects of yourself; the need to come together in unity; may imply stability or support or suggest looking to family for support; *See also* BOY, GIRL, PERSON

Famous person: may indicate a desire for fame; may suggest a specific work that the famous person is in; may suggest you or someone is acting or putting on a show; may indicate you or someone is presenting themselves falsely; may represent a need to be recognized; *See also* IDOL, PERSON

Farm: may represent the need to get back to basics or the simplicity of life; can indicate the animal nature within; may refer to geographical area or location; can suggest animal nature; *See also* CHICK, CHICKEN, COW, ROOSTER

Faucet: outpouring of spirituality; water representing intuitive messages; cleansing of your spirit and soul; a need to cleanse your subconscious; water representing emotions; if faucet is on, body, mind, and spirit are all flowing; if faucet is off, life flow or life force is stalled; if faucet is dripping, you are losing your energy or being drained psychically, physically, and emotionally; leaky or clogged may indicate health problems; can suggest being emotionally turned on or emotionally turned off; *See also* FOUNTAIN, WATER

Feather: represents a sign or a message from heaven; messages from the other side; angelic presence; common "gift" from angels; as in "birds of a feather flock together," like-minded people join together; as in "feather in the cap," just one more accomplishment; may represent what we show or outer appearance; *See also* BIRD

Feet: See FOOT/FEET, SPORT SOCKS

Fence: can indicate putting up physical or emotional boundaries; may represent an argument between you and a close friend or family member; may indicate a decision to keep people away or to separate yourself; protecting yourself from the outside; as in "on the fence," unable to make a decision; segregating yourself

Fight: may indicate a struggle within; a struggle between your conscious mind and subconscious; can represent a feeling of wrongdoing within or with others; may suggest the need to address subconscious issues; may be associated with a feeling of guilt or a guilty conscience; can represent the need to take another look at something you are getting into, or a new idea or project; can refer to the battle between good and evil, right and wrong, and fighting for what's right; depending upon where the fight is, can indicate problems in relationships in those areas—for instance, workplace, home, bedroom, kitchen, bathroom, etc.

Files/File drawer: may represent storage of information or ideas; may be associated with memory or memories of events and circumstances; can represent the need to organize; may indicate need to research or look something up; as in "keep it in your file for later," may indicate the need to remember a detail or details; can be associated with the Akashic records; depending on location of files/ filing cabinet, can indicate where to lo look for information; *See also* AKASHIC RECORDS

Finger(s): an extension of oneself; reaching for something; depending upon the finger: pointer or index finger may indicate someone "pointing the finger" or placing the blame on you or someone else, or be careful not to point the finger at someone else; middle finger can represent "screw you" or to heck with you; ring finger may refer to an upcoming or recent marriage, divorce, loss of spouse, or the desire to be married; the pinky can indicate the upper class or someone who is snobby or snooty; the thumb may indicate thumbs up, good, or thumbs down, bad; thumb may also suggest needing help or needing a ride; as in "green thumb," may suggest gardening or a gardener; as in "having it at your fingertips," having it available; *See also* HAND

Finish line/Checkered flag: reaching the end; the completion of a project; a job well done; winning the race; a successful end to something; may indicate a competition within oneself or with others

Fire: may represent hell; may symbolize a burning desire or a burning need; may be associated with anger or rage; can indicate something that is all-consuming, destructive; making room for rebirth, clearing out; as in "she's on fire," she's great; as in "she's hot," she's very good-looking; as in "playing with fire," taking a great risk or risking something without reason; as in "setting the world on fire," implies great success; as in "under fire," being scrutinized or blamed or yelled at; as in "fire away," go ahead and ask questions; may indicate a hot or important topic; *See also* FIREPLACE, HELL, SMOKE, STOVE

Fireplace: may represent the warmth or stability of hearth and home; can indicate hunger or eating or consuming something; a need to feed yourself spiritually; may represent passion or desire; depending on mantel décor, may suggest a specific holiday or time of year; may suggest a fire within; *See also* FIRE

Fireworks: may indicate explosive energy; can represent an explosive argument; can be a celebration of a job well done or the completion of a project; can indicate a positive outcome; may represent holidays or the Fourth of July; may represent happiness or joy

Fish: as with Christianity, represents belief in Jesus or a symbol for Christ; as in "teach a man to fish," may indicate need to learn to change life; as in "something's fishy," indicates something is not quite right or not quite honest or truthful; as in "fishing for something," indicates someone looking for answers or sneakily trying to get answers; as in "cold fish," may indicate frigidity or standoffishness; *See also* ANGELFISH, BLUEFISH, CATFISH, DOLPHIN, EEL, GOLDFISH, SHARK, TROUT, WHALE

Flag: may be indicative of a belief in something; may indicate the follower of something; may represent a specific country or origin; can represent international travel or international affairs; may be indicative of one's identity; represents what one stands for; depending on the flag color: black, death or sadness; white, surrender or peace; yellow, caution or quarantine; red, stop or danger; green, go or go for it; checkered, the finish line or end of something; as in "flagging someone down," getting someone's attention; *See also* FLAGPOLE, VICTORY BANNER

Flagpole: may indicate waving a banner for, or standing up for, something you believe in; can represent an idea; may represent a belief system; depending upon where the flag is: all the way down, something is not fulfilled or an idea has not yet taken off; half mast, literal death or the death of an idea; all the way up, the birth of an idea; *See also* FLAG, VICTORY BANNER

Flashlight: shining a light on something; calling attention to something; the need to spotlight something; a bright idea; looking for something; lighting the way; signifies a direction or a path that you are taking

Flowers: may represent nature; may be a gift, physically or metaphysically; spiritual good wishes from the other side; may indicate a gift or talent in oneself blossoming; may signify sexuality; growth of gifts; *See also* FLOWERS (MIXED), IRIS, LILY, ROSE, VASE, WILD-FLOWERS

Flowers (mixed): representing the chakras; can suggest happiness; may indicate diversity; *See also* FLOWERS

Fly (insect): something that is annoying; may represent a nagging feeling or something that is nagging you; as in "fly in the ointment," there is something that is causing a problem; *See also* BUG/INSECT, DRAGONFLY, MOSQUITO

Flying: may represent freedom; can represent the need to get away or to fly away; may represent someone who is ungrounded; can indicate astral travel or the ability to leave one's body and travel purely as spirit; may represent unfettered freedom or joy; may indicate spirituality; may represent rising above an issue; can symbolize upcoming travel plans; as in "fly off the handle," can indicate a loss of control; can suggest happiness or success; *See also* AIRPLANE, FLYING SAUCER/UFO, JET

Flying saucer/UFO: may indicate something that is foreign to you; flying high; an unconscious or subconscious fear of the unknown; may represent aliens; may represent the feeling of not fitting in; *See also* ALIEN, FLYING

Fog: may indicate the inability to see through the fog; something is not quite clear; something is foggy or blocked out; may indicate the inability to separate issues or see circumstances clearly; the presence of a messenger from the other side; may indicate cloudy or confused state of mind

Food: may represent your relationship with food; depending upon different foods, may mean different dietary issues or different chakra associations; may relate to indulging or overindulging; may represent a need for control or being out of control, as with anorexia or bulimia; may be phallic or sexual, depending on the type of food; may represent different seasons or holidays—e.g., pumpkins: fall or Halloween; turkey or cranberries: fall or Thanksgiving; plum pudding or Christmas cookies: Christmas or winter; fresh peaches or vegetables: spring/summer; or watermelon: summer; as in "in a jam," getting stuck in a bad spot; as in "only crumbs," receiving only a little; as in "buttering up," falsely praised; as in "a piece of cake," easy; as in "he's a ham," he's silly or seeking attention; as in "bread of life," basis of all life; as in "food for thought," someone's ideas or thoughts about something; as in "tall drink of water," someone attractive; *See also* APPLE, BANANA, BIRTHDAY CAKE, CAKE, CUPCAKE, FRUIT, GOURD, GRAIN, GRAPES, JELL-O, TEA/TEA BAG

Foot/Feet: time to step into action; groundedness or a need to be grounded; direction in life; as in "putting your foot down," standing your ground; as in "swept off one's feet," to be overwhelmed with emotion; as in "best foot forward," giving it all you've got; as in "one foot in the grave," on your way to dying; as in "put your foot in your mouth," saying the wrong thing; *See also* TOES

Football: may indicate a game or the game of life; may point to the actual sport of football; note what's happening in the game: ball dropped or fumbled may point to missed opportunity, touchdown may suggest reaching an important goal or triumphing over adversity; may suggest passing responsibility or problems to someone else; *See also* ATHLETE, SPORT SOCKS

Forehead: indicative of thought or brain power; suggesting intelligence; a thought or idea in one's mind; can relate to the third eye or sixth chakra; clairvoyance; *See also* HEAD

Forest: as in "can't see the forest for the trees," paying too much attention to little details and missing the big or greater picture; representing nature; may refer to old ideas, old growth or new ideas, new growth; can suggest the north; feeling like part of a group as opposed to feeling alone; healing energy; *See also* TREE

Fork: may represent mealtime; may refer to the devil's pitchfork; can indicate eating, or a need to review diet and nutrition; may suggest the need to separate into smaller bites or portions; as in "fork it over," give it up or give it to someone; *See also* FORK IN THE ROAD

Fork in the road: a decision needs to be made; the need to mull over the situation and make a choice; may represent the difficulty of reaching a decision; can represent going in a good or bad direction; may suggest two situations, ideas, or opportunities; *See also* FORK, ROAD/STREET

Fort Knox: represents the wealth or financial condition of the United States; represents money/gold; may suggest something that is safe, secure, or locked up; may indicate a need to review finances or investments; may represent someone who is closed up or closed off materially or emotionally; a storehouse for your materials

Fossil: associated with old or ancient times, objects, beings, or animals; can represent the need to review past experiences or pull information from the past or past memories; representative of someone or something that is antique; may refer to prehistoric or dinosaur times; relic from the past

Fountain: burst of emotion; overwhelming emotions; excitement; as in the "fountain of youth," can suggest vitality and liveliness; fountain as a source of all knowledge, spirituality; may suggest a message from the other side; *See also* FAUCET, WATER

Four-leaf clover: may represent luck or good fortune; green suggesting heart chakra; may represent St. Patrick's Day

France: may represent visit to or a visitor from France; suggests "French things" or images that come to one's own mind when thinking of France, such as the Eiffel Tower; *See also* CONTINENT/COUNTRY

Frog: as in "hop to it," get it going or get started; as in "frog in the throat," suggests difficulty with communication or talking; ability to leap over obstacles; as in Cinderella, can represent enchantment or magic; may represent the need to cleanse or clean; *See also* ANIMALS

Fruit: as in the "fruit of your labor," represents the accomplishment for your hard work; depending upon particular fruit, can indicate need for specific vitamins in diet; may suggest different chakras based on color of fruit; *See also* APPLE, BANANA, FOOD, GRAPES

Funeral/Funeral procession: may suggest a literal death; often suggests transition or change; as with the "Death card" in tarot, may indicate the end of something so another thing can begin; to bury or get rid of something that's no longer useful; may represent physical, mental, or emotional loss; *See also* CASKET, DEAD PERSON/DEATH, HEARSE

Furnace: *See* HOUSE

Furniture: can suggest personality of a person; may refer to a person's state of mind; can indicate one's ideas, thoughts, or opinions; can suggest decisions or personal preference; may suggest a variety of traits based on type of furniture and state of furniture; can refer to an era or period of time; *See also* CHAIR, DESK, MATTRESS, TABLE

Fuse: as in "blow a fuse," getting very upset; a power conduit; may represent an explosion of energy; may suggest being under pressure

Game (board game): may suggest someone is "playing games" with you or not being entirely honest with you; may indicate a need to tap into your inner child; can represent your current life experiences; may suggest friendly competition or the thrill of the game; may indicate a game plan or path or route to follow; may refer to current group activities or work or home life; *See also* GAME (ELECTRONIC)

Game (electronic): may also represent proficiency with computers or technology; may indicate a programmer or electrician or someone with electronic skills; may represent focus and determination, or alternatively, frustration; may indicate technical training; *See also* GAME (BOARD GAME)

Gandhi, Mahatma: symbolic of peace and cooperation; nonviolence and passive resistance; may indicate someone who has given up all worldly possessions in pursuit of a greater peace for the world; physically may represent someone who is bald or someone who is prayerful; may refer to India or someone from or going to India; may represent a need for meditation

Ganesh: Hindu god of wisdom, success, and learning; symbolized by elephant head on body of man; may suggest Hinduism; may represent a need for meditation

Gang: may indicate danger; may suggest someone who is part of a group; may represent fighting or war; may represent an extremely dysfunctional family; may indicate a group of people against you; *See also* GANGSTER, PERSON

Gangster: may represent crooked or untrustworthy parts of yourself or someone else; may indicate deception or evil deeds; *See also* GANG, PERSON

Garbage/Garbage can: may suggest a need to get rid of or throw out things no longer necessary in your life; may represent something or someone that has no value to you or is worthless; may indicate that something you've lost has been discarded or thrown away accidentally; may indicate a need to cleanse or purge yourself physically, emotionally, mentally, or spiritually

Garden (flowers): may indicate growth, spirituality; as in "reap what you sow," you get what you deserve; depending on what is growing in the garden, which flowers/colors, etc., can suggest various chakras need attending to; may represent hard work to achieve accomplishments; can indicate a need to plant your seeds wisely or planning ahead; *See also* FLOWERS, TREE, VASE, WILDFLOWERS

Garden (vegetable): may suggest the need for vegetables or vitamins; depending upon what is happening, can suggest different areas in your life that need attention: e.g., watering can indicate areas in your life that need nurturing, weeding can indicate the need to weed people or situations from your life; may indicate dietary changes are necessary; *See also* FOOD, GARDEN (FLOWERS)

Gate: an entry to a new idea or situation; alternatively, an exit or an escape route from something that no longer works in your life or that is not positive or productive; may represent a doorway to new information or knowledge; may suggest a way to avoid obstacles in your life

Gemini (born May 21–June 20): the sign of the twin and the third sign in the zodiac, ruled by the third house of communication; can see and act out both sides of everything, the yin and the yang; generally love to talk and share information; usually bright, quick-witted, and imaginative; can be the life of the party; curious and interested in a lot, it's hard to follow through with anything; sometimes finds it difficult to take a stand; *See also* ZODIAC/ASTROLOGICAL SIGN

Gemstones: *See* JEWELS/GEMSTONES

Genie: representing wish fulfillment; as in "genie in a bottle," finding a magical object and being granted three wishes; as in "be careful what you wish for because you just might get it," be sure what you have in mind is what you actually wish for or desire to manifest; may represent magic or magic within oneself; may represent the boundless abilities to manifest whatever is wanted in life; may indicate help from the other side, spirit guides, or your inner self

Germany: may indicate journey to or a visitor from Germany; can suggest any images that come to mind when thinking of Germany; may represent various German foods, such as sauerkraut or schnitzel; based on particular feeling or symbol of Germany, can indicate the Holocaust, Adolf Hitler, or the horrific Nazi era in German history; *See also* CONTINENT/COUNTRY

Ghost: may represent communication from the other side or spirit communication; can indicate the presence of spirit or the presence of someone who has passed on; can be associated with your own shadows, fears, or thoughts of the past; you may have to look through what is there in order to understand what's really in front of you; can refer to unfinished business; may indicate Halloween; *See also* DEAD PERSON/DEATH, HEARSE, PERSON

Giant: may represent something or someone that is very prevalent in your life or that stands out or above other things; something that is larger than life; something or someone that you have to deal with; being overwhelmed by an issue or person in your life; depending on person, may suggest a huge ego; can suggest a big event coming up or being spotlighted

Gift: may indicate an actual gift coming your way or a present; may be a suggestion to look inside at your own gifts or talents; can represent a gift from the other side; may suggest the need to give a gift or compliment to someone else; may represent the need to develop any gifts you have; may represent a celebration or achievement

Giraffe: may represent something that is a long distance away; may represent the throat, the will, or the throat chakra, communication; may suggest a distance or disconnect from emotions to thought; can represent something that is out of reach or just out of reach; may suggest the need to nurture your throat and your voice; may represent someone who works with their communication chakra; *See also* ANIMALS

Girl: may indicate a child; may represent new ideas or new birth, literal or spiritual; associated with femininity; may represent an actual person; pay attention to how the girl is dressed, what she is doing, etc.; *See also* CHICK, KIDS/CHILDREN, PERSON

Gladiator: suggests powerful, strong emotions; may suggest an inner battle or conflict; may represent someone or something that you are or have been battling against; can relate to a current struggle or conflict around you; *See also* PERSON

Glass: depending upon condition of glass, seeing something clearly or a clear representation of a situation or idea; alternatively, having a skewed vision when glass is dirty or distorted; feeling either trapped or protected from reality or a situation that is present in your life; colored glass can represent spirituality; as in seeing things through rose-colored glasses, may suggest seeing things as better than they are; if drinking glass, note whether glass is full or empty or half-full or half-empty; pay attention to type of glass, such as water, wine goblet, champagne flute, etc.; *See also* MUG

Glasses: how you see the world and what's around you; take a look at your situation: what do you see?; may indicate a need to use your clairvoyance; as in "looking at the world with rose-colored glasses," mistakenly thinking everything is just fine

Gloves: the need to cover up; suggesting winter weather or cold; the need to hide something; hand something over; handiwork; something you can put your hands into or hands on; as in "handle with kid gloves," be very careful; *See also* HAND

Glue: that which holds something together; a project or idea gelling or coming together; may indicate a sticky situation; depending upon feeling, may suggest someone who is stuck in something or somewhere or unable to move forward

Goat: as in "stubborn as a goat," unwavering stubbornness; associated with astrological sign Capricorn; as in "gets my goat," irritating; if bloody goat's head, may be associated with devil worship; *See also* ANIMALS

God: divine intervention or divine guidance; depending upon religious beliefs, can indicate need to worship or pray; may refer to importance of idea or situation; can suggest the supreme, omnipotent being is present; may suggest situation is "heavenly"; can indicate the beginning of time, the creation of all that is; may suggest a time to ask God for help; *See also* Chapter 7: "Religion, Spirituality, Culture, and Symbols"

Golden fishes: *See* FISH and Chapter 7: "Religion, Spirituality, Culture, and Symbols"

Golden Gate Bridge: may refer to California, specifically San Francisco; may suggest connecting two ideas or two people or two structures; can indicate a bridging of feelings; may refer to a bridge or path to the other side; can suggest a bridge to the past or past lives; as in "bridging the distance," may indicate a coming together of friends or ideas; may refer to a channel of information from the other side; *See also* BRIDGE

Goldfish: as with gold, can indicate spiritual enlightenment; wisdom; small details are significant; *See also* FISH

Gonads: a male or a male presence; may refer to someone who is arrogant or conceited; may represent a feeling of inadequacy or lack of confidence; may represent sex or sexuality; may indicate fertility or pregnancy; desire to procreate; alternatively, may refer to a lack of sex drive; *See also* BOY, PHALLUS

Goose: indicating someone who is loud; someone who is "silly as a goose"; being in touch or needing to be in touch with your silly side; as in "your goose is cooked," could represent you've been busted or caught in some way; trouble is waiting for you; someone is getting ready to yell at or reprimand you; as in "golden goose," representing a windfall of money; as in "goose egg," a big zero; *See also* BIRD

Gopher: may indicate presence of the actual animal; may refer to someone who is industrious or who works with the earth, such as a farmer; can indicate a tunnel structure or infrastructure; may suggest a need to dig deeper into the situation; may indicate shows or movies with specific cartoon gophers, e.g., from *Loony Tunes* or many of the *Winnie the Pooh* features or *Caddyshack*; may suggest something that is pesky or annoying or something or someone that you know is present but that keeps hiding from sight; also, as in "Gopher protocol," may suggest computer technology software or may refer to computers; *See also* ANIMALS

Gorilla: may suggest actual animal; can indicate presence of large energy or force; may indicate strength in situation or matter; may suggest intelligence where it's not expected; may refer to someone who is vegetarian, as gorillas are predominately herbivorous; can refer to someone who is mute or communicates through sign language; *See also* GORILLA

Gourd: can refer to time of year, i.e.: fall, Thanksgiving, or Halloween; may refer to Native Americans or an Indian spirit guide; may refer to something that can be recycled or reused; may suggest the transformation from one thing to another; may suggest either climbing toward something or trailing behind in some way; *See also* FOOD

Graduation gown/cap: may suggest celebration; the actual graduation from a school or school of higher education; may refer to graduating to another level of understanding spiritually; can indicate a need or desire to return to school or resume your studies or begin learning something new; a desire to increase your knowledge; may represent a professor or teacher; may refer to a commencement or beginning of something new; alternatively may suggest the completion of something; *See also* DIPLOMA, SCHOOL

Grain: may refer to nutrition or nutritional value; can indicate the beginning of something; as in "grain of sand," may represent something that is one small but integral part of a larger group; may represent crops or farming or wheat; may suggest allergy to wheat; may suggest a complex system or life that appears very simple; may represent a need to look beyond what you can see openly; *See also* FOOD

Grapes: may indicate the need to eat grapes; possibly a need for vitamins A and C; may refer to the color purple (crown) or green (heart) in the chakra system; may refer to wine or vineyards; can indicate a bunch or clusters of something or clusters of people; may suggest a pack-type mentality or group of people; may refer to a wine cellar; *See also* FOOD, FRUIT

Grass: may suggest growth or regrowth or rebirth; may indicate freshness; may indicate every blade of grass is individual yet necessary to the whole; may suggest the need to ground yourself in nature; can refer to the green (heart) chakra; as with lawn, may indicate area of pride or neglect depending on type of lawn, representing pride or neglect of oneself or emotions; as in "grassroots," can suggest rock and roll music; also as in "grassroots," can suggest getting back to fundamentals in politics, or a local/community-based political movement; may refer to marijuana or someone who uses marijuana

Grave: something is buried; something is dead to you or lifeless or unmoving; may indicate a communication from beyond; can represent actual death or losing someone; represents the past or leaving something in the past; as in "grave importance," can indicate something of great urgency; as in "one foot in the grave," can suggest someone close to or nearing death

Greenhouse: may represent growth or rebirth; may indicate new ideas or the cultivation of new ideas; may represent spiritual growth or the nurturing of spirit; can indicate a healthy house or community

Guitar: may suggest music; can be associated with clairaudience or clear hearing; may indicate a need to listen to the music or face the music; can indicate a musician or the need to practice; *See also* IN-STRUMENT, MUSIC

Gun: as in "under the gun," can represent being rushed or forced into hurrying; may represent anger or violence; phallic symbol; may suggest aggression; can indicate war or warring parties; may be associated with fear or danger; can indicate a personal attack

Gym: may suggest exercise or physical fitness; can suggest sports or group activities; may indicate school activities or sports; may represent socialization

Gypsy: related to fortunetelling, mystics, or magic; travelers, either passing through or leaving; may suggest a desire or need to travel or move often; can indicate nomads or nomadic existence; may suggest heritage; *See also* CRYSTAL BALL

Hair: may represent intellect or ideas; may be associated with the crown chakra on top of the head; may be associated with ego or sense of self; may represent how one feels or presents themselves or how one is seen by others; as in the Bible's Samson, represents great strength or vitality or the source of great strength; as in "got by the short hairs," having under tight control; as in "splitting hairs," minor argument or disagreement; as in "hair of the dog," drinking the same alcohol to make you feel better that caused you to be intoxicated the day before; as in "hair-raising experience," being in a scary situation; type of hair or state of hair: straight, long, neat can suggest everything is in order or controlled; full, long, and wavy may represent someone who has many tasks going on at once; too much hair can suggest someone or something is out of control or may indicate increased sexuality; knotted hair may represent chaos or confusion; no hair or bald may represent feeling naked or exposed; coloring or cutting can indicate the need for or the act of changing one's mind or making a decision; blow-drying may suggest a need to blow out clutter or confusion or something that is blowing your mind; straightening may suggest a need to control or tame; *See also* HEAD

Halloween (party): feeling like nothing is as it seems; everyone is hiding behind something else; pay attention to type of costume: ghost, witch, devil, angel, cat, dog, etc.; *See also* COSTUME, JACK-O'-LANTERN

Halo: *See* Chapter 7: "Religion, Spirituality, Culture, and Symbols"

Hammer: pounding away at something, or something that pounds or irritates; striking a blow; building or creating either literally or mentally, such as an idea; may represent male aggression; phallic symbol; as in "bring the hammer down," it's time to do your task now or else you'll be in trouble

Hand: relating to one's identity or sense of self; may indicate type of job, as in someone working with their hands; may suggest service for others; depending on position of hands, may represent: yoga (mudra hand positions), begging or asking for or needing help (holding hands open and out), "screw you" (middle finger upright), deafness or sign language (hands in classic signing formation), partnership or agreement (handshake); as in "biting the hand that feeds you," turning on the one who helps you; as in "giving a hand up," helping someone on their path to accomplishing something; as in "handout," receiving a donation or desiring something for nothing; as in "forcing his hand," pushing someone to the point of making their move or making a decision; as in "eating out of someone's hand," someone having total power or control over another person or being obedient to someone; as in "getting out of hand," something getting out of control; as in "laying on of hands," using universal or God energy to heal; as in "living hand to mouth," living paycheck to paycheck; as in "handing over," giving the responsibility or project or task to someone else; as in "lay your hands on," getting control of or finding something; as in "hands down," without contest or without dispute; as in "too many hands in the pot," too many people in charge or involved; *See also* FINGER(S), PERSON

Handkerchief: may represent getting rid of something; clearing out your system, specifically sinuses; reminiscent of things from the past; may indicate sadness as with crying; may represent emotion or an emotional experience or situation; might indicate allergies

Handwriting: may represent communication from the other side; can suggest communication such as a letter or note; depending upon handwriting, may represent foreign language; can represent expressing oneself or sense of identity; as in "the writing on the wall," recognizing something that is inevitably coming

Harbor: water representing spirituality or emotions; as in "ship has come in," something good has happened; may suggest arrival of important information or relevant idea or insight; can suggest safety, comfort, security, or a safe haven; *See also* BOAT, WATER

Hat: may represent protection from outside influences; may suggest an idea or opinion about something; can represent what's currently on your mind or what you are thinking about; as in "hat's off to you," acknowledging someone's achievement; as in "wearing many hats," having many different jobs or responsibilities; as in "throwing your hat in the ring," participating in the activity; depending upon type of hat, may represent different type of job, sport, or activity; *See also* HEAD, HELMET

Hawk: dedicated; perseverance; a need for reconnaissance; fast, keen senses; swift and rapid over long distances; feminine energy/presence/message; message from mother; deliberate actions; *See also* BIRD

Hay: represents farming, farm land, horses; as in "needle in a haystack," looking for something extremely difficult to find; as in "time to hit the hay," it's time to go to sleep; may represent fiber or a need for dietary fiber

Head: may represent an idea, thought, or state of mind; may refer to intelligence or intellect; associated with the sixth chakra; associated with the seventh chakra or crown chakra; may represent the need to open your chakras to receive messages; as in "get out of your head," stop thinking about something so much; as in "headstrong," being stubborn or strong-willed; as in "in over your head," in a situation that's out of control or out of your hands; as in "heads up," a warning to pay attention; as in "heads or tails," flipping a coin for a decision; as in "head and shoulders above the rest," much better than any other choice; as in "coming to a head," the situation is coming to a close or the situation is getting ready to explode; as in "went to her head," it made her egotistical; as in "she's out of her head," she's crazy; as in "head over heels," being out of control toward or for something or someone; as in "it's all in your head," you're making it up; *See also* FOREHEAD, HAT, HELMET, PERSON

Headless person: may be associated with losing your head over a situation or someone else losing their head; may indicate having not concrete thoughts or ideas; may suggest you or someone not thinking straight; may refer to Halloween or the Headless Horseman

Headlights: may refer to an actual car or motorcycle; lighting your way; as in "seeing the light," coming to understand a situation; illuminating your path or journey through life; may refer to shining a light or spotlight on a situation or direction; may suggest helping you to see your way through a situation

Hearse: may represent an actual death or funeral; can suggest a journey to the afterlife; may represent the path to a literal death; can be a warning to take care of yourself, your health, and physical well-being; may represent the "death" of a car; *See also* CASKET, DEAD PERSON/DEATH, FUNERAL/FUNERAL PROCESSION, GHOST

Heart: may represent someone's emotions; may suggest love, feelings, emotions; can refer to a relationship; associated with fourth chakra or heart chakra; may suggest energetic healing is needed; as in "broken heart," may represent extreme sadness over a broken relationship; as in "the heart of the matter," what's really important in the situation; as in "wearing his heart on his sleeve," means letting everyone see how he feels; as in "a person after my own heart," someone wanting the same thing you want; as in "doesn't have the heart for it," has no desire to pursue or stay engaged in something; as in "to lose heart," to give up; a heart with three swords through it may represent being unfaithful, as with the Three of Swords in tarot; *See also* Chapter 8: "Tarot Symbols"

Heater: may represent a situation that is heating up; as in "a heated argument," may suggest aggravation or frustration; alternatively, can suggest warmth from someone or something; as in "turning on the heat," may represent making something more intense or harder; as in "he's hot," may indicate he's really good looking; as in "a really hot relationship," may suggest a very passionate, sexual couple

Heaven: may represent the presence of, or messages from, angels; can suggest communication from the afterlife; may represent spirituality; can refer to messages from the higher self; represents harmony, perfection, love, joy, happiness; heaven is known as "the House of God"; great or supreme place of afterlife; idyllic, tranquil resting place; as in "that's heaven" or a "slice of heaven" or a "little piece of heaven," means perfection or having your own piece of bliss; may suggest a visit from someone who is deceased

Hedge: having a protective barrier; feeling either fenced in or feeling a need or desire to keep others out; as in "hedging a bet," placing wagers in a way to minimize loss; may refer to what you show others or more importantly what you keep hidden from others; as in "hedge fund," investments; may represent hinting or not wanting to reveal whole truth

Heel: needing to grind something out; putting something in the past; as in "he's a heel," he's a jerk or a coldhearted person; as in "falling head over heels in love," uncontrollable feelings of love; as in "hot on your heels," to be right behind someone; *See also* FOOT/FEET

Helicopter: *See* AIRPLANE, FLYING, JET

Hell: a period of stress or a stressful time; a state of extreme suffering or misery; something evil is present; feeling guilty about something; away from God; as in "this is hell," this is very difficult; as in "come hell or high water," forging forward regardless of difficulties; as in "hell to pay," there will be serious trouble for the actions; as in "hell in a handbasket," everything is falling apart or plans are deteriorating; as in "give him hell," give him a hard time; as in "for the hell of it," do something just to do it; *See also* FIRE

Helmet: protection from external sources; protecting your thoughts or ideas from damage; may suggest being hardheaded or stubborn; can refer to sports such as football, cycling, lacrosse, baseball, etc.; depending on type of helmet, may imply soldiers or war or motorcycle rider; *See also* HAT, HEAD

Hematite: may suggest grounding or a need to ground your energy; may relate to foundation or stability; may prevent negative energy; *See also* JEWELS/GEMSTONES

Hen: as in "cackle like a hen," constant talking or laughing; as in "old hen," an older woman; may also indicate the pecking order of something or someone; someone who is being annoying or nagging; *See also* BIRD

Highchair: may represent childhood or childish ways; may refer to inner child; may represent miniature or small-minded thoughts or ideas; may indicate childish eating habits; *See also* CHAIR, FURNITURE

Hill: reaching a higher level of spirituality or a higher level of spiritual understanding; may represent an obstacle or hurdle in life; may suggest something better on the other side of the hill; may represent a need to look at life or a situation from a different perspective; may suggest a need to pay attention to how you accomplish something; as in "it's not worth a hill of beans," it's not worth anything or it's not important; as in "over the hill," being past your prime in age or past your best years; *See also* MOUNTAIN

Hobo/Bum: may represent feeling inadequate or worthless; may suggest feeling left out in the cold; may suggest homelessness or someone who wanders from place to place; may indicate someone losing their way or falling off their path through life; may represent someone who needs help; *See also* PERSON

Horse: may represent power or strength; can suggest freedom; may suggest a message or communication; type of message may be determined by type of horse: wild horse, instinctual message or one that is out of control or needs to be contained; winged horse, spiritual message or message from beyond; racehorse, message of great urgency or one that needs a quick response; the color of horse may also be relevant: black horse may suggest negative or sad message; white horse may suggest spiritual or angelic message; a spotted or painted horse may suggest an exciting or creative message; a tan or brown horse may suggest a message from someone who has crossed over or may suggest a message that is from someone who has walked the earth or even from your higher self; as in "horse of a different color," someone who is different; as in "putting the horse before the cart," doing something out of order; as in "she's on her high horse," she's being egotistical or conceited; as in "horsing around," fooling around; as in "don't look a gift horse in the mouth," don't question the value of your good fortune, and be grateful for what's given to you; *See also* ANIMALS, HORSE AND BUGGY

Horse and buggy: may represent a time of relaxation; something from the past; may indicate the "olden days"; can suggest specific place that has horse and buggy rides, such as New York City; may refer to Amish people, culture, or area; *See also* ANIMALS, HORSE

Hose: associated with water or emotions; may suggest control of emotions; can indicate area in a car or a person that needs attention; may refer to male sexuality or phallic symbol; *See also* CAR/AUTO-MOBILE, PERSON, PHALLUS, WATER

Hospital: may represent an illness or accident; may represent a place of healing; can indicate something needs attending to or needs healing; may represent someone who works as a healer: e.g., a nurse or doctor; *See also* AMBULANCE, DOCTOR, EMERGENCY ROOM, NURSE

House: may refer to how we show ourselves to the world; can represent the physical body; may indicate attention is needed in an area of the body; depending on the area of the house, may represent messages: *front of house*: what we show the world; *front porch*: watching the world, being in two parts of awareness or two states of emotion; *back of house*: what we put behind or what we keep private; *living room*: normal or comfortable or usual living space; *bedroom*:

relating to relationships, sexuality; *attic*: what we think about or higher consciousness; *basement*: what we store away, storehouse of knowledge, lower or base desires, sexuality; *bathroom*: what we rid ourselves of or dispose of, cleansing the physical self or spiritual self, clearing out; *kitchen*: nutrition or diet needs to be looked at, or things may be heating up, or focus on nurturing physical, spiritual self; *dining room*: nutrition or diet needs to be looked at, where we show our public self; *family room*: relaxation, defenses are down or at rest; *windows*: portal to the soul; *plumbing*: elimination, or getting rid of things we no longer need or a flow of emotions; *furnace*: representing heated emotions, anger, rage; *boiler*: situation is boiling over, heated situation; *yard*: how we present ourselves to the world; *roof*: higher self or higher awareness or connection to spirit; *See also* ATTIC, BASEMENT, BATHROOM, BEDROOM, CASTLE, CLOSET, DINING ROOM, DOOR, FURNACE, LIVING ROOM, PIPE (PLUMBING), PORCH, ROOF, STAIRS, STOVE

Ice: may refer to something or someone that is frozen; can suggest emotional detachment or frigidity or frozen solid emotionally; may indicate sexual frigidity; melting ice may mean letting go of past emotional attachments or the old ways are no longer available or useful; as in "break the ice," start a conversation to get to know someone; as in "ice cold" or "cold as ice," unemotional; as in "on thin ice," in a dangerous spot or one more mistake or wrong step and it's all over; *See also* WATER

Idol: worshipping something or someone; putting someone on a pedestal; may indicate false adulation or hero worship; may suggest famous singer(s) from television show *American Idol*; *See also* FAMOUS PERSON, PERSON

Indian (Native American): may represent various Indian tribes or Native Americans in general; often represents communication from a spirit guide; may suggest living off the land or living harmoniously in nature; may represent a spiritual journey or natural spirituality; as in "Indian giver," giving something and then taking it back; as in "Indian summer," warm weather in the fall or winter; *See also* ARROW

Infant: See BABY, BOY, GIRL, PERSON

Insect: See BUG/INSECT

Instrument: may represent music; may refer to particular instrument or melody; can suggest the need for music in your life; as in "instrument for change," may represent a catalyst or a suggestion to change something or someone in your life; may suggest heavenly or spiritually tuning in; *See also* CYMBALS, DRUM(S), GUITAR, KEYBOARD, MUSIC

Iris: may represent spirituality; extension of one's spirit or soul; birth of psychic awareness; *See also* FLOWERS

Iron: to smooth away any problems; to flatten out any issues; there may be pressing issues; may suggest strength, stubbornness, or inflexibility; as in "iron out problems," work out any issues that may be present; may represent straightening out oneself; may suggest improving your appearance

Island: surrounding yourself with emotion; may indicate isolating yourself and your emotions from everyone and everything else; may suggest an isolated thought or idea; may refer to a vacation or vacation spot; *See also* CONTINENT/COUNTRY

Italy: can suggest travel to or from Italy or a visitor from Italy; may refer to typical Italian food; may indicate a person of Italian descent; as with all foreign countries, may represent the unknown; may represent what people think of when imagining Italy: e.g., Venice, the Leaning Tower of Pisa, Rome, the Vatican, the Pope; *See also* CONTINENT/COUNTRY

Ivory: may refer to something that is hard and smooth; may indicate something or someone precious; may indicate something that is not quite clear; as in "ivory tower," may suggest aloofness; *See also* Chapter 5: "Color Symbolism"

Jacket/coat: represents that which protects you; suggests insulation from the outside; may suggest how you show yourself to the outside world

Jack-o'-lantern: represents Halloween; can indicate mystery or even the occult; depending on "face" of the jack-o'-lantern, may represent various emotions; *See also* HALLOWEEN (PARTY), PUMPKIN

Jade: may represent healing energy; can indicate China; can suggest life energy, power, and protection; representing love and serenity; *See also* JEWELS/GEMSTONES

Jail/Prison: represents being confined, imprisoned, penalized, or punished; may suggest feeling trapped or unable to do what you want; loss of freedom or having another's will imposed upon you; could suggest a warning you are in the wrong

Japan: can suggest travel to or from Japan or a visitor from Japan; may refer to typical Japanese food; may indicate a person of Japanese or Asian descent; as with all foreign countries, may represent the unknown; depending on image, may represent specific group of Japanese entertainers known as Geisha girls; may represent what people think of when imagining Japan; *See also* CONTINENT/COUNTRY

Jaw: having to do with communications; communicating needs or desires; depending upon set of jaw in image, may suggest different emotions: stiff jaw: anger or stubbornness; wide-open jaw: awe or surprise or even disbelief; may represent a need to talk to someone; may also symbolize pondering an idea internally; *See also* FACE

Jeans: may suggest relaxation; typically representative of a casual feeling or gathering or relaxed time; depending upon image, may indicate type of profession: e.g., carpenter, cowboy, mechanic, etc.; may suggest something or someone durable

Jell-O: may represent something or someone that is unstable or easily moved; can suggest a shaky foundation or idea; something that has not yet solidified or gelled; may indicate an idea or thought that has not yet been completed; may represent adding gelatin to the diet to increase collagen proteins to help the skin become firm and smooth; *See also* FOOD

Jesus, Jesus Christ: *See* Chapter 7: "Religion, Spirituality, Culture, and Symbols"

Jet: going somewhere fast; taking the fast way; a big or grand project; *See also* AIRPLANE, FLYING

Jewelry: may indicate power or wealth or material success; may be associated with values or spiritual wisdom; may suggest relationships or promises or an agreement between two people; *See also* BRACELET, NECKLACE, RING, WATCH

Jewels/Gemstones: See AMETHYSTS, CRYSTAL, DIAMONDS, EMERALDS, HEMATITE, JADE, LAPIS LAZULI, MOONSTONE, OPALS, PEARLS, QUARTZ, ROSE QUARTZ, RUBIES, SAPPHIRES, TOPAZ, TURQUOISE

Jockey: may represent betting or gambling; can suggest a coming message; can represent feeling small; may indicate an actual jockey or horseback rider; *See also* HORSE

Judge: may represent critiquing yourself or others; may suggest analyzing the situation, idea, or person; can suggest a more powerful authority; may be associated with your higher self criticizing or evaluating your everyday self; an indication of fairness or right and wrong; *See also* JURY

Jungle: may represent that which is wild; can suggest a steamy or hot situation; may represent an overabundance of growth or possibilities or ideas; can be associated with lush, dense vegetation; can suggest jungle location; may indicate jungle life, animals, plants; *See also* ANIMALS

Jury: indicative of judging someone else; having many people against one person; may represent being judgmental; can suggest criticizing oneself or someone else; may represent feeling as though you are being judged; representing peers not agreeing with you; may suggest trials and tribulations through life; can indicate fair play or being forced to be fair; *See also* JUDGE

Kali: See BANNER, FLAG, and Chapter 7: "Religion, Spirituality, Culture, and Symbols"

Kangaroo: may be associated with Australia; may indicate jumping around from place to place; can refer to moving often or consistently; may indicate an unstable or unpredictable outcome; unstable force in life; can indicate the desire to fight or punch out; can indicate the desire to retreat or check out of something in life; *See also* ANIMALS

Key: may be associated with an actual home or new house; may be associated with a new car; as in "the key to," can indicate the answer to life, the problem, etc.; as in "holds the key," may indicate someone or something has the means to unlock all the answers; can indicate potential; may represent the unlocking of your subconscious; may indicate holding something private or keeping someone away

Keyboard: may represent music, as with piano or organ keyboard; can suggest a need to listen to music, or listen to the message in the music; may indicate being in control of your own life symphony; may represent computers, as with computer keyboards; can suggest having everything you need to know at your fingertips; may represent a logical system; *See also* COMPUTER, INSTRUMENT, MUSIC

Kids/Children: may suggest childlike innocence; can represent playfulness or playing; may indicate feeling childlike; may represent the need to not take life too seriously; can represent pregnancy or the birth of a child; may represent your inner child; *See also* BOY, GIRL, PERSON

Kimono: may indicate Japan or Japanese things; can represent beauty; something that covers or protects; may represent something foreign

King: may represent a literal king; may indicate someone who is in charge; can indicate feeling in control; may represent a dictator or a boss; as in "king of the hill," may represent someone above all others; may be associated with tarot cards; *See also* Chapter 8: "Tarot Symbols"

Kiss: See LIPS

Kitchen: may indicate the nurturing of your body, spirit, mind; can suggest something is heating up; may suggest a need to look at dietary and nutritional intake and make some adjustments; *See also* HOUSE, OVEN

Knees: may represent submission or service to someone; may indicate worshipping someone or something; as in "bring him to his knees," to force or overpower into submission; as in "fall on your knees," to beg for forgiveness; as in "on bended knee," to pray or ask for one's hand; as in "taken out at the knees," to stop someone's progress; *See also* LEG

Knife: may represent cutting, slicing, or dividing something in your life or out of your life; may suggest a need to separate from something or someone; may indicate anger, hostility, or aggression; can represent male aggression, phallic symbol; as in "cuts like a knife," sharp words that hurt like a physical wound; as in "stabbed in the back," betrayed by someone trusted; as in "under the knife," under scrutiny or actual surgery; *See also* LANCE, SAW, SWORD

Knight: may represent standing up for what's yours; can indicate fighting for what's right or what you believe in; may suggest medieval time period; as in "knight in shining armor," someone coming in to save the day; as in "knight in shining armor on a white horse," the perfect person who will sweep you off your feet and marry you just in time to save you from yourself or others or a situation; *See also* Chapter 8: "Tarot Symbols

Knot: can represent trouble or confusion; can indicate a mess or chaos; as in a Celtic knot, may indicate spirituality intertwining with physicality; may represent a problem or entanglement; as in "tying the knot," getting married; may suggest a firm or chaotic union or partnership; *See also* CELTIC KNOT, ENDLESS KNOT

Koran: represents spiritual wisdom; sacred and holy Muslim text; words of God; may suggest the reciting of something magnificent and important

Ladder: may represent construction or home improvements; as in "one step at a time," can indicate a steady progression; able to overcome a situation; as in "stairway to heaven," climbing toward heaven; may represent moving toward spirituality; as in "taken down a rung," can indicate being put back in your place by someone or being demoted; a missing rung can indicate missing a step or a misstep in the process

Lake: may represent a pool of emotion or spiritual reservoir; may suggest a tranquil place or a period of rest; may indicate a time of reflection of self or situation; depending on the visual image and the feeling about the lake: a muddy lake may suggest cloudy or uncertain spirituality, intuition, or unclear emotions; a lake densely surrounded by trees may indicate protection from external pressures or alternatively may suggest emotional claustrophobia or feeling trapped emotionally; a clear warm lake may indicate a happy emotional state; and a scary or dark lake may represent being "in over your head"; *See also* POND, POOL, WATER

Lamb: may represent childlike innocence; may indicate purity, tenderness, or wholesomeness; may be associated with Easter or Passover; as in "Lamb of God," may represent a child of God or a sacrificial lamb; *See also* ANIMALS

Lamp: may represent shining a light on someone or something; may suggest awareness or illuminating an insight; a lamp switched on may represent an idea; a lamp switched off may indicate no thought on the matter; a lamp turning on may suggest a new idea; a lamp turning off may refer to the end of an idea, or not understanding an idea; *See also* LIGHT, LIGHT BULB, LIGHTHOUSE

Lance: a pointed suggestion or something you need to think about now; if lance is pointed at you, it may represent someone blaming you; may indicate aggression or male aggression (*see also* PHALLUS); as in "taking a stab at something," taking a chance at something; may represent a stabbing pain or injury; *See also* KNIFE, SWORD

Lapis lazuli: may suggest psychic ability, intuition, or insight; can suggest psychic messages; can indicate clairvoyance; *See also* JEWELS/GEMSTONES

Las Vegas: may suggest gambling or betting; may indicate someone with a gambling addiction; can represent good luck or good fortune or, alternatively, bad luck or misfortune; may represent something that is shiny or attractive on the outside, but not as appealing on the inside; may indicate an actual trip to or someone living in or moving to Las Vegas; *See also* CARDS, ROULETTE WHEEL, SLOT MACHINE

Leaf/Leaves: may represent growth, or growth of new idea(s); can suggest healing; depending on the season: winter leaves can indicate something dried out or dead, and a time for rest, rejuvenation, dormancy, or the ending of a situation or period; spring leaves: new ideas, new growth, new beginnings; summer leaves: full insight, lush or dense growth, happiness; autumn leaves: old ideas making way for new ones, the end of an age or time; pay attention to what's happening with the leaves: raking leaves may suggest gathering of ideas; blowing leaves can mean getting rid of unwanted or old ideas; jumping in a pile of leaves suggests fun, childlike activity, enjoyment; *See also* TREE

Leg: may represent a physical leg or something about the leg needs attention; may indicate support or foundation; may suggest the beliefs or principles one's life is structured upon; as in "pulling my leg," making a joke or teasing; as in "break a leg," well wishes for a successful performance; as in "shake a leg," get moving, hurry up; as in "on his last leg," he won't last much longer, on his way to dying; *See also* KNEES, PANTS

Leo (born July 23–August 22): the sign of the lion and the fifth sign in the zodiac, ruled by the fifth house of pleasure; like the king of the jungle, lives with a flair for the royally dramatic; a magnanimous leader who enjoys being center stage in work and in life; "what you see is what you get" attitude; can unconsciously hurt those around them or warmly help and care for them; a fire sign that survives at all costs and a lioness that protects her young; can be narcissistic; *See also* ZODIAC/ASTROLOGICAL SIGN

Letter/Mail: may represent a correspondence or message; can suggest a coming idea or suggestion; may suggest information from someone else or a different perspective; can refer to a need to share an idea or insight or intuitive awareness with someone else

Libra (born September 23–October 22): the sign of the scales and the seventh sign in the zodiac, ruled by the seventh house of relationships; balance is very important; when out of balance, does not fare well; known as diplomatic, they help others above themselves; need to be careful not to forego own personal needs when taking care of others; a charming host, they intuit others' needs before they ask; can be keen strategists; at times fickle and indecisive; intuitive and able to see the reason behind acts; *See also* ZODIAC/ASTROLOGICAL SIGNS

Library: may refer to an area of expansive knowledge; may indicate a need to research something or a need to look into something more in depth; can represent the Akashic Records; may suggest higher knowledge or knowledge from a higher source; *See also* AKASHIC RECORDS, BOOK

License: can indicate qualifications or authority to do business: e.g., contractor's license, driver's license, medical license; may represent a need for further training; as in "poetic license," to write what you want or do something other than what's expected

Life jacket/Vest: may suggest a feeling of security or protection; may indicate feeling like something or someone needs saving; may represent insulation from or defense against something that may harm or hurt; may represent feeling as though you need help or assistance in order to stay afloat in life

Light: may be associated with "God's light"; may indicate an important idea or a moment of inspiration; illuminating what's important; may represent knowing or moment of knowing; can suggest knowledge from a higher source or from intuition; as in "let there be light," let creation begin; as in "bring to light," bring into awareness; as in "light from above," God's love or help; as in "to make light of," to lessen the significance of something or an event; as in "to light into," to yell at; *See also* LAMP, LIGHT BULB, LIGHTHOUSE

Light bulb: may represent an idea; someone who is bright or intelligent; may indicate the coming of a message; may represent a flash of intuition or insight; *See also* LAMP, LIGHT, LIGHTHOUSE

Lighthouse: may suggest an illuminated path or something or someone illuminating the way; may represent spiritual guidance and direction; may suggest something or someone able to rise up or rise above a person or situation; may indicate a direction for a journey, spiritual or physical; can refer to the ocean or boating; *See also* LAMP, LIGHT, LIGHT BULB

Lightning bolt: may represent a warning or a warning sign for an upcoming event or person; may suggest a breakthrough in an idea or thought or insight; can represent electricity; may represent an explosive situation or emotional outburst; as with lightning rods, may indicate something or someone you are attracted to or something or someone who is attracted to you

Lily: purity; new beginnings or rebirth; can refer to actual person named Lily; *See also* FLOWER

Lion: may represent courage or strength; can indicate the need to hunt for answers; associated with the sign Leo; as in "king of the jungle," the boss or leader or person in charge; as in "getting the lion's share," getting more than anyone else or more than your share; as in "putting your head in the lion's mouth," putting yourself in danger; depending on image, can relate to various emotions or personalities or qualities from works such as *The Wizard of Oz*, *The Lion King*, *The Chronicles of Narnia*, and *The Emperor's New Clothes*; *See also* ANIMALS, ZODIAC/ASTROLOGICAL SIGN-LEO

Lips: may represent communication or the need to communicate; can indicate there is something to say or something needing to be said, or a need to speak up for yourself; as in "keep a stiff upper lip," be brave; as in "bite your lip," don't say anything or keep it to yourself; as in "don't give me any lip," don't talk back to me; if pouting lips, something wanted or missing; may refer to iconic personality or band member, as with Aerosmith or the Rolling Stones; *See also* LIPS (KISSING)

Lips (kissing): may suggest love or passion; may refer to a relationship; can indicate the need to communicate feelings of love or desire; as in "kiss of death," an act that guarantees death or dying; as in "sealed with a kiss," sent with love; *See also* LIPS

Living room: with a casual living room can suggest casual or relaxing atmosphere; may suggest an area where you are open or relaxed, defenses down; with a formal living room can suggest an area where you entertain outsiders or friends; may suggest how you feel at the moment or what you are thinking about or how you are living at the moment; *See also* HOUSE

Lizard: may suggest the ability to escape; may indicate regrowth or evolutionary change; may represent listening intently or looking in all different directions; may suggest an extra-perceptive sensitivity to vibrations or energy; can indicate the ability to be still or even blend into surroundings; may suggest something hidden or camouflaged

Lobster: may indicate something with a hard exterior or emotions but soft interior; may indicate focus or spiritual focus; alternatively, may suggest a bottom-feeder, someone who forages for nutrition or spiritual nourishment; *See also* CRAB

Log: *See* WOOD (LOG)

Lotus flower: *See* FLOWERS and Chapter 7: "Religion, Spirituality, Culture, and Symbols"

Luggage/Suitcase: may indicate a trip or journey; may represent what we take with us or traits we take with us; may suggest an upcoming vacation or that a vacation is necessary; may represent material possessions in hand or needed; may represent what we bring to a relationship; *See also* BAG, PURSE/POCKETBOOK

Lumber: *See* WOOD (LUMBER)

Lungs: may indicate a need to meditate; may suggest needing to breathe or stop and take a breath; clinically, may indicate a need to look at or examine lungs; if lungs are dirty, may indicate some form of pulmonary disease, emphysema, or smoking; *See also* PERSON

Machine: represents mechanical movements or having no individual or personal thought; may suggest automatic functions of the body; may suggest lack of, or numbness to, emotion or feeling

Madonna (biblical): represents motherhood; mother of Christ; nurturing, loving, caring; can indicate that which is taken on faith

Madonna (singer): may represent freedom of expression; can suggest sexuality or independence; may suggest creativity or musical creativity

Magazine: can suggest current events or a need to stay informed; may represent the need to connect to the outside world; depending on magazine, may indicate different areas in your life; the advertisements may be suggestive of looking for something different in your life; *See also* BOOK

Maggot: may indicate feeding off of others; might represent the end result of cause-and-effect occurrences; may indicate rot or decay or disease; can indicate end of cycle; destroying or consuming to make room for new; *See also* BUG/INSECT

Magician: may refer to having magical or mystical powers; can suggest being able to change the unchangeable; may indicate there is more to something than you expect or more to a situation than meets the eye; can indicate a magical change or idea; may suggest an intuitive communication or flash of insight; can indicate creating something out of nothing; may refer to tarot cards, major arcana card 1; *See also* Chapter 8: "Tarot Symbols"

Magnet: may suggest a powerful force or a powerful attraction; can indicate someone or something that is drawn to someone or something else; may indicate opposition or having two opposing forces; may suggest having to accept the negative with the positive in order to have balance; can indicate or refer to yin yang (*see* chapter 7); may suggest someone with bipolar disorder or who is manic depressive; may be a time to look at what you have around you or have attracted to you

Magnifying glass: can indicate a need to look more closely at someone or something or a situation; may suggest a need to inspect or examine an idea more closely; may represent looking at something for what it's worth; can indicate opening your eyes to a situation; may indicate a need to reflect upon or look at your true desires

Maid: may indicate a need to clean up after yourself; can suggest it's time to take charge of your own situation; it may be a time to clean up a mess or straighten out a situation; might indicate a time for cleaning out spiritually to open yourself up to new messages or new or higher learning; can indicate a need to get rid of the cobwebs of the mind; can literally mean it's time to hire a maid or housekeeper; can indicate one who waits on others; *See also* PERSON

Mail: See LETTER/MAIL

Mandala: may indicate psychic wholeness; can refer to order or the archetype of order; may represent oneself, past, present, future; may represent colors; *See also* Chapter 5: "Color Symbolism"

Mattress: may relate to unfinished relationships; can indicate a need to rest; may represent sexuality or the act of sex; mattress without linens may suggest "dirty" or "nasty" sex; mattress tightly bound may indicate lack of sex; *See also* BED, BEDROOM, FURNITURE

Mermaid: may represent the unknown; can indicate that which is fantastical or magical; can suggest someone with powerful intuition; may represent ultimate female beauty; powerful woman; can indicate someone who is seductive or someone who is being seduced; as with "sirens," may suggest seduction of someone who is dazed and blind to being swindled or lied to; may indicate a love of women and the ocean; may suggest a mysterious woman

Microphone: may indicate a desire to sing; suggests communication; may represent a hidden vocal talent; may indicate a need to have your voice or your thoughts or opinions heard; may be associated with the fifth or communication chakra; might represent an actual singer or someone who uses a microphone; can suggest receiving messages through television or radio; may indicate a need to speak up or speak loudly so people may hear what you have to say; may suggest a need to share your ideas with others; *See also* RADIO, TELEVISION

Mirror: can suggest a period of reflection; it may be time to look in the mirror and recognize what you are doing or what the situation is around you; may be time for self-reflection; may be associated with a big ego or, alternatively, lack of self-esteem

Money: may represent something of value or valuables; may represent wealth; may indicate financial success or the success of a future venture; may represent a financial windfall; may relate to a money-making concept or idea; can suggest what you get for working hard; may represent something desired, or something to be desired; as in "in the money," a success; as in "money hungry," interested only in money

Monkey: may represent a jungle; can indicate a playful side; may represent a desire to play; can indicate immaturity; may represent intelligence or someone who is clever; may represent ability to adapt and flow smoothly; as in "monkey on my back," can indicate something that is annoying; something or someone that is addictive; as in "stop monkeying around," stop fooling around and be serious; *See also* ANIMALS

Moon: may relate to feminine energy; may suggest various cycles including menstrual, psychological, gardening, etc.; may relate to intuition or intuitive messages; may represent feelings or emotions; may refer to tarot cards, major arcana card 18; *See also* Chapter 8: "Tarot Symbols"

Moonstone: often indicative of feminine energy; can indicate fertility or menstruation; may suggest emotions or an emotional state; *See also* JEWELS/GEMSTONES

Mosquito: may represent something that is irritating; can suggest something that sucks the life out of you; may indicate something or someone that feeds on others; can represent blood disease or diseases spread by mosquitoes, such as malaria or West Nile virus; *See also* BUG/INSECT, FLY

Motor: See CAR/AUTOMOBILE, ENGINE, MOTORCYCLE

Motorcycle: can relate to something that is exhilarating but dangerous; may indicate a need for excitement; may suggest a need for balance; can represent youth, freedom, or courage; may represent being part of a group; *See also* CAR/AUTOMOBILE, ENGINE

Mountain: may represent a huge obstacle or enormous challenge to surmount; may suggest reaching a higher level of awareness or spirituality; may indicate a heightened state of awareness or seeing things from a new height or level; going up the mountain may suggest climbing toward a new goal or taking a new journey; going down the mountain can relate to an obstacle successfully overcome or the end of a journey; as in "making a mountain out of a molehill," making something big out of something little; *See also* HILL

Mouse: may represent feeling small or insignificant; may be associated with something unseen in the house; may suggest a mousy quality or lack of confidence; can indicate squeezing into tight situations; can indicate the inability to speak up or speak loudly enough that others hear your opinions, thoughts; *See also* ANIMALS

Mug: may represent warm drinks such as coffee, tea, hot chocolate, hot cider; may represent comfort gleaned from sharing a cup of coffee; can indicate a container for emotions, warm indicating happiness and contentedness; *See also* GLASS

Music: may represent the creation of something in tune with or tuned in to life; may suggest it's time to listen to the music; may indicate a need to recognize the order or discipline needed to create something great or a masterpiece; may represent the music of your life; *See also* CYMBALS, DRUM(S), INSTRUMENT, GUITAR

Native American: See INDIAN (NATIVE AMERICAN)

Necklace: may relate to the way a person presents themselves, what they show the world; may be associated with the fourth or heart chakra or the fifth or communication chakra; may suggest any burdens or ideas held; *See also* JEWELRY

Needle: may suggest a need to focus and get to the point of things; can indicate a need to sew things up and finish your projects; as in "needle in a haystack," can suggest looking for something that's very difficult to find; can suggest a need for sharp insight; may refer to your third eye or psychic sight

Net: can suggest feeling trapped or claustrophobic; alternatively, as with safety net, may indicate a feeling of security; can suggest a support system; may refer to the Internet or that answers can be found on the Internet; may refer to all of the separate strands that come together to make up the cohesive whole; may indicate you need to support yourself

Noose: can indicate feeling choked or choking on your words or values or principles, etc.; may suggest being hung up on something; can represent a bad idea or a bad decision; can indicate feeling strung up, trapped, or stuck with something not wanted; may suggest being hung up on a feeling or belief; can refer to the Hanged Man tarot card, major arcana card 12

Nose: may suggest being nosey or sticking your nose in where it doesn't belong; may indicate a specific smell or an enhanced sense of smell; may suggest something that smells bad or is smelly; as in "won by a nose," just barely won or just barely the winner; as in "right on the nose," exactly right or the exact amount; as in "look down the nose," demonstrate distaste for something or someone; as in "turn up one's nose," act better than someone else or disinterested; as in "under your nose," happening right in front of you without you noticing; as in "lead by the nose," to have control over someone; as in "putting his nose out of joint," offending him; as in "she's nosy," she's interested in things that have nothing to do with her; as in "cut your nose off to spite your face," doing something that will negatively affect you even more later; as in "pay through the nose," pay more than it's worth or too much; as in "follow your nose," do what you think is best at the time; as in "the nose knows," trusting your sense of smell; *See also* FACE

Nun: See Chapter 7: "Religion, Spirituality, Culture, and Symbols"

Nurse: may indicate someone who is actually a nurse; may represent a healer or someone possessing healing ability; may suggest someone who needs healing; may suggest a need to look at your own health or health issues; *See also* AMBULANCE, DOCTOR, EMERGENCY ROOM, HOSPITAL

Ocean: may indicate a great depth of emotion or intuition; can suggest deep spirituality; may indicate a journey or trip across the ocean;

may represent femininity or feminine energy; may suggest a meaningful experience; *See also* WATER

Octopus: may suggest having many hands in many different areas; may suggest an attachment or an unhealthy attachment; may indicate something that's holding on; may refer to something or someone stuck to something; *See also* ANIMALS

Olive branch: *See* Chapter 7: "Religion, Spirituality, Culture, and Symbols"

Oneself: can indicate the need to review your life, what you're doing, where you're going; can represent a mirror image or time to look in the mirror; can represent the need to celebrate your life and who you are; *See also* PERSON

Opals: may indicate spirituality or a higher level of spirituality or consciousness; may indicate an angelic presence; *See also* JEWELS/GEMSTONES

Oven: may refer to the brewing of new ideas; can suggest emotions are heating up; may represent a need to move around so you don't get burned; can suggest a need to let ideas or situations heat up slowly so they don't become charred and ruined; as in "bun in the oven," there may be a literal pregnancy; *See also* KITCHEN

Owl: may represent clear vision or sight; may represent being able to see in the dark; can suggest knowledge or someone who is wise; can suggest clairvoyance or connection to clairvoyance; represents clear seeing; seeing things that are hidden or are in the dark; being comfortable in the nighttime; looking for guidance from a wise person; pay attention to someone who is wise; may suggest finding your way; *See also* BIRD

Pants: may represent the lower chakras; can indicate sexuality or desire; may suggest how one presents themselves and their identity to the world; as in "she wears the pants," she's in charge; *See also* LEG

Parachute: may represent an escape plan; can suggest leaping to safety; can indicate a way or need to slow down in life; as in "golden parachute," may represent planning for something or retirement

Parade: may represent working together to form a stream of consciousness or a long process; a united front to show the public; may suggest childhood or nostalgia; can represent a holiday, depending on type of parade

Parasol: See UMBRELLA and Chapter 7: "Religion, Spirituality, Culture, and Symbols"

Path: may represent your path or journey in life; may indicate a new direction to travel; may suggest what course you are on or a new course; can indicate a spiritual journey

Peace sign: can suggest a time of peace, love, and happiness; may represent a need to remove your ego and put your energy into the greater good; may represent a veteran or the 1960s and 1970s; can indicate happy times ahead; may suggest it's time to chill out and let things happen

Pearls: can suggest old wealth or old money; may relate to classic or classy style; as with the pearl in the oyster, may represent inner beauty or wisdom; *See also* JEWELS/GEMSTONES

Pen: may represent the flow of information; may suggest writing a letter or communication to someone; can indicate getting your ideas down on paper or solidifying your ideas; may be a suggestion that it's time to write; *See also* PENCIL

Pencil: may suggest a need to get thoughts down on paper; similar to PEN, but less permanent or less important: pencil can be erased, ideas can be changed, it is not written in stone; may represent working with numbers, accounting, or mathematics; if carpenter's or contractor's pencil, can indicate someone or something in the building profession; *See also* PEN

Pentagram: See Chapter 7: "Religion, Spirituality, Culture, and Symbols"

Person: may represent how you see yourself or specific aspects about yourself; may represent a specific person you know; may suggest qualities you'd like or qualities you wish you had that someone else possesses; if an authority figure, it could indicate a need to follow their instructions or be dutiful; if a spiritual figure, it may suggest it's time to open your intuition and spiritual wisdom; if a foreign person, may represent the unknown or a specific region or a fear of the unknown; other specific people may suggest what they are known for or recognized for or how they dress or how they act; *See also* BOY, GIRL, GLADIATOR, HAND, HEAD, HOBO/BUM, HOSE, KIDS/CHILDREN, MAID

Person (dead): *See* DEAD BODIES, DEAD PERSON/DEATH, GHOST

Person (family): *See* FAMILY

Person (famous): *See* FAMOUS PERSON, IDOL, PERSON

Person (gang): *See* GANG, GANGSTER, PERSON

Person (headless): *See* HEADLESS PERSON

Person (oneself): *See* ONESELF

Phallus: may be associated with male sexuality; may represent force or pressure; may relate to aggression or bullying; as in "cocky," may suggest conceit or selfishness; may represent an extension of oneself; *See also* BOY, GONADS

Piano: *See* KEYBOARD

Picture (hazy): an unclear idea or unclear thought; something that hasn't come to fruition yet; an idea that is not yet fully formed

Picture (landscape): may represent looking to the horizon or seeing what's on the horizon; can indicate getting back to nature

Picture (on wall): may represent memories or family; may represent creativity or what we enjoy; can refer to one's tastes; may represent beauty; can refer to a specific person, place, or item in picture; *See also* PICTURE FRAME

Picture frame: may represent how we hold our family or our memories; may suggest framing an idea; something that surrounds; may suggest lending importance to someone or something

Pig: may represent something or someone that is extremely dirty or filthy; may suggest someone who is greedy, takes what does not belong to them; often associated with someone who is morally or socially inappropriate; as in "making a pig of yourself," taking too much or what's not yours to take; as in "pigheaded," stubborn and unyielding; as in "hog wild," someone who is acting crazy or overly excited; as in "whole hog," going all out for something or someone; as in "a pig in a poke," not knowing much about something or something that is not adequately valued; *See also* ANIMALS

Pipe (plumbing): may represent your elimination or digestive system; may suggest a need to clean or clear out that which is no longer needed or necessary; may indicate a plumbing situation in your house that needs addressing; may suggest a need for a physical or checkup to make sure everything is working as it should be; *See also* HOUSE

Pipe (smoking): may represent an older gentleman, such as father or grandfather; may suggest something that is smelly; may be associated with relaxation, reading, thought, or introspection; may indicate being addicted to nicotine; *See also* CIGARETTE

Pisces (born February 19–March 20): the sign of the fish and the twelfth sign in the zodiac, ruled by the twelfth house of the subconscious; spiritual and creative; need to ground in reality; easily lose direction; easily go with the flow; generally intuitive, charitable, and compassionate; tendency to live in denial about any problems or trouble; *See also* ZODIAC/ASTROLOGICAL SIGN

Planet: may represent the human race or humanity; may suggest an association with aliens or life on other planets; may relate to vast spirituality or connecting to another plane of existence; can represent thoughts or dreams that are in the far distance in time or location

Plant (flowering): may represent nature or nurturing in nature; may indicate the growth or birth of ideas; may suggest a period of success; can indicate the moment of recognition for an idea; may represent a blooming talent or ability; may represent a soul blossoming in nature; *See also* FLOWER, GARDEN, PLANT (GREEN), TREE, VASE

Plant (green): may represent healing energy; may represent new growth or fresh ideas; may suggest spirituality; may indicate being rooted in a belief or situation; *See also* GARDEN, PLANT (FLOWERING), TREE

Playground: may suggest a time to revisit your inner child; can indicate school, a return to school, or teaching; may refer to a need to play; can refer to playing the game of life; alternatively, can suggest someone who is being childish; if specifically a swing, can suggest going back and forth about an idea or situation; if specifically a slide, can suggest sliding into something quickly and smoothly; *See also* SCHOOL

Plumbing: *See* PIPE (PLUMBING)

Police: may represent someone in authority over you; may suggest safety or security; can indicate the need to be saved or to save yourself; may represent the need to evaluate your life and make sure you are being honest and truthful to yourself and others; may indicate an actual person you know; can indicate a problem with authority figures

Pond: may suggest a period of reflection or the need to mentally reflect on your life; can indicate an emotional time in your life; may indicate a spiritual reservoir; may suggest storage of or storing up emotions; *See also* LAKE, POOL, WATER

Pool: may represent an emotional or spiritual feeling or time; can indicate storing up emotions; may represent your current feelings or state of mind; may indicate manufactured emotions; may indicate a need to pool together resources or friends; *See also* LAKE, POND, WATER

Porch: may represent temporary security; can indicate opening to something new; may represent being in between situations, environments, or ideas; *See also* HOUSE

Possum: may suggest all is not what it seems; may represent fooling yourself or being fooled by others; can indicate you or someone else is pretending to be someone you're not; as in "playing possum," pretending to be dead; *See also* ANIMALS

Praying hands: *See* Chapter 7: "Religion, Spirituality, Culture, and Symbols"

Priest: *See* Chapter 7: "Religion, Spirituality, Culture, and Symbols"

Prison: *See* JAIL/PRISON

Pumpkin: can indicate autumn; may represent Halloween or even Thanksgiving; can represent memories of childhood or pumpkin pie or family; may refer to the first Thanksgiving or pilgrims and Native Americans; *See also* JACK-O'-LANTERN

Puppet: may indicate feeling controlled by others; may represent allowing yourself to be or feeling as though you are being manipulated by others; may suggest someone who is controlled by the whims of someone else; may suggest feeling like a "dummy"

Purse/Pocketbook: may indicate that which we carry daily; can suggest what we need; may represent how we shoulder our responsibilities; a fancy bag can represent putting on a show; an old or ratty bag, avoidance or ignoring responsibilities; may represent female sexual anatomy; can represent how we show ourselves to the world or how we represent ourselves; may suggest independence; *See also* BAG, LUGGAGE/SUITCASE

Quartz: may suggest the amplification of whatever it comes into contact with; may represent clearing and clarity; may represent vision; *See also* JEWELS/GEMSTONES

Rabbit: may represent Easter; as in "hop to it," get going; may suggest hopping from place to place; may represent timidity or meekness; may suggest being overly sexual or having an abundance of sex; *See also* ANIMALS

Radio: may indicate communication or spirit communication; may represent a need to broadcast or send out information; can indicate messages or awareness from the higher self; can suggest clairaudience or the need to develop clear psychic hearing; may suggest a need to listen; can represent music, entertainment, or someone who is on the radio; *See also* SPEAKER, TELEVISION

Rain: may represent a flow of emotions or an outpouring of emotion; as in "let the rain pour down," let your emotions flow out without restriction; if flooding, may indicate being inundated or overwhelmed with emotion; if light mist, may represent clouded emotions or the inability to understand feelings; may represent falling or feeling as though you are falling; may indicate the need to cleanse physically, emotionally, or spiritually; can refer to a lazy, rainy day; as in "it's raining cats and dogs," may suggest pouring rain or being inundated by emotion; *See also* WATER, SNOW

Rainbow: can refer to the chakra system; may suggest that through adversity comes beauty and achievement; can suggest the levels of diversity needed to achieve strength and unity; may refer to sexual orientation; *See also* Chapter 5: "Color Symbolism" and Chapter 6: "Chakra and Aura Symbolism"

Rat: may represent someone who is sneaky or untrustworthy; as in "dirty rat," someone who lies or does something behind your back; as in "rat you out," someone who is tattling on you; as in "I smell a rat," I think there is something wrong or someone not quite right; can suggest someone who feasts on whatever you leave behind; may represent someone who is sadistic or cruel; *See also* ANIMALS, MOUSE

Refrigerator: may represent something in cold storage or preserving something; can indicate a chilly attitude; may represent someone who is sexually frigid; may suggest a need to save something for future use; can refer to food, diet, or nutrition; *See also* HOUSE, KITCHEN

Ring/Wedding/Engagement: may suggest a union or partnership or agreement; can indicate an engagement, marriage, actual wedding, or someone who is married; if wedding/engagement ring is off, can indicate a separation or divorce; *See also* JEWELRY

Road/Street: may suggest you are on a journey; can indicate a need to avoid potholes or obstacles in your path ahead; may suggest a need to review where you've come from and where you're going; as in "the road less traveled," can indicate taking a tougher course but one that may be more beneficial in the long run; can suggest staying in your truth; can indicate a need to be careful not to veer off your path; as in "take the high road or the take the low road," may suggest choosing the more responsible versus least responsible way; See also FORK IN THE ROAD

Robin: related to first or root chakra; representing fame; a feeling of pride; feeling popular or your idea or your career will be popular; *See also* BIRD

Rock: can indicate strength and stability; can suggest a solid foundation; if a specific type of rock, may indicate metaphysical or spiritual connection; may suggest a connection to the earth; can refer to a feeling of heaviness; as in "sink like a rock," can suggest a quick fall metaphorically or physically

Roller coaster: may indicate life, or life's challenges; may refer to life's ups and downs; what goes up must come down or you must be down in order to go up; there are many twists and turns coming your way; may indicate queasiness; may indicate anxious feelings, never knowing what's coming up next

Roof: may represent a higher power; can represent your higher self or higher thought; what protects you or shields you physically, psychically, emotionally, or spiritually; may represent security; as in "the roof is on fire," can indicate the inability to keep a lid on things or keep a situation contained; as in "bringing down the roof," can represent excitement or a great performance; *See also* HOUSE

Rooster: feeling confident and courageous; having courage; politically strong; needing to crow or express yourself; puffing out your chest with confidence; exaggerating your strength and confidence; may suggest a morning person; can indicate a positive new day is coming; can indicate the need to wake up to a situation; *See also* BIRD, CHICK, CHICKEN, FARM

Rope: may suggest something that ties or binds; may represent something that holds firmly or securely; may indicate something that connects; as in "she's at the end of her rope," she's done, she's overwhelmed; as in "just enough rope to hang herself," just enough leeway to allow her to make a mistake; as in "he knows the ropes," he knows what to do in the situation or position

Rosary/Rosary beads: See Chapter 7: "Religion, Spirituality, Culture, and Symbols"

Rose: may suggest passion, love, or harmony among partners; may represent a message of love from the other side; as in "a rose by any other name is still a rose," it doesn't matter if you call it something else, it will always be beautiful like a rose; colored roses—red: love, passion; white: purity, forgiveness; yellow: friendship; pink: sweetness; blue: stalled emotion or communication; violet: enlightenment or spiritual awareness; *See also* FLOWERS

Rose quartz: often represents universal love; associated with the heart chakra; *See also* JEWELS/GEMSTONES

Roulette wheel: may represent gambling or someone with a gambling addiction; may indicate taking a chance on something or someone; may suggest the odds are against success; may represent the spinning wheel of life; may represent life cycles or the end of a cycle; *See also* CARDS, LAS VEGAS, SLOT MACHINE

Rubies: may represent passionate love; strong, powerful energy; may represent compassion; can suggest a strong foundation; *See also* JEWELS/GEMSTONES

Rug: See CARPET/RUG

Sagittarius (born November 22–December 21): the sign of the archer/centaur and the ninth sign in the zodiac, ruled by the ninth house of philosophy and religion; always aiming toward heaven; always on a quest for knowledge; looking for the meaning to life and are happier when others agree with their point of view; travelers, who enjoy the outdoors or outdoor activities; tendency to speak their mind or their truth without realizing they may be hurting someone's feelings; feeling of "if only there were enough money, life would be good"; *See also* ZODIAC/ASTROLOGICAL SIGN

Sand: may represent an unsure or unstable foundation; as in "sands of time," can indicate the passage of time; as with sand in an hourglass, may represent time running out; may relate to the physical self; *See also* BEACH

Sapphires: may indicate communication or messages; often associated with the fifth or communication chakra; may suggest someone who is strong-willed; *See also* JEWELS/GEMSTONES

Saw: may represent a need to cut something out of your life or cut something away from you; may indicate a need to separate yourself from someone or something; may indicate the use of tools; may suggest male aggression or anger (*See also* PHALLUS); may refer to construction or a construction worker; *See also* KNIFE

School: may represent a need to learn—spiritually, metaphysically, or academically; can indicate someone in school or going back to school; may represent a need for higher learning; can indicate some kind of teacher; can represent a need to learn lessons or life lessons; may suggest expanding one's consciousness; may represent unresolved issues or issues from the past; as in "school of fish," can suggest a group that keeps together or works as an efficient whole; *See also* PLAYGROUND

Scorpio (born October 23–November 21): the sign of the scorpion and the eighth sign in the zodiac, ruled by the eighth house of the birth/life/death cycle; intuitive, intense, and passionate; tendency to sting when hurt or when someone tries to probe too deeply into emotions; need constant reassurance, so they keep moving to find it; they are curious and are therefore good investigators or detectives; people are generally drawn to them, but if they are too close, they get the stinger; *See also* ZODIAC/ASTROLOGICAL SIGN

Scrolls: may represent ancient wisdom; can represent information from the Akashic Records; can indicate an important message; may suggest religious records or books; may represent the Dead Sea Scrolls, the ancient religious writings from various times between about 150 BCE and 70 CE; *See also* AKASHIC RECORDS

Shark: may represent someone who is out to get you; someone or something powerful, strong, and sometimes dangerous; may indicate someone ready to attack or someone who is sneaky; *See also* FISH

Shirt: may represent what you show to the world; may indicate a need to protect yourself from outside influences; depending on type of shirt, may represent occupation: white-collar executive, blue-collar manual laborer, uniform, medical professional, and so on; as in "give you the shirt off my back," giving you whatever I have; as in "keep your shirt on," be patient, just wait a minute; as in "losing one's shirt," losing everything

Shop: See STORE

Shower: may indicate a need to cleanse physically, spiritually, emotionally; can represent inspiration or intuition; may suggest eliminating from your life dirt or that which is dirty; may suggest being open to metaphysical communication; *See also* BATHROOM, BATH/BATHTUB, SINK

Sign: may suggest a synchronistic event; can indicate a direction you need to go in life; may represent a message from the universe; can suggest you need to pay attention; may indicate a need to stop and think about what the sign represents; depending on the sign, can indicate something specific such as that a stop sign means stop

Sink: may represent a need to wash away any worries; can suggest cleaning any unneeded emotions; as in "down the drain," waste of money or resources; *See also* BATHROOM, BATH/BATHTUB, SHOWER, WASHING MACHINE

Skunk: may represent something smelly or that something stinks; can indicate pushing people away or driving people off; may suggest a tendency to form a barrier around oneself to keep others from getting too close; can refer to something you have said or done that is keeping others from you; alternatively, may suggest feeling a need to protect oneself; may indicate things aren't always as they seem; may represent seeing things in black and white; can indicate anger or aggressive tendencies; *See also* ANIMALS

Slot machine: may suggest taking a chance or gambling on something; can indicate a constant money drain or waste of money; can refer to Las Vegas or Atlantic City; can suggest luck or someone who is lucky; *See also* CARDS, LAS VEGAS, ROULETTE WHEEL

Smiley face: may suggest a happy time; can indicate a need to put on a happy face for everyone to see; can indicate pure joy; can suggest a childlike, pure happiness; can suggest the universe is smiling upon you in appreciation for who you are and what you are accomplishing; can refer to pure delight

Smoke: may suggest something that is hazy or an unclear situation; as in "behind a smokescreen," might represent someone hiding behind something; as in "dreams going up in smoke," dreams floating away; as in "smoke something out," force something into the open or find out a secret; as in "up in smoke," losing something or an opportunity lost; *See also* FIRE

Smoking: See CIGARETTE, FIRE, PIPE (SMOKING)

Snail: may suggest moving slowly through life; can indicate being slow and methodical; may represent what you're waiting for may not come for a long while; can suggest a need to speed up or hurry up; as in "at a snail's pace," taking your time; *See also* ANIMAL

Snake: indicates transformation and transmutation; as in "he's a snake," someone who is not trustworthy or "slimy"; someone who is constantly changing; adaptation to environment; as in the Bible, temptation or the fall of man; also can refer to wisdom and healing; may refer to male, as in phallic symbol; as in "snake in the grass," someone or something that is hidden or not quite in the open and dangerous or treacherous; as in "shedding your skin," can indicate renewal, transition, or transformation; *See also* ANIMAL

Sneakers: may indicate a need to step into action; can suggest it's time to get moving, no more dragging your feet; may refer to an exercise program or sports; can suggest putting your plan into motion now; may indicate that running away from your issues won't get you to the finish line; as in "run with it," may suggest a need to devise a strategy and run with it; alternatively, may refer to something or someone working behind the scenes in a devious way or sneaking around behind your back; *See also* ATHLETE, SPORT SOCKS

Snow: associated with emotions; can represent frozen emotions; may indicate someone who is cold or frigid; as in "snowed over," can represent being lied to or overpowered by a situation or emotion; may represent childhood, memories of sledding, or ice skating; can refer to time of year, winter, or geographical location such as Alaska; may represent purity; *See also* RAIN, WATER

Socks (athletic): See ATHLETE, SNEAKERS, SPORT SOCKS

Sparrow: connected to fifth or communication chakra; known for being small but vocal; traveling great distances but always returning home; traveling in groups; never alone; can be a message that you're never alone, you have the security of the group; small but worthy; *See also* BIRD

Speaker: can suggest a message from the other side; a psychic connection; may indicate communications; can indicate a need to tune in to your clairaudience; may represent a need or an attempt to get your attention; *See also* RADIO, TELEVISION

Spider: may suggest someone who is deceitful; one who spins a dangerous web; as in "black widow," someone who destroys or kills their spouse or partner; may indicate someone or something with a dangerous bite; creating a web may indicate security; can suggest creativity or revisiting your creative side; *See also* BUG/INSECT

Sport socks: may indicate exercise or someone who is physically fit; alternatively, may represent someone who needs to exercise; may indicate a particular sport or activity; can refer to an athlete; *See also* ATHLETE, FOOTBALL, SNEAKERS

Square: can indicate something that is contained; may suggest someone who lives life oblivious or out of synch with what's cool in life; as in "three square meals a day," three balanced meals; as in "squared away," everything is all set; as in "square peg in a round hole," trying to fit something in where it doesn't fit; as in "fair and square," everything's even; as in "squared off," getting ready for a fight; may represent a foundation or security

Squirrel: can indicate gathering or a gatherer; may represent hoarding or saving for the future; can be a time for investment; hard-working; can indicate someone who is looking to the future; simple person; as in "squirrely," someone who is dodgy; can represent an annoyance or someone who is annoying; *See also* ANIMALS

Stairs: may suggest climbing to success or rising up to another level; may indicate taking a spiritual journey; as in "one step at a time," taking it easy, going one pace at a time; as in "stairway to heaven," may represent a spiritual path toward good; *See also* HOUSE

Stage: may suggest a performance or performing; can indicate what is shown externally; may represent a need to be the center of attention or the star; may represent a need to pay attention to what's being presented or shown; can indicate what is rehearsed or prepared; may refer to how you perceive yourself or your surroundings

Staple/Stapler: may represent holding everything together; may indicate binding or the need to be bound together; may refer to office work or desk work

Star(s): may indicate the vastness of life and existence; may represent dreams and wishes; may represent psychic ability or intuition; can indicate a famous person; may represent someone who wants to be a star or famous; may suggest someone who needs to be the center of attention; as in "thank your lucky stars," be very grateful; as in "catch a shooting star," have all the happiness and excitement you need; *See also* Chapter 7: "Religion, Spirituality, Culture, and Symbols"

Star of David: See Chapter 7: "Religion, Spirituality, Culture, and Symbols"

Statue: may represent feeling frozen or being stuck; may suggest immobility or the inability to progress; may indicate being put on a pedestal or honored in some way

Stone: may indicate something strong; can represent something or someone that can withstand time; as in "stone cold," having no feeling; as in "no stone unturned," look everywhere; as in "he's a stoner," he smokes a lot of marijuana; as in "don't cast stones," don't talk about someone else in a derogatory way; *See also* JEWELS/ GEMSTONES

Store: may suggest everything in the world is yours to choose from; can indicate a need to browse or peruse through various options;

can refer to feeling as though your life is on display; may suggest needing to look for what you want; as in "store of emotions," can indicate keeping your emotions hidden; can suggest putting something away and not worrying about it until it's necessary to take it out again

Stork: new baby is coming; may represent or birth of a new idea; needing support and balance on what appears to be a shaky foundation; spiritual support; delivering a message or a present; *See also* BIRD

Storm: may represent a tumultuous time; can suggest a time of chaos or confusion; may indicate arguments or upheaval; can indicate difficulties; may represent challenges that have to be worked through; may represent a period of unrest

Stove: may suggest something getting heated or heating up; can indicate cooking or an idea that is cooking up; may indicate family gatherings; as in "if you can't stand the heat, get out of the kitchen," if you can't handle the difficulties, don't get involved; as in "put it on the back burner," do it later; *See also* FIRE, HOUSE, KITCHEN

Suitcase: *See* LUGGAGE/SUITCASE

Sun: may indicate the actual need to get outdoors or get vitamin D; can suggest being in the sunlight or spotlight; may represent a bright message from heaven; can indicate creation of something new; can refer to illuminating something or someone; as in "a place in the sun," can represent your time to stand out or excel; *See also* SUNSHINE and Chapter 8: "Tarot Symbols"

Sunshine: may suggest a time to be outdoors; a need to shine in your life; being recognized or noticed; may represent a new idea or relationship; message from above; *See also* SUN

Swastika: *See* Chapter 7: "Religion, Spirituality, Culture, and Symbols"

Sword: may represent cutting through to the heart or center of the matter; can indicate keeping someone or something away; may represent quick-witted personality; someone who cuts with their words; can indicate male aggression (*See also* PHALLUS); *See also* AX, KNIFE, LANCE, and Chapter 8: "Tarot Symbols"

Table: may represent choices we make; can indicate a need to look at diet or nutritional choices; may represent a family gathering; can represent mealtime or holiday meals; may refer to stability or the leveling off of something; as in "lay it all on the table," share all secrets or tell everything; *See also* FURNITURE, HOUSE

Taurus (born April 20–May 20): the sign of the bull and the second sign of the zodiac, ruled by the second house of material possessions; will keep going because they are very determined; practical and sensible, they enjoy comfortable living and surroundings; usually gentle but stubborn when sense of peace is challenged; can be stable to the point of being boring; need to stop and appreciate beauty; *See also* ZODIAC/ASTROLOGICAL SIGN

Tea/Tea bag: may represent the need to drink tea for health; can indicate a need to remain alert or stay awake or energize yourself; may refer to what tea brings to mind, as in socialization, relaxation, waking up, etc.; if tea bag is open, may suggest reading tea leaves or fortunetelling; type of container may be indicative of message: a broken mug/glass can represent a period of unrest; a small or tiny vessel may indicate a need to cut back on consumption of stimulants or caffeine; a glass of iced tea may refer to a summer day of relaxation and harmony; *See also* FOOD

Tear/Teardrop: may indicate sadness; can suggest a welling up or overwhelming emotion; may represent a need to flush one's vision to see clearly; if tattooed, can suggest a murder or murderer, as with some gang initiations/rites; *See also* WATER

Teeth: See TOOTH/TEETH, PERSON

Telephone: may represent communication or hearing from someone; can indicate a message or spiritual message from beyond; may suggest a need to contact someone; may indicate a long-awaited call is coming your way; a ringing phone may refer to a need to listen or pay attention, or a message is coming; a phone off the hook may represent someone who is not available, is unwilling to listen, or is busy; *See also* Chapter 4: "How We Receive Symbols"

Television: may represent communication from a distance or spirit communication; can refer to a specific actor or actress; may indicate a story or drama unfolding; can indicate certain parts of life to be addressed; someone who is a star or wants to be a star or be treated like a star; can indicate broadcasting of ideas, people, or events; *See also* MICROPHONE, RADIO, SPEAKER

Temple: See Chapter 7: "Religion, Spirituality, Culture, and Symbols"

Third eye: associated with clairvoyance; psychically seeing; may represent ESP or extrasensory perception; that which is mystical or unknown; having "second sight" or "sixth sense"; representing psychic awareness or intuitive ability; the sixth chakra; *See also* EYES and Chapter 6: "Chakra and Aura Symbolism"

Throat: may represent a need to communicate; can indicate having a hard time speaking your mind; may represent someone who works with their voice, such as a speaker, singer, actor, reporter, or teacher; can indicate a message or message you give; can indicate music or vocal ability; may indicate a need to check thyroid or thyroid disease; *See also* PERSON and Chapter 6: "Chakra and Aura Symbolism"

Tiger: may represent swiftness or swift action; may suggest ferocity or someone who is, or a situation that is, ferocious or audacious; may represent power or someone who is powerful; can indicate a maternal or nurturing disposition; may represent sensuality; as in "can't change their stripes," may indicate someone who is unable or unwilling to change; as in "Tony the Tiger," may represent cereal; *See also* ANIMALS, LION

Tissues: may represent sadness or misery; may indicate a need to dry your tears and move on; can suggest a sad time or event; may represent someone or something that is depressed; may suggest misery or a miserable event; can indicate a cold or flu

Toes: may represent an extension of oneself; can indicate a need to get sure footing or stability; may suggest an alternative way to grasp something or get hold of something; *See also* FOOT/FEET, PERSON

Toilet: may represent that which we dispose of or rid ourselves of; may refer to a clearing out spiritually or physically; may suggest something that is no longer necessary; as in "in the toilet," may represent someone who has gone downhill or is no longer at the top of their game; *See also* BATHROOM, HOUSE

Tooth/Teeth: may represent a need to start something new; can indicate power or strength; can represent aggression; as in "sink your teeth into it," get involved with it; if losing teeth or teeth falling out, may represent losing control over someone or a situation or may suggest an inability to speak your truth or lack of communication; may suggest a need to visit a dentist or someone who is a dentist; may also represent the first or base or root chakra

Topaz: may represent knowledge; can suggest a need to focus; may indicate a need to heal; *See also* JEWELS/GEMSTONES

Train: may represent a need to move forward; can indicate travel or commute to or from home; may indicate training of some type; as in "silver bullet train," may indicate propelling extremely fast in life or in a career; as in "hard to stop a train," hard to slow down the momentum of something

Trampoline: may represent jumping from one place to another; can indicate a need to stop jumping around; may suggest returning to the same idea or lesson repeatedly; may represent a need for exercise; can indicate someone who is "flipping out"

Treasure vase: *See* VASE and Chapter 7: "Religion, Spirituality, Culture, and Symbols"

Tree: may represent growth or healing; can represent the connection from earth to heaven; may indicate psychic growth; as in "tree of life," suggests all living things are connected and encompassed in the universe; *See also* FOREST, LEAF/LEAVES, PLANT (GREEN), WOOD

Triangle: may represent body, mind, spirit; can indicate either equality or inequality; may represent solidness or balance; may represent the number 3 or what three represents; can indicate pointing toward heaven or pointing toward materialistic or physical properties; may represent the pyramids; can represent a trilogy or a threesome; *See also* Chapter 8: "Tarot Symbols"

Trout: relaxation; may suggest lake or lakeside; picnic; *See also* FISH

Truck: may represent movement or forward movement; can suggest a need for power or aggression; can represent that which holds or transports something; transporting your thoughts or ideas; can indicate type of work or profession, depending on type of truck; as in "keep on trucking," can indicate to keep moving or keep going on your path; as in "broken-down pickup," may refer to a specific or general country music song

Turkey: can indicate blessings shared or a bountiful harvest; may represent a holiday meal, specifically Thanksgiving; may represent someone who is more comfortable in a group; may represent spirituality; as in "you're a turkey," you're acting silly and ridiculous; *See also* BIRD

Turquoise: a powerful and empowering stone; can indicate a connection to the spiritual world, or spiritual messages; suggests communication; can represent a need to walk the walk and talk the talk; also suggests protection and healing; often associated with the fifth or communication chakra; can indicate the presence of Native Americans or Native American guide(s); *See also* JEWELS/GEM-STONES

Turtle: may represent ancient wisdom; can represent a tendency to hide inside one's shell, sheltering from outside sources; may suggest awakening or opening to opportunities; can indicate motherhood; *See also* ANIMALS

Twin towers: may represent duality or twins; represents New York City; may suggest two hands reaching toward the heavens; as in 9/11, can suggest terrorists or a terrorist attack; can indicate loss of life or sadness; can indicate a journey or visitor from or to New York or New York City

UFO: *See* FLYING SAUCER/UFO

Umbrella: may represent shielding from the elements; can relate to having everything covered; being spiritually protected, or surrounded by spiritual energy; can refer to rain; may suggest a need to protect yourself; protection from emotions

United States of America: can represent the American Dream; can indicate Americans or America; may suggest freedom or the quest for
freedom or democracy; CONTINENT/COUNTRY

Vase (empty): may represent a vessel or that which holds something;
can indicate spirituality; may suggest being void or empty of emotion; femininity; *See also* FLOWERS, GARDEN (FLOWERS),
PLANT (FLOWERING), VASE (WITH FLOWERS)

Vase (with flowers): may represent a vessel or that which holds something; can indicate spirituality; may suggest being full of emotion;
depending on type of flowers, can indicate particular emotion; may
refer to chakra system; femininity; *See also* FLOWERS, GARDEN
(FLOWERS), PLANT (FLOWERING), VASE (EMPTY)

Vegetables: may suggest a need to get back to nature; can indicate a
need to add more vegetables to diet; depending on type or color,
can relate to various chakras; may suggest phallus, depending on
shape of vegetable; *See also* FOOD, GARDEN (VEGETABLE),
GOURD, PUMPKIN

Victory banner: *See* FLAG and Chapter 7: "Religion, Spirituality, Culture, and Symbols"

Virgo (born August 23–September 22): the sign of the virgin and the
sixth sign of the zodiac, ruled by the sixth house of health; modest and efficient; largely noted for their attention to detail; balanced
and fair, yet picky; neat freaks with a messy closet somewhere; need
to not be so critical of themselves and others; *See also* ZODIAC/
ASTROLOGICAL SIGN

Vishnu: *See* Chapter 7: "Religion, Spirituality, Culture, and Symbols"

Washing machine: may suggest you are emotionally going through the
wringer; may indicate it's time to clean up a situation; may suggest
feeling wishy-washy; can indicate needing to purge what you no
longer need; may refer to ridding yourself of debris that has been
hanging on; may suggest that although the process feels disruptive,
the final outcome will be great; may indicate it's time to come clean;
See also SINK

Watch: usually suggests time, may be the passing of time or an actual time; can indicate better times to come; can represent downtime is needed; can suggest time is running out; *See also* JEWELRY

Water: indicative of emotions and emotional states; can represent the unconscious or the conscious or the stream of consciousness; may suggest cleansing, purifying, or renewing; can indicate feeling over-whelmed or drowning; as in "in hot water," may indicate someone in trouble; as in "all washed up," can indicate being through with something, or no longer significant in some way; spirituality and spiritual wisdom; *See also* BEACH, HARBOR, HOSE, ICE, LAKE, OCEAN, POND, POOL, RAIN, TEAR/TEARDROP, WATER BOT-TLE, WATERFALL

Water bottle: may indicate a need to hydrate or dehydration; can sug-gest bottling up emotions or holding various emotions in; may rep-resent a need to open up or express yourself; *See also* WATER

Waterfall: may represent an overwhelming or active emotion; can refer to a powerful or forceful emotion; a powerful stream of con-sciousness; may suggest an inability to stop an outpouring of emo-tion; may represent a sadness; may indicate drowning; can suggest cleansing, purifying, or renewing; *See also* WATER

Wedding: See RING

Whale: may indicate something big to talk about; as in "whale of a tale," can indicate exaggeration or an overdone story; may refer to the literary classic *Moby Dick*; with gambling, may refer to a big spender; *See also* ANIMALS

Wheel: can indicate the cycle or circle of life; may represent the begin-ning of a new era in time; can indicate travel or transportation or the ability to move forward and navigate; can represent a spiritual or psychic mandala; as in "wheel of fortune," may represent various opportunities or changes in fortune; may represent ups and downs or inconsistencies; as in a "third wheel," may represent an odd man out or someone left out; as in "a squeaky wheel gets the grease," someone who complains gets attention; *See also* Chapter 7: "Religion, Spirituality, Culture, and Symbols"

Wildflowers: wildness; excitement; natural; untamed or unrefined talents or abilities; *See also* FLOWERS

Windows: *See* HOUSE

Wood (log): represents stability or stability being cut down; can refer to a fire or fireplace; may represent life or pieces of life; can indicate waste; may suggest nature; may refer to a lumberjack or farmer; *See also* TREE, WOOD (LUMBER)

Wood (lumber): represents building or construction; can refer to rebuilding or the structure of life; can indicate a need to create or construct something; *See also* TREE, WOOD (LOG)

Yin-Yang symbol: *See* Chapter 7: "Religion, Spirituality, Culture, and Symbols"

Zebra: may represent a need to blend in or be camouflaged; can indicate individuality; may refer to an ability to exist within a group but to continue individuality; may refer to Africa or a visit or visitor to or from Africa; may indicate blending in is beneficial; *See also* ANIMALS

Zodiac/Astrological sign: represents a system based on planetary or stellar positioning; refers to the twelve astrological signs based on dates of birth; may represent specific energy patterns; may be indicative of expression or modes of expression; refers to specific characteristics or traits based on where you fall in the zodiac or your astrological sign. *See also* AQUARIUS, ARIES, CANCER, CAPRICORN, GEMINI, LEO, LIBRA, PISCES, SAGITTARIUS, SCORPIO, TAURUS, VIRGO

Zoo: may represent a combination of different personalities; can indicate an ordered chaos; may suggest a menagerie; can represent feeling on public display; may represent feeling caged or trapped; *See also* ANIMALS, JUNGLE

Bibliography and Recommended Reading

Andrews, Ted. *How to Meet & Work with Spirit Guides*. St. Paul, MN: Llewellyn Publications, 2002.

———. *How to See and Read the Aura*. St. Paul, MN: Llewellyn Publications, 2002.

The Anima Project. Online at http://www.animaproject.org.

Browne, Sylvia. *Phenomenon: Everything You Need to Know about the Paranormal*. New York: Dutton, 2005.

Buffum, Jude, and Paul Kepple. *The Housewives Tarot*. Philadelphia: Quirk Books, 2004.

Byrne, Rhonda. *The Secret*. New York: Atria Books, 2006.

Calabrese, Adrian. *Sacred Signs: Hear, See & Believe Messages from the Universe*. Woodbury, MN: Llewellyn Publications, 2006.

Choquette, Sonia. *Ask Your Guides: Connecting to Your Divine Support System*. Carlsbad, CA: Hay House, 2006.

Cloninger, Susan. *Theories of Personality: Understanding Persons*, fifth edition. Upper Saddle River, NJ: Pearson Prentice Hall, 2007.

Dale, Cyndi. *The Subtle Body: An Encyclopedia of Your Energetic Anatomy*. Boulder, CO: Sounds True, Inc., 2009.

Denning, Melita, and Osborne Phillips. *Practical Guide to Psychic Powers: Awaken Your Sixth Sense*. St. Paul, MN: Llewellyn Publications, 2000.

"The Eight Auspicious Symbols." Buddha Dharma Education Association and Buddha Net. Online at http://www.buddhanet.net/e-learning/history/b8symbol.htm.

Greer, Mary K. *Mary K. Greer's 21 Ways to Read a Tarot Card*. Woodbury, MN: Llewellyn Publications, 2006.

———. *Tarot for Your Self: A Workbook for Personal Transformation*, second edition. Pompton Plains, NJ: New Page Books, 2002.

Harper, Elizabeth. *Wishing: How to Fulfill Your Heart's Desires*. New York: Atria Books, 2008.

Holland, John. *Psychic Navigator: Harnessing Your Inner Guidance*. Carlsbad, CA: Hay House, 2004.

Jung, Carl Gustav, ed. *Man and His Symbols*. Garden City, NY: Doubleday, 1964.

Kumar, Nitin. "The Eight Auspicious Symbols of Buddhism: A Study in Spiritual Evolution." ExoticIndia.com (October 2003). Online at http://www.exoticindiaart.com/article/symbols.

Louis, Anthony. *Tarot Plain and Simple*. St. Paul, MN: Llewellyn Publications, 2002.

Mark, Barbara, and Trudy Griswold. *Angelspeake: How to Talk with Your Angels*. New York: Simon & Schuster, 1995.

Microsoft Encarta College Dictionary. New York: St. Martin's Press, 2001.

Morehouse, David. *Psychic Warrior: Inside the CIA's Stargate Program*. New York: St. Martin's Press, 1996.

Pollack, Rachel. *The Complete Illustrated Guide to Tarot*. New York: Gramercy Books, 2004.

———. *Seventy-Eight Degrees of Wisdom: A Book of Tarot*. San Francisco: Red Wheel/Weiser, 2007.

Steiner, Rudolf. *Guardian Angels: Connecting with Our Spiritual Guides and Helpers.* Forest Row, UK: Rudolf Steiner Press, 2001.

Sucheta, and Craig Howel. "About Kwan Yin." MyKwanYin.com. Online at http://www.mykwanyin.com/kwgoddess.html.

Todeschi, Kevin J. *The Encyclopedia of Symbolism.* New York: Berkley Publishing Group, 1995.

Waite, Arthur Edward, and Pamela Colman Smith. *The Rider-Waite Tarot Deck.* Stamford, CT: U.S. Games Systems, Inc., 1971. Originally published in 1909.

"Who Is Buddha?" Aboutbuddha.org. Online at http://www.aboutbuddha.org/english/who-is-buddha.htm/.

Wittgenstein, Ludwig. *Tractatus Logico-Philosophicus.* (Translated by C. K. Ogden.) New York: Harcourt, Brace & Company, 1922.

To Write to the Author

If you wish to contact the author or would like more information about this book, please write to the author in care of Llewellyn Worldwide Ltd. and we will forward your request. Both the author and publisher appreciate hearing from you and learning of your enjoyment of this book and how it has helped you. Llewellyn Worldwide Ltd. cannot guarantee that every letter written to the author can be answered, but all will be forwarded. Please write to:

Melanie Barnum
℅ Llewellyn Worldwide
2143 Wooddale Drive
Woodbury, MN 55125-2989

Please enclose a self-addressed stamped envelope for reply,
or $1.00 to cover costs. If outside the USA, enclose
an international postal reply coupon.

Many of Llewellyn's authors have websites with additional information and resources. For more information, please visit our website at http://www.llewellyn.com.